# JOURNAL FOR THE STUDY OF THE NEW TESTAMENT
## SUPPLEMENT SERIES
# 115

*Executive Editor*
Stanley E. Porter

Sheffield Academic Press
Sheffield

# The Old Testament
# in the Book of Revelation

## Steve Moyise

Journal for the Study of the New Testament
Supplement Series 115

Copyright © 1995 Sheffield Academic Press

Published by
Sheffield Academic Press Ltd
Mansion House
19 Kingfield Road
Sheffield, S11 9AS
England


Typeset by Sheffield Academic Press
and
Printed on acid-free paper in Great Britain
by Bookcraft
Midsomer Norton, Somerset


British Library Cataloguing in Publication Data

A catalogue record for this book is available
from the British Library


ISBN 1-85075-554-X

# CONTENTS

## ACKNOWLEDGMENTS

First, my thanks go to Professor Frances Young, who taught me as an undergraduate and supervised my doctorate. My six-year association with the theology department of Birmingham University was a very happy one. I am also indebted to the critical comments of Dr Paul Joyce and Dr George Brooke, which led to many improvements. Some of the ideas were first presented at the annual seminar (Hawarden, N. Wales) on the use of the OT in the NT. I am grateful for the encouragement and friendship shown to me by its convener, Dr Lionel North, and its members. Completion of the book was largely the result of study leave granted to me by the St Albans Ministerial Training Scheme. I am particularly grateful to the scheme's principal, the Revd Geoff Gillard, who urged me to 'get it finished' and covered my work while I was away. It is to him that I would like to dedicate this book.

# ABBREVIATIONS

| | |
|---|---|
| AB | *Anchor Bible* |
| BA | *Biblical Archaeologist* |
| BASOR | *Bulletin of the American Schools of Oriental Research* |
| BAGD | W. Bauer, W.F. Arndt and F.W. Gingrich, *A Greek–English Lexicon of the New Testament* |
| BDB | F. Brown, S.R. Driver and C.A. Briggs, *A Hebrew and English Lexicon of the Old Testament* |
| BDF | F. Blass, A. Debrunner and R.W. Funk, *A Greek Grammar of the New Testament and other Early Christian Literature* |
| BFCT | Beiträge zur Förderung christlicher Theologie |
| *Bib* | *Biblica* |
| BNTC | Black's New Testament Commentaries |
| BZNW | Beihefte zur *ZNW* |
| *CBQ* | *Catholic Biblical Quarterly* |
| DJD | Discoveries in the Judaean Desert |
| *Eccl. Hist.* | Eusebius, *The Ecclesiastical History* |
| *Exp Tim* | *Expository Times* |
| FOTL | The Forms of the Old Testament Literature |
| FRLANT | Forschungen zur Religion und Literatur des Alten und Neuen Testaments |
| *HTR* | *Harvard Theological Review* |
| ICC | International Critical Commentary |
| *Int* | *Interpretation* |
| *JBL* | *Journal of Biblical Literature* |
| *JJS* | *Journal for Jewish Studies* |
| *JSJ* | *Journal for the Study of Judaism* |
| *JSNT* | *Journal for the Study of the New Testament* |
| JSNTSup | *Journal for the Study of the New Testament*, Supplement Series |
| JSOT | *Journal for the Study of the Old Testament* |
| JSOTSup | *Journal for the Study of the Old Testament*, Supplement Series |
| JSPSup | *Journal for the Study of the Pseudepigrapha*, Supplement Series |
| *JTS* | *Journal of Theological Studies* |
| LS | H.G. Liddell and R. Scott, *A Greek-English Lexicon* |
| MNTC | Moffatt New Testament Commentary |
| NA[26] | Nestle–Aland, *Novum Testamentum Graece*, 26th edn |
| NCB | New Century Bible |

| NICNT | New International Commentary on the New Testament |
|---|---|
| NovT | *Novum Testamentum* |
| NovTSup | *Novum Testamentum*, Supplements |
| NRT | *La nouvelle revue théologique* |
| NTS | *New Testament Studies* |
| RB | *Revue biblique* |
| RevQ | *Revue de Qumrân* |
| RivB | *Rivista biblica* |
| SBLMS | Society of Biblical Literature Monograph Series |
| SJT | *Scottish Journal of Theology* |
| SNTSMS | Society for New Testament Studies Monograph Series |
| TDNT | G. Kittel and G. Friedrich (eds.), *Theological Dictionary of the New Testament* |
| TNTC | Tyndale New Testament Commentaries |
| UBSGNT | *United Bible Societies Greek New Testament* |
| VT | *Vetus Testamentum* |
| VTSup | *Vetus Testamentum*, Supplements |
| WBC | Word Biblical Commentary |
| ZNW | *Zeitschrift für die neutestamentliche Wissenschaft* |

Chapter 1

INTRODUCTION

During the early part of this century, studies on the use of the Old
Testament in the New Testament focused on parallels found in Rabbinic
works.[1] This was of value as it showed that the New Testament authors
did not operate in a vacuum but were part of a continuous tradition of
interpreting Scripture. Unfortunately, the date of these sources (several
centuries after the Christian era) meant that one could never be sure
whether they were representative of how things were in the New
Testament period. The discovery of the Dead Sea Scrolls (DSS), however, changed all this.[2] It has now become possible to make comparisons
with a collection of writings that span the New Testament period and
even use some of the same texts.[3] Interest has revolved around three
areas, each of which deserves introduction and discussion.

*Text-Form of the Quotations*

Why is it that some quotations agree exactly with the Masoretic Text
(MT) or Septuagint (LXX), whereas others are very different? Was it
lapse of memory on the part of the author, or were there a number of
different text-traditions in circulation? The question is made particularly
interesting by the fact that some of these differences are crucial to the
author's argument. Did the author choose the text that best suited his

---

1. J. Bonsirven, *Exégèse rabbinique et exégèse paulinienne* (Paris: Beauchesne,
1939); W.D. Davies, *Paul and Rabbinic Judaism: Some Rabbinic Elements in Pauline
Theology* (London: SPCK, 4th edn, 1981 [1948]); A. Schlatter, *Das alte Testament in
der johanneischen Apokalypse* (BFCT 16.6; Gütersloh: Bertelsmann, 1912).

2. For a brief introduction, see the latest edition of Y. Yadin, *The Message of the
Scrolls* (with a new Introduction by J.H. Charlesworth; New York: Crossroad, 1992).

3. For example, the use of 2 Sam. 7.14 in 2 Cor. 6.18; Heb. 1.5; Rev. 21.7 and
4QFlor 10–11.

12    *The Old Testament in the Book of Revelation*

argument or did he actually modify an existing text so that it said what he wanted it to say?[4]

*Respect for Context*

There has been much debate as to whether the authors (New Testament or DSS) were interested in the original context of their quotations.[5] Part of the 'argument from prophecy' was that the new movement was able to give the true meaning of Scripture and this ability was thought to originate with the founder:

> Then he opened their minds to understand the scriptures, and he said to them, 'Thus it is written, that the Messiah is to suffer and to rise from the dead on the third day...' (Lk. 24.45-46).

> and God told Habakkuk to write down that which would happen to the final generation, but He did not make known to him when time would come to an end. And as for that which He said, *That he who reads may read it speedily*: interpreted this concerns the Teacher of Righteousness, to whom God made known all the mysteries of the words of His servants the Prophets (1QpHab 7.1-5, trans. Vermes).

Such a view contrasts sharply with the historical consciousness of our own age. For example, many of the interpretations offered in the New Testament depend on the hearer/reader knowing about the coming of Christ, the birth of the Church and the inclusion of the Gentiles. They are meanings that the ancient people could not possibly have given to the texts. Thus Grollenberg deduces from the quotations in Matthew that 'the first Christians were not concerned with what the authors of the ancient text had wanted to say. That is something that we moderns ask about. They inferred the meaning of the ancient text from the events brought about by God in which they themselves were involved.'[6] On the other hand, it must surely be maintained that these beliefs did not arise in a vacuum but in minds that had already been significantly moulded by the Scriptures. Borgen says, 'Since the Old Testament was the thought-world in which Jesus, the disciples and the other first

4. For a recent study, see C.D. Stanley, *Paul and the Language of Scripture: Citation Technique in the Pauline Epistles and Contemporary Literature* (SNTSMS 74; Cambridge: Cambridge University Press, 1992).
5. See my article, 'Does the New Testament Quote the Old Testament out of Context?', *Anvil* 11 (1994), pp. 133-43.
6. L. Grollenberg, *Unexpected Messiah* (London: SCM Press, 1988), p. 7.

Christians lived, and since the Old Testament was woven into the very fabric of Jewish institutions and Jewish ways of life, it therefore determined the theological issues raised to a large extent, either negatively or positively'.[7]

### Exegetical Methods of the Author

In the face of the above, attempts were made to try and understand the principles or techniques used by the author in order to move from text to interpretation.[8] Were authors free to make the text mean whatever they liked, or were there rules (like the rabbinic *middôt*) that governed such exegesis? It might be thought that the claim to divine inspiration would rule out the use of fixed methods of exegesis, but this is not necessarily the case. Authors still have to persuade others to accept their interpretations.

With all this interest and activity, it is somewhat surprising that Schlatter's work (1912) remained the only scholarly book on John's use of Scripture until 1984.[9] Trudinger[10] (1963) and Ozanne[11] (1964) both produced dissertations on the language of John's allusions, but these were never published. Articles appeared in Italian,[12] French[13] and

7. P. Borgen, 'Response', *NTS* 23 (1976–77), p. 68.

8. See G.J. Brooke, *Exegesis at Qumran: 4Q Florilegium in its Jewish Context* (JSOTSup 29, Sheffield: JSOT Press, 1985).

9. G.K. Beale, *The Use of Daniel in Jewish Apocalyptic Literature and in the Revelation of St John* (Lanham, MD: University Press of America, 1984).

10. L. Trudinger, 'The Text of the Old Testament in the Book of Revelation' (ThD Dissertation, Boston University, 1963).

11. C.G. Ozanne, 'The Influence of the Text and Language of the Old Testament on the Book of Revelation' (PhD Thesis, University of Manchester, 1964).

12. A. Lancellotti, 'L'Antico Testamento nell'Apocalisse', *RivB* 14 (1966), pp. 369-84; A. Gangemi, 'L'utilizzazione del Deutero-Isaia nell'Apocalisse di Giovanni', *Euntes Docete* 27 (1974), pp. 109-44; B. Marconcini, 'L'utilizzazione del T.M. nelle citazioni Isaiane dell'Apocalisse', *RivB* 24 (1976), pp. 113-36; G. Deiana, 'Utilizzazione del libro di Geremia in alcuni brani dell'Apocalisse', *Lateranum* 48 (1982), pp. 125-37. I am indebted to J.-P. Ruiz, *Ezekiel in the Apocalypse: The Transformation of Prophetic Language in Revelation 16:17–19:10* (European University Studies 23; Frankfurt: Peter Lang, 1989), pp. 78-90, for his review of Italian scholarship.

13. M.E. Boismard, '"L'Apocalypse" ou "Les Apocalypses" de St Jean', *RB* 56 (1949), pp. 507-41; J. Cambier, 'Les images de l'Ancien Testament dans l'Apocalypse de Saint Jean', *NRT* 77 (1955), pp. 113-22; A. Vanhoye, 'L'utilisation

German,[14] but very little was published in English.[15] As Beale says in his Festschrift article, 'In comparison with the rest of the New Testament, the use of the Old Testament in the Apocalypse of John has not been given a proportionate amount of attention'.[16]

The main reason for this neglect concerns John's particular style of using the Old Testament. Works like the Gospels or Paul's major epistles are easily compared with the Damascus Rule (CD), the Habakkuk pesher (1QpHab) or the florilegium (4QFlor) because they all contain explicit Old Testament quotations.[17] The book of Revelation, however, never uses introductory formulae to introduce its Old Testament references, but weaves its words and phrases into its own composition. The index of allusions and quotations in the back of the *United Bible Societies Greek New Testament* reveals that Revelation contains more Old Testament allusions than any other New Testament book, but it does not record a single quotation.[18] The total number of quotations and allusions listed in *UBSGNT* for Romans, Matthew, Hebrews and Revelation is illustrated in the following graphs. No great claim for objectivity is being made for these since (a) deciding what constitutes an allusion is itself a very subjective affair and (b) *UBSGNT* does not take into account the length of the quotation/allusion. For example, in the book of Hebrews, it only records two quotations and four allusions from Jeremiah, which disguises the fact that one of the quotations runs to 131 words (Heb. 8.8-12 = Jer. 31.31-34). Nevertheless, it is interesting to compare the overall shape of the graphs. Romans, Matthew and Hebrews have the highest number from the Pentateuch (particularly

du livre d'Ezéchiel dans l'Apocalypse', *Bib* 43 (1962), pp. 436-76.

14. E. Lohse, 'Die alttestamentliche Sprache des Sehers Johannes', *ZNW* 52 (1961), pp. 122-26.

15. The first to appear was Trudinger's summary of his thesis, 'Some Observations concerning the Text of the Old Testament in the Book of Revelation', *JTS* 17 (1966), pp. 82-88. A short book appeared in 1972 by F. Jenkins, *The Old Testament in the Book of Revelation* (Grand Rapids: Eerdmans, 1972) but this was for a popular audience. In the early eighties, there were articles by Lust and Goulder (see Bibliography).

16. 'Revelation', in *It is Written: Scripture Citing Scripture* (FS B. Lindars; ed. D.A. Carson and H.G.M. Williamson; Cambridge: Cambridge University Press, 1988), p. 318.

17. The first works to use the material from the DSS were K. Stendahl on Matthew (1954) and E. Ellis on Paul (1957).

18. *UBSGNT*, 3rd edn, pp. 897-911.

Hebrews). Next come either Psalms or Isaiah; there are very few from Jeremiah, Ezekiel or Daniel, with a slight increase for the minor prophets (notably in Matthew).

QUOTATIONS AND ALLUSIONS IN CERTAIN NEW TESTAMENT BOOKS

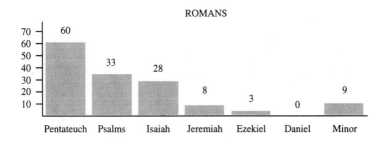

ROMANS

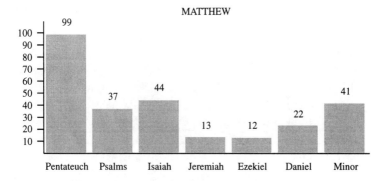

MATTHEW

In contrast, the graph of Revelation is almost the opposite, peaking in the middle rather than the ends (only Jeremiah spoils this). Thus whilst no claim for objectivity can be made for these graphs, it is nevertheless interesting that John's choice of scriptures is substantially different from Romans, Matthew and Hebrews. It would appear that his primary interest was not the Torah but the prophetic literature, along with the worship language of the Psalms.

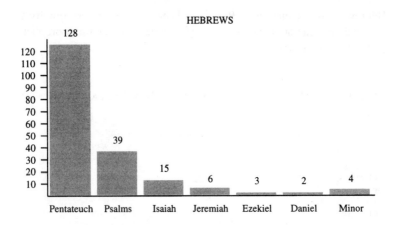

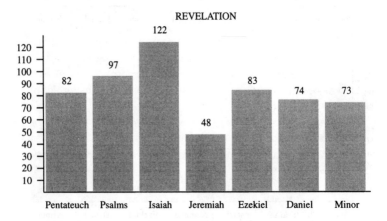

Previous studies on John's use of the Old Testament have been aware that we are dealing with allusions rather than quotations, but they try to get around this by distinguishing between allusions and echoes.[19] The

19. G.K. Beale proposes a distinction between 'clear', 'probable' and 'possible' allusions. The first is when the wording is almost the same as the source, has the same general meaning and could not reasonably have come from anywhere else. The second is less precise but contains an idea which is uniquely traceable to that text. The third is better referred to as an 'echo' and is of a much more general nature. See 'A Reconsideration of the Text of Daniel in the Apocalypse', *Bib* 67 (1986), pp. 539-43. A. Vanhoye divides them into 'Utilisation certaine' and 'Contacts littéraires', which in turn are divided into 'fidèle' and 'libre' for the first and 'plus probants' and 'moins probants' for the second ('L'utilisation', pp. 473-76).

aim has been to avoid the sort of subjectivity that Sandmel[20] has called 'parallelomania', by dealing with a smaller group of allusions that can more or less be treated as quotations. For example, Charles uses the differences between John's allusions and the LXX (which he refers to as o′) to conclude that 'our author draws his materials directly from the Hebrew (or Aramaic) text, and apparently never solely from o′ or any other version'.[21] Thus John's use of ἐξαλείφω in Rev. 7.17 instead of the LXX's ἀφαιρέω (Isa. 25.8) means that we must 'maintain our author's independence of the LXX'.[22] His use of αἴρω in Rev. 10.5 instead of the ὑψόω of the Greek versions (Dan. 12.7) leads him to conclude that 'our author did not use the Versions but the Hebrew of Daniel, which he rendered freely to suit his purpose'.[23] His use of νικάω in Rev. 11.7 and 13.7 (one of John's favourite words) instead of Theodotion's ἰσχύω (Dan. 7.21) points in the same direction.[24] The implication is that John would have followed the LXX more closely, had he known it. But is this true? Was it John's purpose to quote texts accurately, whether from Greek or Semitic sources? Most commentators think not. Indeed, even Charles says that John used the 'Hebrew of Daniel, which he rendered freely to suit his purpose'. Differences from the LXX are likely to arise from John's particular way of using Scripture, rather than constituting proof that he is following a Semitic text.[25]

When it comes to analysing John's use of Scripture, there is clearly some value in trying to distinguish between allusions that are virtually certain and the countless echoes or literary parallels that various scholars

20. S. Sandmel, 'Parallelomania', *JBL* 81 (1962), pp. 1-13.

21. R.H. Charles, *A Critical and Exegetical Commentary on the Revelation of St John* (ICC; Edinburgh: T. & T. Clark, 1920), I, p. lxvi.

22. *Revelation*, I, p. 217.

23. *Revelation*, I, p. 263.

24. *Revelation*, I, p. 286.

25. A full discussion of this can be found in ch. 7 of my thesis, 'The Use of the Old Testament in the Book of Revelation' (University of Birmingham, 1994). The conclusion reached there is that John makes use of both Greek and Semitic sources and is not solely dependent on either the Greek (*contra* Swete) or the Hebrew (*contra* Ozanne). Various scholars have tried to show that John prefers the Hebrew (e.g. Trudinger) or that his use of it is different from his use of Greek texts. For example, Charles distinguishes between *drawing directly* on the Hebrew, and simply being *influenced by* the Greek. I argue in my thesis that such a view can only be maintained by extensive special pleading.

have suggested. Thus Fekkes[26] considers all the allusions to Isaiah that
have been proposed and then categorizes them into 'Certain/Virtually
Certain', 'Probable/Possible' and 'Unlikely/Doubtful'. He says that the
advantages of this delimiting approach are twofold. First, the elimination
of doubtful parallels and the corresponding confirmation of certain texts
paves the way for a better appreciation and evaluation of those Isaiah
passages which lie at the heart of John's prophetic message. Secondly,
more conviction can be attached to conclusions based on these accepted
texts.[27]

This is useful, but it cannot be the complete solution since, as with any
work of art, it is often the subtle nuances that separate it from other
members of the genre. After all, we would not expect a music critic to
limit his or her comments to the loudest instruments in the orchestra!
Literary and aesthetic criteria are now regularly used in biblical
scholarship to supplement historical study, but 'Use of the Old
Testament in the New Testament' studies have largely remained within
the historical-critical paradigm. One of the aims of this book is to
investigate whether the literary concept of 'intertextuality' can shed any
light on John's allusive use of Scripture. The term was first coined by
Julia Kristeva[28] in 1969 and concerns the way that texts interact with
their subtexts. The underlying principle is simple. Alluding to a past
work sets up a link or correspondence between the two contexts. The
reader is asked to follow the current text while being mindful of a
previous context (or contexts). This inevitably leads to a tension, since
context is vital for meaning. As Michael Worten and Judith Still state in

26. J. Fekkes, *Isaiah and Prophetic Traditions in the Book of Revelation:
Visionary Antecedents and their Development* (JSNTSup 93; Sheffield: JSOT Press,
1994).

27. *Isaiah and Prophetic Traditions*, p. 281. Trudinger, despite the absence of
introductory formulae, believes that he can isolate a group of accurate allusions which
deserve to be called 'quotations'. His criterion is the presence of 'word combinations
in a form in which one would not have used them had it not been for a knowledge of
their occurrence in this particular form in another source' ('Observations', p. 84).
See further, J. Paulien, 'Elusive Allusions: The Problematic Use of the Old Testament
in Revelation', *BR* 33 (1988), pp. 37-53.

28. 'Word, Dialogue and Novel' was written in 1966 and appeared in *Séméiotiké*
in 1969. It was translated in *Desire in Language: A Semiotic Approach to Literature
and Art* (ed. L.S. Roudiez; New York: Columbia University Press, 1980) and is now
conveniently found in *The Kristeva Reader* (ed. T. Moi; Oxford: Columbia
University Press, 1986).

their introductory essay on intertextuality, 'every quotation distorts and redefines the "primary" utterance by relocating it within another linguistic and cultural context'.[29] On the other hand, the quoted text does not accept this 'relocation' without a fight (so to speak), but reminds the reader that it once belonged to a different context. A dynamic is thereby established in which the new affects the old and the old affects the new.

The significance of this for 'Use of the Old Testament in the New Testament' studies is two-fold. First, it gives a rather different perspective to the observation that some of the Old Testament quotations are taken out of context. As Worten and Still observe, all quotations are out of context in the sense that they have been relocated 'within another linguistic and cultural context'. Now since context is essential for meaning, there is in fact no possibility that a quotation can bear the same meaning in a new composition as it did in the old. The actual words might be the same but all the factors that affect interpretation have changed. For example, in response to a question about the greatest commandment (Mk 12.28-34), Jesus quotes Deut. 6.4 ('love the Lord your God') and Lev. 19.18 ('love your neighbour as yourself'). On one level, Jesus is simply directing the enquirer to two Old Testament texts that answer his question. However, Christians down the ages have found tremendous significance in the bringing together of these two commands as a summary of the Law. By placing them in such close juxtaposition, the reader/hearer is asked to interpret each in the light of the other. Love for God must not be interpreted as turning away from one's fellow human beings, nor vice versa. The new context has a significant effect on the interpretation.

Secondly, the presence of a quotation or allusion means that the clues that enable interpretation to take place are coming from two separate sources. Like a radio dial that is incorrectly tuned, the listener hears several 'voices' simultaneously and may have to choose which to concentrate on. The effect with the radio dial is usually annoyance, but if an author has consciously chosen a particular quotation or allusion, we can expect the interaction to be more productive. Thus the relevant question concerning the presence of Old Testament quotations or allusions in the New Testament is not, 'has the author respected the context', but 'in what ways do the two contexts interact?' Or, continuing the 'sound

29. M. Worten and J. Still, 'Introduction', *Intertextuality: Theories and Practices* (Manchester: Manchester University Press, 1990), p. 11.

waves' metaphor, has the author chosen a quotation or allusion which leads to 'harmonies', or does it simply produce 'interference'?

Nevertheless, this study is not going to start with 'intertextuality' and attempt to 'apply' it to the book of Revelation. Rather, it will progress inductively, drawing conclusions from a set of case studies, bringing in comparisons with the Dead Sea Scrolls and then, and only then, seeing if intertextuality is able to illuminate John's use of Scripture. There are two reasons for this. First, there is always the danger of anachronism when using modern theories to interpret ancient texts. Ancient people did not think as we think, and what may appear obvious to us may not have been obvious to them. This can be seen when modern scholars categorize particular uses of Scripture as 'arbitrary' or 'non-contextual'. It may appear 'arbitrary' to us, but in the author's mind, some word, image or even sound might have made it an obvious choice. Indeed, such connections might well have operated at an unconscious level.[30] Meaning is thus not dictated by the original context in any easy to define way—but this is not to say that we can safely ignore that context.

The second reason for beginning with a number of case studies is that this is how the research was actually carried out. A number of positive conclusions emerged from the case studies but also a number of difficult questions. For example, why is it that John makes numerous allusions to the 'new temple' section of Ezekiel 40–48, while specifically denying that the new Jerusalem contains such a thing as a temple building? Why is that he juxtaposes images of power ('Lion of Judah') with images of mortality ('slain Lamb') or divine attributes ('first and the last') with Christian tradition about Christ's death? Why is it that he hears one thing (144,000) but sees another (great multitude)? It was clear that what was needed was some way of describing an interaction of images or voices, as Richard Hays had discovered in his *Echoes of Scripture in the Letters of Paul*.[31] Like Hays, the sensitive treatment of echoes in Milton by John Hollander[32] and in Renaissance poetry by Thomas

---

30. Some would want to restrict the use of the word 'allusion' to conscious choice and use the word 'echo' or even 'literary parallel' for anything else. However, this could easily lead to some form of the 'intentional fallacy'. It is better to admit that the 'volume' of a particular echo will depend on the reader (including the possibility that some will not hear it at all) than to try and judge whether the author intended it or not.

31. R.B. Hays, *Echoes of Scripture in the Letters of Paul* (New Haven: Yale University Press, 1989).

32. J. Hollander, *The Figure of Echo: A Mode of Allusion in Milton and After* (Berkeley: University of California Press, 1981).

Greene[33] proved inspiring. My debt to them and to Richard Hays will become clear in Chapter 6.

For these two reasons, it seemed best to adhere to the original order, even though the 'Easter faith' now permeates the whole. Thus the book begins with a series of case studies. The first (Chapter 2) looks at the use of Scripture in the messages to the seven churches (Rev. 2–3). This was chosen for two reasons. First, there has not been a major study on John's use of Scripture in the seven messages. Secondly, it is of particular interest because many scholars believe that the images used in the messages were chosen because of their relevance to the local churches. However, it is also clear that many of the images derive from the Old Testament and a number of them have already occurred in the inaugural vision (Rev. 1.12-18). This gives a unique opportunity for asking: which has priority, the Old Testament context or the contemporary situation? Ramsay[34] and Hemer[35] argue that John's desire to allude to local conditions led him to particular texts. For example, the metal industry at Thyatira led John to 'smelting' texts like Dan.10.6 ('eyes like flaming torches...legs like the gleam of burnished bronze'), which were then used to construct the vision (even though the vision now comes first in Revelation). The focus in Chapter 2 will be whether the evidence supports this or whether it is more likely that the vision came first (as a mosaic of Scripture texts), some of which were then applied to the seven churches.[36]

33. T.M. Greene, *The Light in Troy: Imitation and Discovery in Renaissance Poetry* (New Haven: Yale University Press, 1982).

34. W.M. Ramsay, *The Letters to the Seven Churches of Asia and their Place in the Plan of the Apocalypse* (London: Hodder & Stoughton, 1904).

35. C.J. Hemer, *The Letters to the Seven Churches of Asia in their Local Setting* (JSNTSup 11, Sheffield: JSOT Press, 1986).

36. Farrer holds the extreme view that the seven messages are an exposition of the inaugural vision and so bear no relationship to the places addressed. Noting how the seven seals and the seven trumpets are subdivided into a four and a three, he argues that the first four messages work back through the vision (seven stars = 1.20, first and the last = 1.17, sharp sword = 1.16, feet and eyes = 1.14-15). The fifth (Sardis) then returns to 1.20 (seven stars) with Philadelphia and Laodicea based on 1.18 (keys) and 1.5 (faithful witness), respectively. His analysis demonstrates the close links between the first chapter and the seven messages but his theory does not stand up to scrutiny. For example, it is by no means obvious that the title to Ephesus or Sardis is based on the explanation of the stars in 1.20. One or both of them could derive from the first mention of the 'seven stars' in 1.16. Nor is it clear that the messages fall into a four/ three pattern. Indeed, the position of the 'anyone who has an ear' clause suggests a

John's use of Daniel offers a similar challenge. Does he use only those parts of the book that fit in with his own prophetic vision or has his own vision been influenced by the book of Daniel? Beale argues that certain chapters of Revelation (1, 4–5, 13, 17) are a midrash on Daniel 7 and that John meets the needs of the recipients by locating their situation within the prophetic scheme of that book. Other scholars believe that his use of other texts, such as Ezekiel and Isaiah, show that he has a standpoint outside of the book of Daniel and uses various texts in order to express his own viewpoint.[37] As well as examining these theories, I will begin in Chapter 3 to formulate some of the techniques used by John in his handling of Old Testament texts.

The fourth chapter is on John's use of Ezekiel and is mainly concerned with hermeneutical questions. In particular, the extensive parallels between key sections of the two books (Ezek. 1–3//Rev. 4–5; Ezek. 9–10//Rev. 7–8; Ezek. 16, 23//Rev. 17; Ezek. 26–28//Rev. 18; Ezek. 38–48//Rev. 20–22) are coupled with extensive differences. The latter have caused Vogelgesang[38] to call Revelation an 'anti-apocalypse'. He believes that John applies a consistent hermeneutical strategy (which he calls 'democratization') to the book of Ezekiel, stripping it of its particularistic elements and making it accessible to all. On the other hand, Ruiz looks to a number of 'hermeneutical imperatives' that are embedded in the text, which are designed to force the reader to engage actively in a 'dialogue with the text and with the texts within the text'.[39] It is becoming clear that John is neither a slave to the Old Testament texts nor can he make them mean whatever he wants them to mean. Any description of John's use of Scripture must do justice to both the continuities and the discontinuities.

Chapter 5 investigates the use of Scripture at Qumran. Its purpose is to see if the direction this study is taking is compatible with uses of Scripture found at Qumran. The DSS now form a large body of

---

three/four pattern. Lastly, even if Farrer's theory were acceptable, it is hardly correct to call the last three messages a second exposition of the vision since it is only the single word 'key' which has a parallel to the vision (Laodicea's 'faithful witness' refers back to the greeting of 1.5). See A. Farrer, *The Revelation of St John the Divine* (Oxford: Clarendon Press, 1964), pp. 70-86.

37.  See the review of Beale's book by A.Y. Collins in *JBL* 105 (1986), pp. 734-35.

38.  J.M. Vogelgesang, 'The Interpretation of Ezekiel in the Book of Revelation' (PhD dissertation, Harvard University, 1985).

39.  *Ezekiel in the Apocalypse*, p. 520.

literature and more is being published all the time.[40] In the space available, discussion will be limited to eight texts, drawn from a variety of documents in order to illustrate different uses of Scripture. Some of these will offer interesting parallels to Revelation, others less so. Nevertheless, it will be seen that the need for an interactive model is not confined to Revelation but could usefully be employed with the DSS (though it is beyond the scope of this book).

This brings us to Chapter 6. Drawing on the work of Mikhail Bakhtin, Kristeva suggests that we should see the interaction of texts as an *'intersection of textual surfaces* rather than a *point'*.[41] Alluding to texts does not result in a single resolution (i.e. a fixed meaning) but a range of possibilities, which the reader tries to order and, to some extent, control. On the view that John's use of Scripture results in a fixed meaning, the task of the reader is to find ways of discovering it. But on the view that John offers us an *intersection of textual surfaces*, the reader has a much more active role to play. As Ellen van Wolde says,

> The writer assigns meaning to his own context and in interaction with other texts he shapes and forms his own text. The reader, in much the same way, assigns meaning to the generated text in interaction with other texts he knows…A writer does not weave a web of meanings that the reader merely has to follow, but…presents them to the reader as a text. The reader reacts to the offer and enters into a dialogue with the possibilities the text has to offer him.[42]

Thus Chapter 6 not only tries to illuminate John's use of Scripture; it also poses questions about the way that the book is read. What is it like to read an allusive text like Revelation? Is the reader left to grapple with an 'intersection of textual surfaces' or is he or she steered into a fixed meaning or resolution? And is this solely the choice of a particular reader or does John's intentions have any bearing on the way the book should be read? The study concludes with an epilogue (Chapter 7), offering a brief assessment of the value of theories of intertextuality for New Testament study.

---

40. See R. Eisenman and M. Wise, *The Dead Sea Scrolls Uncovered* (London: Penguin Books, 1992). For a list of who is working on what, see E. Tov, 'The Unpublished Qumran Texts from Caves 4 and 11', *BA* (June 1992), pp. 94-104.

41. 'Word, Dialogue and Novel', *The Kristeva Reader*, p. 36.

42. E. van Wolde, 'Trendy Intertextuality', in *Intertextuality in Biblical Writings* (FS B. van Iersel; ed. S. Draisma; Kampen: Kok, 1989), pp. 43-49.

## Chapter 2

## THE USE OF SCRIPTURE IN REVELATION 1–3

One of the intriguing questions about John's apocalypse concerns the seven prophetic messages in Revelation 2–3. On the one hand, they appear to be real messages aimed at particular problems in the communities (the lukewarmness at Laodicea, for example). On the other, they are obviously meant to be read by all the churches for they all end with the refrain, 'Let anyone who has an ear listen to what the Spirit is saying to the churches'. Further, the blessing pronounced on both reader and audience in 1.3 ('Blessed is the one who reads aloud the words of the prophecy, and blessed are those who hear'), along with the book's ending at 22.18 ('I warn everyone who hears the words of the prophecy of this book') imply that the whole book is to be read from beginning to end. In view of this, most commentators think that the messages were composed as a unit and were never sent individually to the respective churches.[1]

If this is so, the question arises as to whether the details in the messages actually reflect John's knowledge of the seven churches or are simply a literary device to address the whole church. In favour of the latter is the fact that John addresses precisely seven churches, just as the book goes on to describe seven seals, seven trumpets and seven bowls. When this is coupled with the fact that outside of Revelation 2–3 it is the universal church that is centre stage, with no further mention of individual congregations, the conclusion appears to be that the seven churches are intended to represent the whole church. However, this does not necessarily mean that the messages are fictitious. It is possible that having conceived the scheme of 'sevens', John then used seven

---

1.    A notable exception to this is Charles, *Revelation*, I, pp. 43-47, who claims that the letters were originally written to the individual congregations and later edited by the same author to apply to the universal church.

actual congregations to fulfil his plan.[2] Nevertheless, it must be said that one would have a different view of Paul's letters if it was known that he wrote seven in order to conform to a pre-determined plan.

Another point is the definite way that John speaks of 'the seven churches that are in Asia' (1.4). One might suppose from this that these were the only churches in Asia, but both Acts and Paul's letters show that this was not the case. Alternatively, we might think that these were the leading churches of Asia, but again this does not seem to be true. Thyatira (which receives the longest message) is a relatively insignificant place whereas Colossae, Troas and Magnesia have been passed over. Lastly, it might be suggested that these are the seven churches which were under John's oversight but since they cover such a wide area, it is hard to imagine how this came about. In particular, the epistle to the Colossians shows that a close relationship existed between that church, the author of the canonical letter and the church at Laodicea (Col. 4.13-14). How could it be that John's oversight extended from Ephesus to Laodicea but did not include either Colossae or Hierapolis? The obvious conclusion is that the definite nature of the address to 'the seven churches that are in Asia' is intended to be representative and means something like 'to the Church in all its fullness and diversity'.

On the other hand, if the seven churches simply represent the universal church, it is strange that the various errors mentioned in the messages are scarcely differentiated. One could see the usefulness in a sort of 'typology of errors' but the error of the Nicolaitans, Jezebel and those who follow the teaching of Balaam is much the same thing (inciting fornication and idolatry).[3] Further, thanks to the pioneering work of Sir William Ramsay, most commentators accept that the messages do show some knowledge of the various places being addressed. For example, the Laodiceans are exhorted to buy the sort of gold that will really make them rich, white garments to cover their nakedness and salve to anoint their eyes (Rev. 3.18). Ramsay provided external

2. 'The Seer selects such particular churches of Asia and such special features of their condition as afford the best illustration of that state of God's kingdom in the world which is to be the great subject of his prophetic words' (W. Milligan, *The Book of Revelation* [London: Hodder & Stoughton, 1889], p. 36).

3. Farrer says, 'the ingenuity of commentators racking the text to establish the difference of spiritual type as between seven churches is largely misplaced. There is some difference in degree of merit or demerit, but the virtues praised or vices rebuked in all are much the same' (*Revelation*, p. 83).

evidence to show that Laodicea was known for its banking, its woollen industry and its medical school which specialized in opthalmics.[4] This would be something of a coincidence if John had no knowledge of Laodicea. To Thyatira, the only one of the seven known to have had a guild of coppersmiths, the divine speaker is described as having eyes like a 'flame of fire' and feet like 'burnished bronze'. The actual word rendered 'burnished bronze' is χαλκολίβανος (χαλκός = copper, λίβανος = frankincense), which is usually taken to designate some sort of alloy. The word is otherwise unattested and Ramsay conjectured that it was probably a local product of Thyatira. If this is the case, it is significant that it also occurs in John's inaugural vision of 'one like the Son of Man', before we arrive at the seven messages. Ramsay says:

> As to the brief description of the Divine Author, which is prefixed to each of the Seven Letters, there is a special appropriateness in each case to the character or circumstances of the Church which is addressed.[5]

Ramsay also offers an answer for why John addresses these particular seven churches. As a result of his own expeditions, he discovered that each of the cities lies on a trade route. A messenger coming from Patmos would arrive at Ephesus and moving North would come first to Smyrna and then up to Pergamum. If he then turned and descended in a south-easterly direction, he would come to Thyatira, Sardis, Philadelphia and finally Laodicea, where the route back to Ephesus would be due West. Though often called a circular route, its shape is more like that of a triangle (Ephesus, Pergamum, Laodicea) with the other cities acting as stopping off points. Ramsay further conjectured that each of the seven places operated a secondary route allowing for the efficient dissemination of information throughout this part of Asia. Thus according to Ramsay, the reason that John addressed 'the seven churches that are in Asia' is because they formed the seven postal districts for the region.[6]

4. *Letters*, pp. 413-30.
5. *Letters*, p. 198.
6. The view that the order of the letters corresponds to the route taken by the messenger is accepted by most modern commentators; J.P.M. Sweet, *Revelation* (TPI New Testament Commentaries; London: SCM Press; Philadelphia: Trinity Press International, 1990), p. 78; G.B. Caird, *The Revelation of St John the Divine* (BNTC; London: A. & C. Black, 2nd edn, 1984), p. 28; R.H. Mounce, *The Book of Revelation* (NICNT; Grand Rapids: Eerdmans, 1977), p. 76; G.A. Krodel, *Revelation* (Augsburg Commentary on the New Testament; Minneapolis: Augsburg, 1989), p. 94, who says the suggestion is 'as good as any'; also cf. the PhD dissertation of

Ramsay's influence is important for this study because his positive evaluation of John's historical knowledge went hand in hand with his negative evaluation of his use of Scripture. It was axiomatic for Ramsay that all of John's symbols and metaphors derive from his intimate knowledge of local culture. He recognized, of course, that most of the book is filled with apocalyptic images and allusions to Scripture but insisted that 'the Seven Letters are a truer index to the writer's character than any other part of the Apocalypse, because in these letters he is in closer contact with reality than in any other part of the book'.[7]

Allusions to Scripture, which he considered to be almost absent from the seven messages, are part of the 'apocalyptic machinery' which unfortunately engulfed John in the latter part of the book. Thus the descriptions of the 'flaming eyes' and 'bronze feet' have nothing to do with Daniel's vision but were suggested by Thyatira's metal industry. Possession of the key of David, 'who opens and no one will shut, who shuts and no one opens' (Rev. 3.7) is simply a metaphor for the 'open door' of missionary opportunity (as used by Paul), whereas possession of the 'sharp two-edged sword' (Rev. 2.12) is particularly apt for Pergamum because it is the seat of the imperial authority. His position is clearly seen in his comments about the promise of 'hidden manna' given to the church at Pergamum:

> The allusion to the 'hidden manna' is one of the few touches in the Seven Letters derived purely and exclusively from the realm of Jewish belief and superstition. It is not even taken from the Old Testament, but is a witness that some current Jewish superstitions acquired a footing in the early Christian Church.[8]

Ramsay is often quoted in commentaries for showing that John had real knowledge of the seven congregations.[9] However, his position was not that John had recent news of what was happening in the congregations and was therefore responding to the known needs of the recipients. Rather, John's familiarity with the history and geography of each of the places gave him an intuitive knowledge concerning the state of each of the churches. For example, he says that the church at Smyrna is inevitably recipient of the message from him who was 'dead and came

---

L.C. Tengbom, 'Studies in the Interpretation of Revelation Two and Three' (Hartford Seminary Foundation, 1976), p. 101.

7.   *Letters*, p. 277.
8.   *Letters*, p. 308.
9.   For example, in the works mentioned in n. 6 above.

to life' because this is the spirit of Smyrna. It was destroyed in the sixth century BCE and lay dormant for three centuries until it was refounded. The memory of this remains in the city's collective unconscious so that all institutions in Smyrna, including the church, necessarily partake of it. This is why John has the speaker address them with the title, 'These are the words of the first and the last, who was dead and came to life', concerning which, 'All Smyrnaean readers would at once appreciate the striking analogy to the early history of their own city which lies in that form of address'.[10]

Thus it is incorrect to think that Ramsay represents the rationalist 'real letter' approach (i.e. responding to known needs) as opposed to the 'apocalyptic seer'. Ramsay's view is just as 'mystical' as those who imagine John seeing into the future through 'trance-like' visions, but is arrived at in a different way. For Ramsay, meditation on the history and geography of the places allowed John to think 'himself into harmony with the natural influences'[11] that make a place what it is. From this, he was able to discern what state the church *must* be in and write accordingly. Ramsay fully realized that the modern mind would find such a view difficult to accept but insisted that if we wish to understand John's messages, we must be willing to enter into his thought world.

Ramsay's plea is somewhat ironic considering his unwillingness to take John's use of the Old Testament seriously. Given the fact that John describes his visionary experiences in terms of Old Testament theophanies, it is more likely that Scripture provided the inspiration to see into his reader's situation. Nevertheless, Ramsay's work, which has now been updated by Hemer,[12] serves to raise an important issue: Did John move from local conditions to relevant texts or from significant texts to local conditions? Ramsay was quite clear on this question. From the appropriateness of the titles to the places addressed, 'it follows that the complete description of the Divine Author, which is made up of those seven parts, is logically later than the parts, though it comes first in the book'.[13] It is consistent with a prevailing attitude in New Testament scholarship that the

10.  *Letters*, p. 269.
11.  *Letters*, p. 278.
12.  Hemer, *Local Setting*.
13.  *Letters*, p. 198.

place of the Old Testament in the formation of New Testament theology is that of a servant, ready to run to the aid of the gospel whenever it is required, bolstering up arguments, and filling out meaning through evocative allusions, but never acting as the master or leading the way, nor even guiding the process of thought behind the scenes.[14]

The fact that the titles used in the seven messages occur first in the inaugural vision means that we have an almost unique opportunity in the New Testament to test this hypothesis. Did John start from the local situation, move to relevant scriptures and then use these to construct the vision of Rev. 1.12-20? Or did the visionary description come first, some of its phrases then being used to address the seven churches? I will begin by assessing the evidence given by Ramsay and Hemer that the titles came first and were inspired by local conditions.

### The Titles as Local Allusions

To the angel of the church in *Ephesus* write: These are the words of him who holds the seven stars in his right hand, who walks among the seven golden lampstands (Rev. 2.1).

The first message is addressed to Ephesus, either because it was the leading city[15] or perhaps because it was the closest to Patmos. The attributes of the speaker are clearly aimed at establishing a link with the inaugural vision, for John says, 'on turning I saw seven golden lampstands, and in the midst of the lampstands I saw one like the Son of Man' (Rev. 1.12). He then describes his clothing, his head, his hair, his eyes, his feet and his voice, before adding, 'In his right hand he held seven stars' (Rev. 1.16). There does not appear to be any convincing explanation for why Ephesus suggested to John the images of stars or lampstands. Ramsay says it is because

Ephesus, as in practical importance the leading city of the Province Asia, might be said in a sense to be the centre, to be in the midst of the Seven Churches; and the Divine figure that addresses her appropriately holds in

14. B. Lindars, 'The Place of the Old Testament in the Formation of New Testament Theology', *NTS* 23 (1976–7), p. 66.
15. There is some confusion over whether Ephesus or Pergamum was the official capital at this time. Ramsay assumes it was Pergamum (followed by W. Barclay, *The Revelation of St John* [Daily Study Bible; Edinburgh: Saint Andrew Press, rev. edn, 1976], I, p. 87, but Hemer, *Local Setting*, pp. 82-83, says the evidence is ambiguous.

His hand the Seven Stars, which 'are the Seven Churches'. The leading
city can stand for the whole Province, as the Province can stand for the
whole Church.[16]

However, this explanation falters when we note that 'seven stars' also
appears later on in the title to Sardis (see below).

And to the angel of the church in *Smyrna* write: These are the words of the
first and the last, who was dead and came to life (Rev. 2.8).

These words are very similar to the words addressed to John after he
has seen the vision: 'Do not be afraid; I am the first and the last, and the
living one. I was dead, and see, I am alive forever and ever' (Rev. 1.17-
18). The last phrase is clearly an allusion to the resurrection but Ramsay
seeks to make the connection with Smyrna's history more compelling
by insisting that ἐγένετο νεκρὸς καὶ ἔζησεν should be rendered
'became dead and yet lived'. This then fits with his reading of Strabo
that Smyrna lay obliterated for some four centuries (whereas an
inscription suggests that it continued as a village state after the Anatolian
system).[17] According to Ramsay, 'became dead and yet lived' perfectly
describes Smyrna's history so that 'all Smyrnaean readers would at
once appreciate the striking analogy to the early history of their own city
which lies in that form of address'.[18] Hemer is more cautious, calling
Ramsay's rendering of ἐγένετο νεκρὸς καὶ ἔζησεν 'unnecessarily
pedantic' and stating that we 'must recognize that in fact Smyrna had a
more nearly continuous history than Ramsay and his followers have
allowed'.[19]

Ramsay makes no comment about the title 'first and the last'. Most
commentators take it to be a divine title drawn from Isa. 44.6 ('I am the
first and I am the last; besides me there is no god') or Isa. 48.12 ('I am
He; I am the first, and I am the last'). If this is so, then it is remarkable
that a statement concerning the eternity of God is juxtaposed with a
statement about Christ's death and resurrection. The profundity of this
combination weakens the case for supposing that it originated from a
desire to allude to Smyrna's history. Further, if Ramsay wants to argue
for the priority of the local allusion based on the 'yet lived' clause, it is

16. *Letters*, p. 238.
17. *Letters*, p. 270.
18. *Letters*, p. 269.
19. *Local Setting*, p. 76.

surprising that John adds καὶ ὁ ζῶν only when it is supposedly transferred to the vision, for this would have strengthened the local allusion. Though certainty is impossible, it seems more likely that John constructed Rev. 1.17b as a juxtaposition of a divine title and Christian testimony,[20] which he then abbreviated for the letter:

| Rev. 1.17b-18a | Rev. 2.8b |
|---|---|
| ἐγώ εἰμι <u>ὁ πρῶτος καὶ ὁ ἔσχατος</u> | τάδε λέγει <u>ὁ πρῶτος καὶ ὁ ἔσχατος</u> |
| καὶ ὁ ζῶν[21] | |
| καὶ <u>ἐγενόμην νεκρὸς</u> | ὃς <u>ἐγένετο νεκρὸς</u> |
| καὶ ἰδοὺ | |
| <u>ζῶν εἰμι</u> εἰς τοὺς | καὶ <u>ἔζησεν</u>. |
| αἰῶνας τῶν αἰώνων | |

And to the angel of the church in *Pergamum* write: These are the words of him who has the sharp two-edged sword (Rev. 2.12)

As to the two-edged sword, Ramsay believes the point is to show that the author 'wields that power of life and death, which people imagine to be vested in the Proconsul of the Province'.[22] The image is continued in the body of the letter, where the church is given the warning,

Repent then. If not, I will come to you soon and make war against them with the *sword of my mouth* (Rev. 2.16).

The combination of the 'sharp two-edged sword' and 'sword of my mouth' has suggested to many commentators that John is combining two important texts from Isaiah. The first is Isa. 11.4b, which reads, 'he shall strike the earth with the rod of his mouth, and with the breath of his lips he shall kill the wicked'. The LXX speaks of the 'word of his mouth' rather than 'rod of his mouth'. The second is Isa. 49.2a, which reads, 'He made my mouth like a sharp sword'. The two are combined in the inaugural vision, 'and from his mouth came a sharp, two-edged sword' (Rev. 1.16b). They also occur in the parousia vision, once again combined with other Scripture allusions:

From his mouth comes a sharp sword with which to strike down the nations, and he will rule them with a rod of iron; he will tread the winepress of the fury of the wrath of God the Almighty (Rev. 19.15).

20. The following chapters will show that this is not the only occasion that John does this.

21. Omitted by a few MSS possibly because of the parallel in Rev. 2.8.

22. *Letters*, p. 293.

> And the rest were killed by the sword of the rider on the horse, the sword
> that came from his mouth; and all the birds were gorged with their flesh
> (Rev. 19.21).

Thus John's book opens with a vision of Christ, where one of the
images is 'a sharp two-edged sword' coming from his mouth. After the
seals, trumpets and bowls, it draws to a close with a vision of his return,
also with the image of the sword from his mouth. It is interesting that in
both cases, the image belongs to a cluster of Scripture references, which
adds to the evidence that it is itself an allusion to Scripture. As Fekkes[23]
has shown, the image is almost a 'topos' in Jewish writings (*Pss. Sol.*
17.24, 35; 4QpIsa[a] 8-10; 1QSb5 24-25; 2 Thess. 2.8; 4 *Ezra* 13.9-11, 37-
38; *1 Enoch* 62.2). All this makes it very unlikely that it began life as a
local allusion and was then used to construct the inaugural and parousia
visions. It is far more likely to have happened the other way around.

> And to the angel of the church in *Thyatira* write: These are the words of
> the Son of God, who has eyes like a flame of fire, and whose feet are like
> burnished bronze (Rev. 2.18).

Rather strangely, the title 'Son of God' has no parallel in the inaugural
vision and neither Ramsay nor Hemer offer any reason for its presence
in this letter. However, the smelting imagery that follows can be linked
to the guild of χαλκεῖς attested in an inscription.[24] The word that is
here translated 'burnished bronze' is otherwise unattested, but Ramsay
suggests that it is a 'very hard alloyed metal, used for weapons, and under
proper treatment assuming a brilliant polished gleam approximating to
gold'.[25] Hemer says,

> The product, I suggest, was known there as χαλκολίβανος, which I
> *conjecture* to be a 'copulative compound', literally rendered 'copper-zinc',
> λίβανος being an *unrecorded word, perhaps* peculiar to the trade, for a
> metal obtained by distillation, and so derived from the verb λείβω.[26]

The significance of this statement lies in the fact that Dan. 10.5-6, the
source text quoted by most commentators, cannot explain John's choice
of χαλκολίβανος. The Hebrew was rendered χαλκοῦ στίλβοντος by
Theodotion and χαλκὸς ἐξαστράπτων by the LXX. One could of

23. *Isaiah and Prophetic Traditions*, p. 118.
24. Hemer, *Local Setting*, p. 113.
25. *Letters*, p. 329.
26. *Local Setting*, p. 116 (emphasis added).

course argue that χαλκολίβανος is John's own translation of the Hebrew with λίβανος added to χαλκός in order to describe its colour. Mounce[27] suggests that the word derives from κλίβανος (furnace), whereas the Syriac text treats it as a metal from Lebanon. Certainty is clearly impossible but this should be balanced by the conjectural nature of Hemer's proposal (note the use of 'conjecture', 'unrecorded word' and 'perhaps' in the above quotation).

> And to the angel of the church in *Sardis* write: These are the words of him who has the seven spirits of God and the seven stars (Rev. 3.1).

Possession of the seven spirits is not part of the inaugural vision but comes from the introductory greeting of Rev. 1.4 ('Grace to you and peace from him who is and who was and who is to come, and from the seven spirits who are before his throne'). Since the greeting continues with a reference to Jesus Christ, most commentators take this to be John's way of referring to the Holy Spirit, though it is a peculiar expression. Is there some fact about Sardis that would help to explain it? It seems not. Ramsay can only declare that no 'city of Asia at that time showed such a melancholy contrast between past splendour and present decay as Sardis',[28] and so it needs the Spirit, in all its fulness, to revive it. Hemer finds this unconvincing and is willing to admit that both here and elswhere in Revelation, the imagery most likely derives from Zech. 4.2-10.[29]

There is also something rather strange about Ramsay's explanation of the 'seven stars' here. He has already declared that this attribute is particularly appropriate for Ephesus because it is the leading city. Now it is apparently appropriate for Sardis because it is a city in decay. If this is combined with his comment that the promise to Thyatira (to rule with an iron rod) is apt because it was the 'least fitted by nature and by history' to do so,[30] it is difficult not to agree with J. Ramsay Michaels that 'Ramsay's summary of each city's history is shaped by what he already knows of the prophetic message directed to each congregation'.[31]

---

27. *Revelation*, p. 79 n. 41.
28. *Letters*, p. 375.
29. *Local Setting*, p. 142.
30. *Letters*, p. 333.
31. J. Ramsay Michaels, *Interpreting the Book of Revelation* (Grand Rapids: Baker, 1992), p. 38.

> And to the angel of the church in *Philadelphia* write: These are the words
> of the holy one, the true one, who has the key of David, who opens and no
> one will shut, who shuts and no one opens (Rev. 3.7).

Ramsay suggests that the attributes of holiness and truthfulness are
chosen because the Philadelphians have kept his word (Rev. 3.8) and
that the 'picture of Philadelphia that is given in the letter marks it
beyond all others of the Seven as the holy city'.[32] More substantially,
the image of the 'open door' is explained by the unique evangelistic
opportunity afforded by the geographical location of the city:

> Philadelphia must have been pre-eminent among the Seven Cities as the
> missionary Church. We have no other evidence of this; but the situation
> marks out this line of activity as natural, and the letter clearly declares that
> the Philadelphian church acted accordingly.[33]

As Ramsay admits, we have no evidence for this and many commentators dispute that John is using the 'open door' metaphor in the
same way as Paul (1 Cor. 16.9, 2 Cor. 2.12).[34] More important for
John's use of Scripture is the way that the 'open and shut' clauses are
combined with the phrase 'who has the key of David'. This undoubtedly
points to Isa. 22.22, which reads,

> I will place on his shoulder the key of the house of David; he shall open,
> and no one shall shut; he shall shut, and no one shall open.

Now if John had this text in mind, it not only explains the title to the
letter, it may also explain the promise, which says, 'I will make you a
pillar in the temple of my God' (Rev. 3.12), for Isaiah continues, 'I will
fasten him like a peg in a secure place, and he will become a throne of
honour to his ancestral house' (Isa. 22.23). Hemer suggests that John
has been meditating on a number of 'temple texts' (Isa. 60; Ezek. 48;
Isa. 22) and is creatively applying them to the church.[35] The case that
the 'open door' of evangelism suggested Isa. 22.22, which was then
used to construct the title ('key of David') and transferred to the vision
('I have the keys') seems most unlikely.

---

32. *Letters*, p. 402.

33. *Letters*, p. 406. Tengbom says: 'The church seemingly had a wide open
opportunity for missionary activity and it did not fail in carrying out the Lord's great
commission' (*Studies*, p. 387).

34. G.R. Beasley-Murray, *The Book of Revelation* (NCB; London: Marshall,
Morgan & Scott, rev. edn, 1978), p. 100.

35. *Local Setting*, p. 161.

And to the angel of the church in *Laodicea* write: The words of the Amen,
the faithful and true witness, the origin of God's creation (Rev. 3.14).

Ramsay makes no attempt to link these attributes with Laodicea.
Hemer[36] discusses the possibility that they stem from Isa. 65.16 (NEB:
'The God whose name is Amen') and notes Silberman's suggestion that
they derive from a midrash on Prov. 8.22.[37] However, the most striking
parallel is with Col. 1.15, where Christ is described as the 'firstborn of all
creation' (πρωτότοκος πάσης κτίσεως). Since Col. 4.13-14 shows that
there was a link between Colossae and Laodicea, it may be that the
'Colossian heresy' was also present in Laodicea. However, as Hemer
notes, nothing in the letter suggests that John is addressing such a
position. We are left with the conclusion that on our present knowledge
of Laodicea's history, there is no explanation for the attributes given to
the divine speaker in this letter.

*Summary: The Old Testament in the Seven Letters*
The question being considered is whether priority should be given to the
local situation or the Scripture texts. Ramsay, and to a lesser extent
Hemer, argue that the titles were chosen for their special relevance to
the churches and were then used to construct the inaugural vision (even
though the vision comes first in the book). The analysis presented above
shows that this is extremely unlikely for the following reasons:

1.  It can offer no explanation for the titles to the church at
    Laodicea.
2.  It fails to explain why such contrasting cities as Ephesus and
    Sardis share the same title (possession of the seven spirits).
3.  The use of 'sword' in the inaugural vision (Rev. 1) and Christ's
    parousia (Rev. 19) gives it an importance that makes it unlikely
    that it originated as a local allusion. Further, in both cases, it is
    part of a mosaic of Scripture references, which adds to the
    evidence that it is itself an allusion to Scripture (Isa. 11.4, 49.2).
4.  The 'open door' metaphor is hardly sufficient to have sug-
    gested Isa. 22.22 and then to have led on to the use of 'key of
    David' in the title and 'keys of Death and Hades' in the vision.
    It is much more likely that Isa. 22.22 came first.

36. *Local Setting*, p. 184-85.
37. L.H. Silberman, 'Farewell to "O AMHN". A Note on Rev. 3,14', *JBL* 82
(1963), pp. 213-15.

5.  Smyrna's history is insufficient to explain the deliberate linking of a title for God ('first and the last') and testimony to Christ's death and resurrection ('I was dead, and see, I am alive forever and ever'). I will show, in due course, that such juxtapositions are one of John's significant uses of Scripture.

6.  The suggestion that χαλκολίβανος is a product of Thyatira's metal industry remains a speculation. The first attestation of the word in Greek literature is here and it may be that John coined it himself.

7.  It is based on the assumption that local allusions are more important than John's use of the Old Testament. Yet in order to move from local allusions to the description in Rev. 1, the hypothesis has to assume that these local allusions immediately generated Scripture texts (Dan. 10.5-6; Isa. 22.22; Isa. 11.4/ 49.2) which were then combined with other Scripture texts (both in the inaugural vision and the parousia vision), which appears artificial. This does not prove that John began with the Scripture texts, but it shows that they were much more important to John than Ramsay (and to some extent Hemer) are willing to acknowledge.

All this casts casts doubt on the statement by Lindars that the Old Testament always acts as servant and never as master or guide. The use of the same images and attributes in the inaugural vision and the seven messages allowed a unique opportunity to test this thesis and it has proved inadequate. Very little can be said for deriving the attributes from the local situations. Far more probable is that John composed the vision narrative using a mosaic of Scripture texts and then applied what was relevant to the various churches. This does not mean that John's choice of Scriptures was not influenced by the overall purposes of the book—that still has to be investigated. But with respect to local allusions in the seven messages, it is more natural to see John applying already chosen Scripture to the local situations than the local situations suggesting the Scripture texts. In the next chapter, I will consider this question on a larger scale: Was John's use of the book of Daniel like a lens to view the present crisis or did the present crisis lead him to particular parts of Daniel? Before that, having concluded that the inaugural vision is a mosaic of Scripture texts, I will end this chapter by considering its composition in more detail.

### The Old Testament in the Inaugural Vision

| Rev 1.13-16 | Dan. 10.5-6 |
|---|---|
| and in the midst of the lampstands *I saw* one like the Son of *Man*, *clothed with a long robe* and with a *golden sash* across his chest. His head and his hair were white as white wool, white as snow; *his eyes were like a flame of fire, his feet were like burnished bronze*, refined as in a furnace, *and his voice was like the sound* of many waters. In his right hand he held seven stars, and from his mouth came a sharp, two-edged sword, and *his face* was like the sun shining with full force. | *I looked* up and *saw a man clothed in linen*, with a *belt of gold* from Uphaz around his waist. His body was like beryl, *his face* like lightning, *his eyes like flaming* torches, his arms and *legs like* the gleam of *burnished bronze*, *and the sound of his words like* the roar of a multitude. |

Though a variety of texts have been used to construct the inaugural vision, Dan. 10.5-6 stands out as particularly important. With the exception of the face, which comes last in John's vision, both descriptions follow the same order. First is the clothing, which is divided into a linen or ordinary garment, followed by a belt of gold. John then gives a description of his hair, while Daniel describes his body. They both then describe the flaming eyes, followed by the legs like bronze (Daniel includes 'arms'). Then comes a description of his powerful voice, though they use different similes (φωνὴ ὑδάτων πολλῶν in Revelation, φωνὴ ὄχλου in Daniel; cf. Rev. 19.6). Swete[38] believes that John's sojourn on Patmos made the 'waters' metaphor more appropriate than the sound of a multitude but it should be noted that John does tie the sound of a 'multitude' to the sound of 'many waters' later in the book (19.6). The case for dependence on Daniel is increased by the similarity between their responses to the vision:

> When I saw him, I fell at his feet as though *dead*. But he *placed his right hand on me*, saying, *'Do not be afraid...'* (Rev. 1.17).

38. H.B. Swete, *The Apocalypse of St John* (London: Macmillan, 3rd edn, 1911), p. 18.

*and when I heard* the sound of his words, *I fell* into a trance, face to the ground. But then a *hand touched me* and roused me to my hands and knees...He said to me, '*Do not fear*, Daniel...' (Dan. 10.9-12).

Having established the general similarity between the visions, the differences must now be considered. These can be grouped into the following categories:

1. *Further Old Testament Allusions*
Then the man *clothed in linen* (ποδήρης), with the writing case at his side (Ezek. 9.11).

and an Ancient One took his throne, his clothing was *white as snow*, and the *hair of his head like pure wool* (Dan. 7.9).

When they moved, I heard the sound of their wings like the *sound of mighty waters*, like the thunder of the Almighty...(Ezek. 1.24).

And there, the glory of the God of Israel was coming from the east; the *sound was like the sound of mighty waters* (Ezek. 43.2).

he shall strike the earth with the *rod of his mouth* (Isa. 11.4b).
He made my mouth *like a sharp sword* (Isa. 49.2).

'So perish all your enemies, O Lord! But may your friends be *like the sun* as it rises *in its might*' (Judg. 5.31).[39]

2. *Other Additions*
'refined as in a furnace'
'in his right hand he held seven stars'

3. *Omissions*
'Uphaz'.
'His body was like beryl'
'arms'.

4. *Changes*
'*round his breast*'/ 'loins'
'χαλκολίβανος'

1. *Further Old Testament Allusions*
One of the strongest arguments against Ramsay's theory is that it is clear that the vision of Rev. 1.12-20 is a cluster of Scripture references.

---

39. This is the least probable of the allusions. It is based on the Greek of the B text of Judg. 5.31, which reads: ὡς ἔξοδος ἡλίου ἐν δυνάμει αὐτοῦ. John writes, ὡς ὁ ἥλιος φαίνει ἐν τῇ δυνάμει αὐτοῦ. The parallel is listed in the margin of NA[26].

Thus, whatever the starting point, whether the vision of Dan. 10.5-6 or a set of local references, John's method was to weave them into a mosaic of Scripture. Hanson says that 'his use of scripture here is very subtle: the various attributes, words and actions of the risen Christ are drawn from descriptions of angels, from the mysterious "son of man" figure in Daniel 7, and from descriptions of God himself'.[40] John supplements the vision of Dan. 10.5-6 by locating it in the midst of the lampstands (Zech. 4), adding descriptions of his head/hair (Dan. 7) and mouth (Isa. 11, 49), and using other texts to describe his face (Judg. 5) and voice (Ezek. 1). It is like a musician who sets off various instruments in order to produce a full sound. Caird says:

> He constantly echoes the Old Testament writings (without ever actually quoting them), partly because this was the language which came most naturally to him, partly because of the powerful emotive effect of familiar associations, and partly no doubt because his vision had actually taken its form, though not its content, from the permanent furniture of his well-stocked mind.[41]

Caird offers three reasons here for John's extensive use of the Old Testament. First, it is the language that came most naturally to him. Years of listening to the Scriptures read in the synagogue, along with his own study and meditation, gave him a language to express and perhaps interpret his own visionary experience. Secondly, Caird suggests that John uses Scripture for its emotive effect. On the inaugural vision, he declares that this

> is not photographic art. His aim is to set the echoes of memory and association ringing. The humbling sense of the sublime and the majestic which men experience at the sight of a roaring cataract or the midday **sun** is the nearest equivalent to the awe evoked by a vision of the divine.[42]

40. A.T. Hanson, *The Living Utterance of God* (London: Darton, Longman & Todd, 1983), p. 168. He counts 14 allusions in 7 verses and says that there is hardly a New Testament passage to match it. The combination of divine and angelic descriptions might be seen as a difficulty but M.E. Boring says, 'Since John is not thinking metaphysically, this combining of angel-language and God-language in his portrayal of Jesus is not problematical: both serve to express the transcendent glory of the exalted Christ' (*Revelation* [Interpretation: A Bible Commentary for Teaching and Preaching; Louisville: John Knox Press, 1989], p. 83).

41. *Revelation*, p. 74.

42. *Revelation*, pp. 25-26.

For this reason, Caird believes it is unnecessary to compile a list of Old Testament allusions for this would be to 'unweave the rainbow'.[43] This is correct in the sense that the whole is greater than the parts, but appreciation of the vision can only take place if the reader is familiar with the parts. Otherwise the 'echoes of memory and association' are not set ringing.

Thirdly, Caird suggests that the vision had 'actually taken its form... from the permanent furniture of his well-stocked mind'. The suggestion is that visionary experience is not 'wholly out there' but must have points of contact with the visionary's personality. A modern parallel might be the utterances which take place in a Pentecostal church, which are often delivered in the phraseology of the King James Bible. This could be taken as evidence that the utterances are not from God but minds that have been influenced by the text of this great Bible. However, there is no need to insist that these are mutually exclusive explanations. To examine John's literary artistry with the Old Testament does not deny that visionary experience (as he himself claims) is also involved.[44] As Farrer says, 'Revelation reads like a fresh and continuous scriptural meditation, conceived in the very words in which it is written down'.[45]

Caird qualifies his third suggestion by saying that it was the form, rather than the content, which owes so much to the Old Testament. The reason for this seems to be to safeguard the genuinely Christian nature of the book. The Old Testament may have given John a language to express himself but it could not have told him about the death and resurrection of Christ. Fiorenza has a similar concern:

> (John) does not interpret the Old Testament but uses its words, images, phrases, and patterns as a language arsenal in order to make his own theological statement or express his own prophetic vision. He adapts or borrows whole Old Testament sequences as patterns for his original compositions but never refers to the Old Testament as authoritative Scripture.[46]

43. *Revelation*, p. 25.
44. See R. Bauckham, *The Climax of Prophecy: Studies on the Book of Revelation* (Edinburgh: T. & T. Clark, 1993), ch. 1; D.E. Aune, *Prophecy in Early Christianity and the Ancient Mediterranean Word* (Grand Rapids: Eerdmans, 1983); L. Hartman, *Prophecy Interpreted* (ConBNT Series 1; Lund: CWK Gleerup, 1966).
45. *Revelation*, p. 24.
46. E.S. Fiorenza, 'Apokalypsis and Propheteia', in *The Book of Revelation: Justice and Judgment* (Philadelphia: Fortress Press, 1985), p. 135.

The implications of this 'qualification' will be discussed at a later stage. At present, it is enough to point out that both of these scholars acknowledge John's indebtedness to the 'words, images, phrases, and patterns' of the Old Testament. A further point is that most of these 'echoes' reappear later in the book. Thus the Son of Man coming on the clouds appears again in Rev. 14.4; the seven lamps in Revelation 4; the sharp sword in Rev. 19.5. As J.W. Mealy says, 'Revelation consists of a system of references that progressively build up hermeneutical precedents in the text, precedents that precondition the meaning of each new passage in highly significant ways'.[47]

## 2. *Other Additions*

As well as augmenting Daniel's vision with Old Testament allusions, John makes two other additions. The first is his description that the feet were like burnished bronze, 'refined as in a furnace' (ὡς ἐν καμίνῳ πεπυρωμένης).[48] There are several explanations for this. Sweet[49] thinks that it is an allusion to the 'fiery furnace' of Dan. 3.4-6:

> You are commanded, O peoples, nations, and languages, that when you hear the sound of the horn…you are to fall down and worship the golden statue that King Nebuchadnezzar has set up. Whoever does not fall down and worship shall immediately be thrown into a furnace of blazing fire (Theodotion: κάμινον τοῦ πυρὸς τὴν καιομένην)

In support of this is the following. First, the 'ten days' of Rev. 2.10 might be an allusion to Daniel's time of testing (so Ford). Secondly, John is almost certainly alluding to this same verse in Rev. 13.15, where the beast gives power to 'cause those who would not worship the image of the beast to be killed'. Thirdly, the expression 'peoples, nations, and languages' is used frequently in Revelation (5.9; 7.9; 11.9; 13.7; 14.6), though always with a fourth term and never in the same order. Thus it is possible that John is setting the scene of his book by alluding to the fiery furnace of Daniel.

Another possibility is that John wishes to allude to the smelting

---

47. *After the Thousand Years: Resurrection and Judgment in Revelation 20* (JSNTSup 70; Sheffield: JSOT Press, 1992), p. 13.

48. This is the reading of AC and printed by NA[26]. It is one of a number of solecisms where concord between noun and adjective or noun and participle has been neglected (Charles, *Revelation*, I pp. cliii-cliv, lists 20 examples). The variant readings appear to be attempts to correct this (ἐκ καμίνου, πεπυρωμένῳ, πεπυρωμένοι).

49. *Revelation*, p. 72. Also Beale, *Use of Daniel*, p. 161.

industry of Thyatira. The inclusion of χαλκολίβανος and the explicit
mention of ἐν καμίνῳ could mutually support one another. On the
other hand, if there is a link with one of the letters, the letter to Laodicea
is the most likely candidate, with its exhortation (Rev. 3.18) to buy 'gold
refined by fire' (χρυσίον πεπυρωμένον ἐκ πυρὸς). More generally, it
could be that John simply uses 'smelting' imagery in order to heighten
the impact of the words.[50] Thus in Rev. 9.17, the riders of the horses
'wore breastplates the colour of fire' and the angel of Rev. 10.1 has
'legs like pillars of fire'.

The second addition ('in his right hand he held seven stars')
undoubtedly makes way for the seven messages, since 'the mystery of
the seven stars that you saw in my right hand...are the angels of the
seven churches' (Rev. 1.20). There is no consensus as to the origin of
the image. Charles[51] cites Bousset's suggestion that they make up the
constellation of the Bear but then insists that John would have written
τοὺ ἑπτὰ ἀστέρας (*the* seven stars) if he had had this or any other
specific reference in mind. For Charles, there are seven stars simply
because he wants to write to seven churches, a plan inspired by the
sacredness of the number 'seven'. Caird suggests the image derives
from the seven-branched lampstand in Zechariah's vision:

> Once again John is asserting that the church is the new Israel, the true
> people of God, but with this difference: whereas Israel was represented by
> a single candelabra [sic]with seven lamps, the churches are represented by
> seven separate standing lamps; for according to the teaching of the New
> Testament each local congregation of Christians is the church universal in
> all its fulness.[52]

However, he goes on to say that the '**stars** which symbolize **the angels**
are no doubt also the seven planets, pictured as a necklace of glittering
jewels hanging from the hand of the Son of Man'.[53]

---

50. G.R. Driver suggests that the 'smelting imagery' in Ezek. 1 (and subsequently
in Daniel) derives from the exiles' experience of smelting furnaces in Babylon
('Ezekiel's Inaugural Vision', *VT* 1 [1951], pp. 60-62). Consequently, it could be
argued that 'smelting imagery' is part and parcel of such visions and need have no
link with a particular furnace in a particular place.
51. *Revelation*, I, p. 30. Mounce says, 'The number of stars is determined quite
simply by the number of churches to which the Apocalypse is addressed. There is no
need to search for a mythological or astrological background' (*Revelation*, p. 79).
52. *Revelation*, p. 24.
53. *Revelation*, p. 25. Sweet, *Revelation*, p. 71, says, 'The seven planets were a
symbol of heavenly dominion, and *in his right hand he held seven stars* would be

## 3. *Omissions*

Though John expands Daniel's vision to include mention of his head and hair, mouth and face, and the possession of the seven stars in his right hand, he omits the references to his body and arms. The lack of reference to the arms is perhaps understandable in that John wishes to give a specific reference to the right hand, but it is unclear why he omitted mention of the figure's body. It is possible that he took the reference כתרשׁישׁ (NRSV 'beryl') to be a reference to the place of origin (Tarshish) and omitted it for the same reason that he omitted 'Ophaz'. On the other hand, this does not explain why he did not replace it with some other reference. In the light of the change from 'loins' to 'breast' (see below), perhaps he avoided reference to the trunk of the body for reasons of delicacy.

## 4. *Changes*

The change to χαλκολίβανος has already been discussed. As to the golden belt, some scholars think its position is of some significance. Mounce notes that six out of the seven occurrences of ποδήρης in the LXX are associated with the attire of the high priest and that this, 'plus the fact that high girding ("at the breasts") denotes the dignity of an important office, suggests that this part of the description as well is intended to set forth the high-priestly function of Christ'.[54]

### Conclusion

The view that the inaugural vision is a scriptural composition is accepted by most commentators. Similarities with Dan. 10.5-6 suggest that this was the base text or *Vorbild* but the additions and changes show that John was not interested in simply copying Daniel. Rather, by the use of particular words and phrases, it appears that John was intending to create a whole host of inviting connections. It is not impossible that some of the changes (such as χαλκολίβανος) might have been inspired by the desire to make a local allusion, but the weight of evidence suggests that overall priority should be given to the Scripture

read both as a contemptuous dismissal of imperial pretensions, and as a bold assertion of the cosmic significance of the congregations of humble and persecuted people
whom the seven stars represent'.

54. *Revelation*, p. 78. Charles, *Revelation*, I, p. 28, quotes Josephus, *Ant.* 3.7.2:
ποδήρης χιτὼν...ὃν ἐπιζώννυνται κατὰ στῆθος ὀλίγον τῆς μασχάλης
ὑπεράνω τὴν ζώνην περιάγοντες.

texts.[55] As Caird says, John's purpose was to 'set the echoes of memory and association ringing', particularly within the rich storehouse of themes in the prophetic literature. Echoes heard by the majority of commentators are:

| | | |
|---|---|---|
| καὶ ἐν μέσῳ τῶν **λυχνιῶν** | Zech. 4.2 | (ἑπτὰ **λύχνοι**) |
| ὅμοιον **υἱὸν ἀνθρώπου** | Dan 7.13 | (ὡς **υἱὸς ἀνθρώπου**) |
| **ἐνδεδυμένον ποδήρη** καὶ | Ezek. 9.11 | (**ἐνδεδυκὼς** τὸν **ποδήρη**) |
| **περιεζωσμένον** πρὸς τοῖς | Dan. 10.5 | (**περιεζωσμένη**) |
| μαστοῖς **ζώνην χρυσᾶν.** | Dan. 10.5 | (ἐν **χρυσίῳ**) |
| ἡ δὲ **κεφαλὴ αὐτοῦ** καὶ | Dan 7.9 | (θρὶξ τῆς **κεφαλῆς αὐτοῦ**) |
| αἱ **τρίχες λευκαὶ** ὡς **ἔριον** | Dan. 7.9b | (**ὡσεὶ ἔριον** καθαρόν) |
| **λευκὸν** ὡς **χιὼν** καὶ | Dan 7.9a | (**ὡσεὶ χιὼν λευκόν**) |
| οἱ ὀφθαλμοὶ αὐτοῦ ὡς φλὸξ **πυρὸς** | Dan 10.6 | (λαμπάδες **πυρός**) |
| καὶ οἱ **πόδες** αὐτοῦ ὅμοιοι | Dan. 10.6 | (**καὶ οἱ πόδες**—LXX) |
| **χαλκολιβάνῳ** | Dan. 10.6 | (**χαλκοῦ** στίλβοντος) |
| ὡς ἐν καμίνῳ πεπυρωμένης | Dan. 3.6 | (**κάμινον** τοῦ **πυρός**) |
| καὶ ἡ **φωνὴ** αὐτοῦ | Dan. 10.6 | (**καὶ ἡ φωνή**) |
| ὡς **φωνὴ ὑδάτων** πολλῶν, | Ezek.1.24 | (**ὡς φωνὴν ὕδατος πολλοῦ**) |
| | | |
| καὶ ἔχων ἐν τῇ δεξιᾷ χειρὶ αὐτοῦ | ? | |
| ἀστέρας ἑπτὰ | ? | |
| καὶ ἐκ τοῦ **στόματος** αὐτοῦ | Isa. 49.2 | (**στόμα** μου ὡσεί) |
| ῥομφαία δίστομος **ὀξεῖα** | | |
| ἐκπορευομένη | Isa. 49.2 | (μάχαιραν **ὀξεῖαν**) |
| καὶ ἡ ὄψις αὐτοῦ **ὡς ὁ ἥλιος** | Judg. 5.31 | (**ὡς ἔξοδος ἡλίου**—B) |
| **φαίνει ἐν τῇ δυνάμει αὐτοῦ** | Judg. 5.31 | (**ἐν δυνάμει αὐτοῦ**) |

55. For a recent attemot to argue for local references, see C.H.H. Scobie, 'Local References in the Letters to the Seven Churches', *NTS* 39 (1993), pp. 606-24.

## Chapter 3

## JOHN'S USE OF DANIEL

According to Charles,[1] John alludes to twenty-seven different verses in Daniel and these are drawn from eight of its twelve chapters. The distribution is as follows:

| | |
|---|---|
| Dan. 2 (4) | Dan. 7 (11) |
| Dan. 3 (1) | Dan. 8 (1) |
| Dan. 4 (2) | Dan. 10 (3) |
| Dan. 5 (1) | Dan. 12 (4) |

It can be seen from this that by far the most allusions come from Daniel 7, a chapter quoted elsewhere in the New Testament.[2] With the exception of Dan. 5.23 and 8.10, the remaining verses are either related to the Nebuchadnezzar material (Dan. 2–4) or the description and words of the interpreting angel (Dan. 10, 12). John's use of Daniel will therefore be considered under four headings:

1. Nebuchadnezzar material (2.28, 29, 35, 45; 3.6; 4.30, 34).

2. The vision of the 'beasts' and the 'one like a human being' (7.3, 6, 7, 8, 9, 10, 13, 21, 22, 25, 26).

3. The interpreting Angel (10.5, 6, 9; 12.1, 4, 7, 9).

4. Daniel 5.23 and 8.10.

---

1. *Revelation*, I, pp. lxviii-lxxxi. Ozanne adds 3.4, 7, 29; 7.2, 20; 8.2; 9.21 (*Influence*, pp. 66-81).
2. *UBSGNT* lists Mt. 24.30; 26.64; Mk 13.26; 14.62; Lk. 21.27 as quotations and Mt. 19.28; 28.18; Lk. 1.33; 21.8; Jn 12.34; 1 Cor. 6.2 as allusions.

*John's Use of the Nebuchadnezzar Material (Daniel 2–4)*

In the second chapter of Daniel, the author tells how Nebuchadnezzar, king of Babylon, had a distressing dream which none of his magicians or wise men could interpret. The dream consisted of a great statue:

> The head of that statue was of fine gold, its chest and arms of silver, its middle and thighs of bronze, its legs of iron, its feet partly of iron and partly of clay (Dan. 2.32-33).

The dream continues by telling how the feet of iron and clay were broken to pieces by an uncut stone, followed by the bronze, silver and gold parts, so that not a trace of them could be found. Finally, the stone which struck the image became 'a great mountain and filled the whole earth'. The king was greatly troubled and summoned his magicians and wise men to tell him not only the interpretation but also the dream itself. When this proved impossible, the king gave orders that they should all be slain, including Daniel and his friends. In order to avert this crisis, Daniel requests an audience with the king and claims that he is able to give the interpretation. This is granted, and at the appointed time Daniel says to the king:

> No wise men, enchanters, magicians, or diviners can show to the king the mystery that the king is asking, but there is a God in heaven (θεὸς ἐν οὐρανῷ) who reveals (ἀποκαλύπτων) mysteries (μυστήρια), and he has disclosed to King Nebuchadnezzar what will happen at the end of days (ἃ δεῖ γενέσθαι ἐπ' ἐσχάτων τῶν ἡμερῶν)... (2.27-28).

The book of Revelation is also concerned with the revelation of mysteries. It opens with the words:

> The revelation (ἀποκάλυψις) of Jesus Christ, which God gave him to show his servants what must soon take place (ἃ δεῖ γενέσθαι ἐν τάχει) (Rev. 1.1).

The use of both ἀποκάλυψις[3] and ἃ δεῖ γενέσθαι suggests a conscious allusion to Daniel, especially as the explanation given in Rev. 1.20 involves the disclosure of a μυστήριον:

> As for the mystery (μυστήριον) of the seven stars that you saw in my right hand...the seven stars are the angels of the seven churches, and the seven lampstands are the seven churches.

3.   Charles says, 'In Theodotion's rendering of Daniel the verb ἀποκαλύπτειν is used exactly in the sense of the noun ἀποκάλυψις in the title (of John's book)' (*Revelation*, I, p. 5).

That being so, it is of note that John does not follow either the ἐπ' ἐσχάτων τῶν ἡμερῶν of Dan. 2.28 or the μετὰ ταῦτα of 2.45. Instead, he uses the expression ἐν τάχει, from which Ford deduces that the 'crisis appears more urgent in Revelation than in earlier apocalyptic literature'.[4] Beale is more specific:

> what Daniel expected to occur in the distant future—the defeat of cosmic evil and ushering in of the kingdom—John expects to begin in his own generation, and perhaps has already been inaugurated.[5]

The importance of the phrase ἃ δεῖ γενέσθαι, with John's addition of ἐν τάχει, is further emphasized by its repetition at the end of the book:

> These words are trustworthy and true, for the Lord, the God of the spirits of the prophets, has sent his angel to show his servants what must soon take place (ἃ δεῖ γενέσθαι ἐν τάχει)...' (Rev. 22.6).

Thus the book of Revelation begins and ends with a modified allusion[6] to Daniel 2. In between these two references, there are two other places where John alludes to this important phrase. In Rev. 4.1, John is invited to 'Come up here, and I will show you what must take place after this' (ἃ δεῖ γενέσθαι μετὰ ταῦτα). This form agrees exactly with the wording of Dan. 2.45 (Theodotion). The other reference is Rev. 1.19, where John is told to 'write what you have seen, what is, and what is to take place after this'. The Greek is slightly different here (ἃ μέλλει γενέσθαι) and may reflect the diction of Isa. 48.6.[7] Thus not only does the phrase occur at the beginning and end of John's book, it also occurs at important transitions in the text and can be used to divide the book into four sections:[8]

1. Introduction and inaugural vision     (1.1-18)
2. The seven messages to the churches     (1.19–3.22)
3. Apocalyptic visions     (4.1–22.5)
4. Conclusion     (22.6-21)

---

4. J.M. Ford, *Revelation* (AB 38; Garden City: Doubleday, 1975), p. 373.

5. 'Revelation', *Scripture Citing Scripture*, p. 329.

6. Trudinger believes that the expression, even though it only consists of three words, is sufficiently distinctive to be called a quotation. On his analysis, Revelation contains 9 quotations from the book of Daniel, along with 13 allusions (*Text*, p. 42).

7. So J. Moffatt, *Revelation of St John the Divine* (Expositor's Greek Testament 5; London: Hodder & Stoughton, 1910), p. 347; Swete, *Revelation*, p. cxlii.

8. See W.C. van Unnik, 'A Formula Describing Prophecy', *NTS* 9 (1963), pp. 86-94; G.K. Beale, 'The Interpretative Problem of Rev. 1:19', *NovT* 34 (1992), pp. 360-87.

48     *The Old Testament in the Book of Revelation*

In Rev. 20.11, a vision of the great white throne and him who sit
s on it is followed by the statement that 'the earth and the heaven fled
from his presence, and no place was found for them' (καὶ τόπος οὐχ
εὑρέθη αὐτοῖς). These exact words are found in Theodotion's
translation of Dan. 2.35:[9]

> Then the iron, the clay, the bronze, the silver, and the gold, were all broken
> in pieces and became like the chaff of the summer threshing floors; and the
> wind carried them away, so that not a trace of them could be found (καὶ
> τόπος οὐχ εὑρέθη αὐτοῖς).

Another significant use of the Nebuchadnezzar stories comes in Rev.
13.15, where anyone who will not bow down and worship the image of
the beast is to be slain. This is the same sort of threat that the 'peoples,
nations and languages' faced in Daniel 3 and that Daniel's three friends
resisted and emerged victorious:

> when you hear the sound of the horn, pipe, lyre...you are to fall down and
> worship the golden statue that King Nebuchadnezzar has set up. Whoever
> does not fall down and worship shall immediately be thrown into a furnace
> of blazing fire (Dan. 3.5-6).

Opinions differ, however, as to its implications for the setting of
John's book. Charles[10] cites Pliny's letter to Trajan (10.96) to the effect
that shortly after John's time, failure to worship the Emperor's image
was a capital offense. Indeed, according to Eusebius,

> Many were the victims of Domitian's appalling cruelty. At Rome great
> numbers of men distinguished by birth and attainments were for no reason
> at all banished from the country and their property confiscated. Finally, he
> showed himself the successor of Nero in enmity and hostility to God
> (*Eccl. Hist.* 3.17, trans. G.A. Williamson).

9.    A similar phrase occurs in Rev. 12.8 (οὐδὲ τόπος εὑρέθη αὐτῶν) referring
to the dragon and his angels. Charles notes the allusion to Dan. 2.35 but offers no
comment. It is mentioned in NA[26] but not *UBSGNT*. Ozanne recognizes it but his
comments are aimed at discounting it as evidence for John's use of a Greek text:
'The variation between αὐτοῖς and αὐτῶν in Rev. 12.8 (though not in 20.11)
indicates that no direct reference was made to Theod' (*Influence*, p. 77). Such is his
determination to show that John only used Semitic sources.
10.    *Revelation*, I, p. 361. For a different conclusion, see F.G. Downing, 'Pliny's
Prosecutions of Christians: Revelation and 1 Peter', *JSNT* 34 (1988), pp. 105-23.

Indeed, so brightly shone at that time the teaching of our faith that even historians who accepted none of our beliefs unhesitatingly recorded in their pages both the persecution and the martyrdoms to which it led (*Eccl. Hist.* 3.18).

The same emperor ordered the execution of all who were of David's line, and there is an old and firm tradition that a group of heretics accused the descendents of Jude—the brother, humanly speaking, of the Saviour—on the ground that they were of David's line and related to Christ Himself (*Eccl. Hist.* 3.19).

That John wrote at a time of extreme persecution has been repeated in countless commentaries but an increasing number of scholars have doubted whether this is correct. Even in Eusebius, there are signs that it might be exaggerated. Thus Tertullian is quoted as saying that Domitian 'almost equalled Nero in cruelty' but then goes on to add, 'but—I suppose because he had some common sense—he very soon stopped, even recalling those he had banished'.

In the story about the descendents of Jude, far from being executed as relations of Jesus, Eusebius records that 'Domitian found no fault with them, but despising them as beneath his notice let them go free and issued orders terminating the persecution of the Church' (*Eccl. Hist.* 3.20). Thus the evidence of Eusebius is deeply ambiguous. The rest of the evidence comes chiefly from Tacitus, Suetonius and Dio Cassius but according to Krodel, 'they had an ax to grind and they ground it with vengeance after Domitian's death. As persons of senatorial or equestrian rank whose influence Domitian had diminished in the interest of the empire, they lost no time maligning him in every conceivable way once he was dead.'[11]

A close reading of Revelation also casts doubt on a background of intense persecution. Indeed, according to the letters, only one person is specifically mentioned as having lost his life (Rev. 2.13: Antipas), and the problem in many of the churches is laxity and lukewarmness. This has led A.Y. Collins to adopt the phrase 'perceived persecution'. She points

11. *Revelation*, pp. 36-37. He goes on to state that even Domitian's detractors had to admit that he had his good points. Thus Suetonius (Domitian 8.2) admits that he was actually a competent and social-minded administrator. L.L. Thompson says, 'Domitian was no more and no less insistent on divine prerogatives than other emperors and, so far as one can tell, he did not change in any fundamental way the social expressions of imperial religion' (*The Book of Revelation: Apocalypse and Empire* [Oxford: Oxford University Press, 1990], p. 159).

out that a person's response to persecution is not necessarily an accurate guide to its actual intensity. Thus Revelation 'was indeed written in response to a crisis, but one that resulted from the clash between the expectations of John and like-minded Christians and the social reality within which they had to live'.[12] She agrees that a 'crisis' prompted the writing of the book but not one that was obvious from external conditions. It was only evident through the author's angle of vision and the purpose of Revelation is to share that angle of vision with his readers:

> The book of Revelation is not simply a product of a certain social situation, not even a simple response to circumstances. At root is a particular religious view of reality, inherited in large part, which is the framework within which John interpreted his environment.[13]

Before leaving John's use of the Nebuchadnezzar material, there are two further allusions noted by Charles. The first is the phrase 'Babylon the great' (Βαβυλὼν ἡ μεγάλη) in Rev. 14.8:

> Then another angel, a second, followed, saying, 'Fallen, fallen is Babylon the great! (Βαβυλὼν ἡ μεγάλη)... (Rev. 14.8).

> Is this not magnificent Babylon (Βαβυλὼν ἡ μεγάλη), which I have built as a royal capital by my mighty power and for my glorious majesty? (Dan. 4.30).

In this same episode (4.34), Nebuchadnezzar confesses, 'I blessed the Most High, and praised and honoured the one who lives forever' (Theodotion: τῷ ζῶντι εἰς τὸν αἰῶνα). Charles[14] lists this as the source of Rev. 1.18 (ζῶν εἰμι εἰς τοὺς αἰῶνας τῶν αἰώνων), though John is clearly referring to the resurrection of Christ. It may be that he has borrowed the phraseology of Daniel to express this.

---

12. A.Y. Collins, *Crisis and Catharsis: The Power of the Apocalypse* (Philadelphia: Westminster Press, 1984), p. 165. See also A.Y. Collins, 'Vilification and Self-Definition in the Book of Revelation', *HTR* 79 (1986), pp. 308-20.

13. *Crisis and Catharsis*, pp. 106-107. This is similar to the words already quoted on pp. 12-13 by Borgen: 'Since the Old Testament was the thought-world in which Jesus, the disciples and the other first Christians lived, and since the Old Testament was woven into the very fabric of Jewish institutions and Jewish ways of life, it therefore determined the theological issues raised to a large extent, either negatively or positively'.

14. *Revelation*, I, p. 32.

## John's Use of Daniel 7

According to the lists in Charles, John's use of Daniel 7 occurs mainly in Revelation 1, 11, 13 and 20. For Revelation 1, I showed in the previous chapter how John combines phrases from Daniel 7 with Daniel 10 and other scriptures to produce his composite description of the 'one like the Son of Man'. Before that, he combines an allusion to Dan. 7.13 with Zech. 12.10, 12, a combination also found in Mt. 24.30:

> Look! He is coming with (μετά) the clouds; every eye will see him, even those who pierced him; and on his account all the tribes of the earth (πᾶσαι αἱ φυλαὶ τῆς γῆς) will wail (κόψονται) (Rev. 1.7).

> Then the sign of the Son of Man will appear in heaven, and then all the tribes of the earth (πᾶσαι αἱ φυλαὶ τῆς τῆς) will mourn (κόψονται), and they will see 'the Son of Man coming on (ἐπί) the clouds of heaven' with power and great glory (Mt. 24.30).

The use of the phrase πᾶσαι αἱ φυλαὶ τῆς γῆς by both John and Matthew (LXX: ἡ γῆ κατὰ φυλὰς φυλάς) points to a literary connection between them and Swete believes that they both go back to a testimony source.[15] Charles, on the other hand, thinks that John is dependent on Matthew for the combination but has rendered the Old Testament texts for himself, stating that John 'keeps more closely to Daniel and Zechariah and reproduces their text more fully'.[16]

Moving on to Revelation 11, Charles finds three allusions to Daniel 7. The first is in v. 2, where the time reference for the trampling of the city is given as forty-two months (Dan. 7.25). The second and third are both found in v. 7, where the beast is introduced:

> When they have finished their testimony, the beast that comes up (ἀναβαῖνον) from the bottomless pit (ἀβύσσου) will make war on them (ποιήσει μετ' αὐτῶν πόλεμον) and conquer (νικήσει) them and kill them (Rev. 11.7).

> and four great beasts came up (ἀνέβαινον) out of the sea. As I looked, this horn made war (ἐποίει πόλεμον) with the holy ones and was prevailing (ἴσχυσεν) over them (Dan. 7.3, 21).

---

15. *Revelation*, p. 9. Justin speaks of Jesus' second coming ἐπάνω τῶν νεφελῶν, where ὄψεται ὁ λαὸς ὑμῶν καὶ γνωριεῖ εἰς ὅν ἐξεκέντησαν (*Dial. Tryph.* 14.8). See further M. Karrer, *Die Johannesoffenbarung als Brief* (FRLANT 140; Göttingen: Vandenhoeck & Ruprecht, 1986), pp. 121-25.

16. *Revelation*, I, p. 19. Similarly, Ozanne, *Influence*, p. 87.

This use of Daniel 7 is much expanded in Revelation 13, where John describes the persecuting power (Rome) as a beast coming up out of the sea. It has ten horns and seven heads. It is like a leopard but has the feet of a bear and the mouth of a lion. Dominion is given to it and it is allowed to exercise this authority for forty-two months. With its mouth it speaks haughty words (στόμα λαλοῦν μεγάλα), uttering blasphemies against God and making war with the saints (ποιῆσαι πόλεμον μετὰ τῶν ἁγίων). For a time, it even prevails over them. Daniel says:

> and four great *beasts came up out of the sea*...The first was like a *lion* and had eagles' wings...a second one, that looked like a *bear*... another appeared, like a *leopard*...and *dominion was given* to it. After this...a fourth beast...it had *ten horns* (Dan. 7.3-7).

> Then I desired to know the truth...concerning the *ten horns*...and concerning the other horn...that had eyes and a *mouth that spoke arrogantly*...As I looked, this horn *made war with the holy ones* and was *prevailing over them* (Dan. 7.19-21).

> As for the *ten horns*, out of this kingdom ten kings shall arise, and another shall arise after them...*He shall speak words against the Most High*, shall wear out the holy ones...and they shall be given into his power for a time, *two times, and half a time* (Dan. 7.24-25).

Verbal links include the rising from the sea (ἀναβαίνω, θάλασσα), the appearance of the beast(s) (πάρδαλις, ἄρκος, λέων), the ten horns (κέρατα δέκα), the dominion given to it (δίδωμι, ἐξουσία), a mouth speaking haughty words (στόμα λαλοῦν μεγάλα) and its making war with the holy ones (ποιέω, πόλεμος, ἅγιος). Thematic links include the fact that the beast prevails for three and a half years (42 months = time, times and half a time)[17] and that he speaks blasphemies against God. Perhaps of even greater importance is the fact that both Daniel and John

---

17. The Aramaic of Dan. 7.25 uses the dual to speak of 'time, two times, and half a time' (see also Dan. 12.7). In Rev. 11.2, the holy city is trampled for 42 months. In the next verse, the two witnesses are given power to prophesy for 1260 days. In Rev. 12.6, the woman is given safety for 1260 days, which in 12.14 has become 'time, and times, and half a time' (καιρὸν καὶ καιροὺς καὶ ἥμισυ καιροῦ). Charles calls this a mistranslation since the dual is rendered by a simple plural. However, this is also the rendering of Theodotion and LXX, though Charles thinks the expression had become proverbial and is not evidence for John's use of either of these versions (*Revelation*, I, p. 330). Finally, in Rev. 13.5, the beast is given power for 42 months. The duration is clearly meant to link these episodes together, though it is harder to explain the variation in expression (months, days, days, times, months).

use this beast imagery to describe a succession of kings, though John postpones the interpretation until ch. 17:

> And the ten horns that you saw are ten kings who have not yet received a kingdom, but they are to receive authority as kings for one hour...they will make war on the Lamb, and the Lamb will conquer them (Rev. 17.12, 14).

As well as these verbal and thematic links, Beale thinks there are structural parallels also. Thus both the beast from the sea (13.1-10) and the beast from the earth (13.11-18) are introduced in the following manner:

1.    The origin of the beast is described (v. 1a, v. 11a).
2.    Its appearance is described (vv. 1b-2a, v. 11b).
3.    Authority is given to it (v. 2b, v. 12).
4.    It deceives the world into false worship (v. 4, 8, vv. 12b-15).

Beale calls this pattern (presentation, commission, effects) an 'authorization scheme'[18] and believes it is modelled on Dan. 7.13-14:

> I saw one like a human being[2] coming with the clouds of heaven.[1] And he came to the Ancient One and was presented before him. To him was given dominion and glory and kingship,[3] that all peoples, nations, and languages should serve him[4] (Dan. 7.13-14).

Nebuchadnezzar's dream (Dan. 2) was interpreted as standing for a series of kingdoms, usually taken to be those of Babylonia, Media, Persia and Greece, with the latter dividing into the rival Diadochi (Ptolemies and Seleucids). Most commentators accept that Daniel 7 follows a similar scheme,[19] with the four beasts (lion, bear, leopard, fourth with iron teeth, crushing feet and ten horns) also representing successive kingdoms. John's description begins as if he intends to describe Daniel's fourth beast ('I saw a beast rising out of the sea; and on its horns were ten diadems') but then takes features from the other three beasts and in

18.    Beale, *Use of Daniel*, pp. 246ff. This is part of his thesis that certain key chapters of Revelation (1, 4–5, 13, 17) are modelled on Dan. 7, to be discussed later.

19.    J.J. Collins says, 'In view of the sequence of kingdoms presupposed throughout the book, the four kingdoms must be identified as Babylonian, Median, Persian, and Greek' (*Daniel: With an Introduction to Apocalyptic Literature* [FOTL 20; Grand Rapids: Eerdmans, 1984], p. 80. On the other hand, K. Hanhart argues from Rev. 13.2 that they are contemporaneous rather than successive powers: 'The Four Beasts of Daniel's Vision in the Night in the Light of Rev. 13.2', *NTS* 27 (1981), pp. 576-81.

particular, from the little horn that 'made war with the holy ones and was prevailing over them'. As Krodel says,

> John was not interested in portraying the sequence of oppressive empires from the Babylonians to the Hellenistic states, but in evocative images he presented the nature of the empire of the last days in its opposition to God and his people. As the beast, this empire has assumed all the bestial features of the four animals in Daniel.[20]

Finally, Charles believes that the judgment scene of Revelation 20 was influenced by Daniel 7. Parallels include the combination of the many thrones (Rev. 20.4; Dan. 7.9) with the single throne upon which God sits (Rev. 20.11; Dan. 7.9), the opening of books (plural) and the statement that judgment (κρίμα) was given (δίδωμι) to the saints (Rev. 20.4; Dan. 7.22):[21]

> As I watched, thrones were set in place, and an Ancient One took his throne...his throne was fiery flames...The court sat in judgment, and the books were opened...then judgment was given for the holy ones of the Most High, and the time arrived when the holy ones gained possession of the kingdom (Dan. 7.9, 10, 22).

> Then I saw thrones, and those seated on them were given authority to judge...Then I saw a great white throne and the one who sat on it...and books were opened...And the dead were judged according to their works, as recorded in the books (Rev. 20.4, 11, 12).

### John's Use of the Angelic Vision and Interpretation (Daniel 10, 12)

As I demonstrated in the previous chapter, John's inaugural vision is based on Dan. 10.5-6 and supplemented by verses from Isa. 11.4 + 49.2; Ezek. 1.24 + 43.2; Dan. 7.9; Judg. 5.31. His response to the vision is also similar to Daniel's, though slightly less detailed. According to Charles,[22] Daniel's vision of the angel has also affected the description of the seven angels in Rev. 15.6, which are said to be 'robed in pure bright linen, with golden sashes across their chests' (ἐνδεδυμένοι λίνον καθαρὸν

20. *Revelation*, p. 249. A different approach is found in *4 Ezra* 12–13, where the fourth beast is interpreted as the Roman Empire. See R. Bauckham, 'Nero and the Beast', *Climax of Prophecy*, pp. 384-452.

21. See Mealy, *After the Thousand Years*, pp. 102-89; T.F. Glasson, 'The Last Judgment in Rev. 20 and Related Writings', *NTS* 28 (1982), pp. 528-39.

22. *Revelation*, I, p. lxxiii. Some MSS read λίθον, perhaps under the influence of Ezek. 28.13.

λαμπρὸν καὶ περιεζωσμένοι περὶ τὰ στήθη ζώνας χρυσᾶς).

John's use of Daniel 12 can be summarized under three headings. The first is the way that Rev. 10.5-6 is modelled on Dan. 12.7. Charles[23] says that these are the only two places in the Bible where we have this combination of raising the hand and swearing to God:

> The man clothed in linen, who was upstream, raised his right hand and his left hand toward heaven. And I heard him swear by the one who lives forever...(Dan. 12.7).

> Then the angel whom I saw standing on the sea and the land raised his right hand to heaven and swore by him who lives forever and ever (Rev. 10.5-6).

As to the content of what is sworn, the language owes something to Amos 3.7 ('Surely the Lord God does nothing, without revealing his secret to his servants the prophets') but the use of τελέω shows that the Daniel passage is still in mind:

> And I heard him swear by the one who lives forever that it would be for a time, two times, and half a time, and that when the shattering of the power of the holy people comes to an end, all these things would be accomplished (συντελεσθῆναι) (Dan. 12.7b).

> and swore by him who lives forever and ever... 'There will be no more delay, but in the days when the seventh angel is to blow his trumpet, the mystery of God will be fulfilled (ἐτελέσθη), as he announced to his servants the prophets' (Rev. 10.6-7).

The second heading is the notion of sealed and unsealed books. Daniel is told to 'keep the words secret and the book sealed until the time of the end' (12.4). In contrast, John is specifically told,

> Do not seal up the words of the prophecy of this book, for the time is near... (Rev. 22.10).

We have here the same heightening of eschatological expectation as in Rev. 1.1; 22.6, where ἐπ' ἐσχάτων τῶν ἡμερῶν is replaced by ἐν τάχει. Swete[24] comments that the angel's instruction is 'exactly the reverse of that which is given to Daniel', while Charles says, 'As contrasted with Jewish Apocalypses, such as Daniel...1 Enoch... 2 Enoch etc., which were not to be divulged till distant generations, our

23. *Revelation*, I, p. 263.
24. *Revelation*, p. 304.

56     *The Old Testament in the Book of Revelation*

Apocalypse is to be made known by the Seer to his contemporaries'.[25]

Thirdly, John's use of the 'book of life' may owe something to Dan. 12.1, especially in those verses (3.5; 20.15) where he uses the feminine βίβλος. Also in Dan. 12.1 is the statement that there will be a time of anguish 'such as has never occurred since nations first came into existence' (οἵα οὐ γέγονεν ἀφ' οὗ γεγένηται ἔθνος ἐπὶ τῆς γῆς ἕως τοῦ καιροῦ ἐκείνου). Swete[26] cites this as the source of Rev. 16.18, where the earthquake is 'such as had not occurred since people were upon the earth' (οἷος οὐκ ἐγένετο ἀφ'οὗ ἄνθρωπος ἐγένετο ἐπὶ τῆς γῆς).

### John's Use of Daniel 5.23 and 8.10

Dan. 5.23 comes in the 'writing on the wall' incident in the time of Belshazzar. Daniel rebukes the king for using the vessels from the Temple and for praising 'the gods of silver and gold, of bronze, iron, wood, and stone, which do not see or hear or know'. A similar list appears in Rev. 9.20, along with the remark that such things 'cannot see or hear or walk'.

In Dan. 8.10, we read of a little horn which 'grew as high as the host of heaven' and 'threw down to the earth some of the host and some of the stars, and trampled on them'. John does not take up Daniel's 'historical survey' but utilizes the phraseology for the great red dragon's attempted conquest:

> Then another portent appeared in heaven: a great red dragon, with seven heads and ten horns, and seven diadems on his heads. His tail swept down a third of the stars of heaven and threw them to the earth (Rev. 12.3-4).

### Summary

#### 1. *Models of Composition*
John appears to have modelled a number of his vision descriptions on various episodes in Daniel. Our previous chapter showed how the inaugural vision is an expanded version of Dan. 10.5-6. It can now be seen how the 'beast from the sea' in Revelation 13 draws much of its imagery and phrases from the beasts and little horn of Daniel 7. Beale has also drawn attention to the structural parallels between the two chapters. More minor 'models' are:

25. *Revelation*, II, p. 221.
26. *Revelation*, p. cl.

| Rev. 10 | Figure raising hand and swearing | Dan. 12 |
| Rev. 12 | Dragon's revenge | Dan. 8 |
| Rev. 13 | Worship or die | Dan. 3 |
| Rev. 20 | Judgment scene | Dan. 7 |
| Rev. 22 | Command not to seal | Dan. 12 |

## 2. *Use of Imagery and Language*
As well as using parts of Daniel as models of composition, John draws on the language of Daniel to enhance the effect of his composition. The relationship between the two contexts varies. In most cases, some sort of parallel can be detected but the use of Dan. 2.35 in Rev. 20.11 appears to be an exception:

| Rev. 1 | What must soon take place | Dan. 2 |
| Rev. 1 | He who lives for ever | Dan. 4 |
| Rev. 9 | Idols of gold and silver | Dan. 5 |
| Rev. 14 | Babylon the Great | Dan. 4 |
| Rev. 16 | Such as had never been seen since... | Dan. 12 |
| Rev. 20 | No place was found for them | Dan. 2 |

## 3. *Interweaving Texts*
In almost all of the above examples, John's use of Daniel is closely connected with his use of other scriptures. Thus Rev. 1.7 is a composite quotation of Dan. 7.13 and Zech. 12.10, 12. The inaugural vision combines references to Daniel, Ezekiel, Isaiah and Judges. The figure raising his hand and swearing is based on Dan. 12.7 but also draws on Amos 3.7. The judgment scene, like the throne vision in Revelation 4–5, draws on a number of Old Testament passages (Dan. 7; Ezek. 1; Isa. 6) and the epithet 'Babylon the Great' prepares for an extensive use of Ezekiel and Jeremiah in Revelation 17–18. The most exclusive use of Daniel occurs in Revelation 13, where the main source is Daniel 7, though allusions to other texts can still be recognized.[27]

## 4. *Use of Daniel 2.28-29 as Structural Marker*
As well as John's use of the language of Daniel, there is clearly a special use of the phrase ἃ δεῖ γενέσθαι in Rev. 1.1, 19; 4.1; 22.6. These can be used to divide the book into four sections.

---

27. Charles cites Ps. 68.29; Isa. 53.7; Jer. 15.2, *Revelation*, I, pp. lxviii-lxxxi.

## 5. Heightened Eschatological Outlook

In at least two instances, John modifies the language of Daniel in order to heighten the eschatological awareness of his readers. In Rev. 1.1 and 22.6, the phrase ἃ δεῖ γενέθαι is followed immediately by ἐν τάχει and a few verses later by ὁ γὰρ καιρὸς ἐγγύς/ὁ καιρὸς γὰρ ἐγγύς ἐστιν (1.3; 22.10). Second, in distinction from Daniel, who is told to 'keep the words secret and the book sealed until the time of the end' (12.4), John is told not to seal it, 'for the time is near' (ὁ καιρὸς γὰρ ἐγγύς ἐστιν). This heightening of eschatological expectation is of course a commonplace in New Testament writings (Mk 1.15; Rom. 13.11; 1 Cor. 7.29).

These five 'uses' of Daniel suggest a dialectical relationship between the text of Daniel and John's situation, for it would appear that

1. Certain texts like Daniel 7 have affected the way that he perceives the role of the state (cf. Rom. 13 for a different view).
2. Certain texts like Daniel 10 have affected the way that he perceives the person of Christ (even the resurrection appearances are some way off the sort of description found in the inaugural vision).
3. Certain texts like Daniel 2–4 have affected the way that he perceives the situation of his readers/hearers. Whether they were facing an actual persecution or not, it seems clear that John wishes them to see their situation in the light of the life and death struggle of Daniel and his friends.
4. On the other hand, the interweaving of Daniel with other Old Testament texts shows that John has a standpoint which is outside of the book of Daniel. He is not intending to simply reproduce or even update Daniel.
5. The heightened eschatological outlook, as in the rest of the New Testament, is associated with the death and resurrection of Christ. In other words, John's situation has affected how he reads the book of Daniel.
6. John sometimes uses the words of Daniel in quite a different context (e.g. Dan. 2.35; Rev. 20.11) and appears to be minimally influenced by the Danielic context (if at all).
7. John often uses the words of Daniel more than once and in different contexts. This goes against the idea that he is offering a specific interpretation of Daniel.

*Revelation and Daniel according to Gregory Beale*

The scholar who has written the most about John's use of Daniel is Gregory Beale.[28] Beale accepts that John has used Daniel in a variety of ways but thinks that an overall strategy can be discerned. For example, he believes that certain key chapters of Revelation, namely Revelation 1, 4–5, 13 and 17, are a midrash on Daniel 7 and that John's intention is that his readers should see their situation as the fulfilment of the tribulation predicted by Daniel. For Revelation 1, Beale takes a different view of the inaugural vision from the one arrived at in Chapter 2. He claims that it is modelled on Dan. 7.9-10 ('hair of his head like pure wool', 'stream of fire'), which then led to Dan. 10.5-6 by association (the chapters are closely linked) and hence to other scriptures. He describes this process as the operation of a sort of 'hermeneutical magnet', whereby other scriptures are drawn in by catch words or common themes.[29] He supports this view of the inaugural vision by noting that Rev. 1.7 ('Look! He is coming with the clouds') is a clear allusion to Dan. 7.13, while Rev. 1.13 speaks of 'one like the Son of Man'. He closes with a list of parallels between Rev. 1.4-20 and Dan. 7.9–28:[30]

| Revelation | Daniel | Parallel |
|---|---|---|
| 1.4 | 7.9a | God enthroned |
| 1.4 | 7.10b | Heavenly beings around the throne |
| 1.4 | 7.13-14 | Dominion of Christ/Son of man |
| 1.6, 9 | 7.18, 22, 27a | Saints constituted/given a kingdom |
| 1.7a | 7.13 | Son of man coming with the clouds |
| 1.11 | 7.10 | Book associated with judgment |
| 1.12-16 | 7.9-10 | Description of a heavenly figure |
| 1.17a | 7.15 | Seer's reaction |
| 1.17-20 | 7.16ff. | Interpretation of the Vision |

28. His Cambridge dissertation (1980) was subsequently published as *The Use of Daniel in Jewish Apocalyptic Literature and in the Revelation of St John* (Lamham, MD: University Press of America, 1984) and has been followed by a number of articles: 'The Origin of the Title "King of Kings and Lord of Lords" in Revelation 17.14', *NTS* 31 (1985), pp. 618-20; 'A Reconsideration of the Text of Daniel in the Apocalypse', *Bib* 67 (1986), pp. 539-43; 'Revelation', in *It is Written: Scripture Citing Scripture* (FS B. Lindars; ed. D.A. Carson and H.G.M. Williamson; Cambridge: Cambridge University Press, 1988), pp. 318-36; 'The Interpretative Problem of Rev. 1:19', *NovT* 34 (1992), pp. 360-87.

29. *Use of Daniel*, p. 174.

30. *Use of Daniel*, p. 172.

In order to do the same for Revelation 4–5, Beale must refute the consensus view that these chapters are modelled on Ezekiel's throne vision. He attempts to do this by showing that there are a number of features in common with Daniel 7 which cannot be derived from Ezekiel, such as the opening of books (Rev. 5.2-3; Dan. 7.10), the approach of a divine figure (Rev. 5.7; Dan. 7.13-14), the mention of people from every 'tribe and language and people and nation' (Rev. 5.9; Dan. 7.14) and the reign of the saints over the kingdom (Rev. 5.10; Dan. 7.18).[31] This is an impressive list and shows that Daniel 7 has been a significant influence in the composition of Revelation 5. Beale, however, wishes to say more than this. He stresses the fact that John portrays the Lamb as approaching the throne and concludes from this that John intends the reader to see the death and resurrection of Jesus as the fulfilment of Daniel's vision.

Revelation 13 is clearly based on Daniel 7 and few would dispute this. However, Beale wishes to argue the same for the 'harlot' chapter (Rev. 17), where most commentators would see dependence on Isaiah, Jeremiah and Ezekiel.[32] His argument is primarily based on the parallels that exist between Revelation 13 and 17, as well as the structural similarity to Daniel 7 (vision + seer's reaction + interpretation).

Along with this 'midrashic' use of Daniel 7, Beale argues that the use of ἃ δεῖ γενέσθαι at 1.1, 19; 4.1; 22.6 is intended to show that Revelation is to be interpreted within the framework of Daniel 2 and its parallel apocalyptic chapters. His position is summarized as follows:

> if this allusion in Rev. 1.1 is understood by John in the light of the escha-
> tological context of Daniel 2—and there is good reason to believe that this
> is the case—then he may be asserting that the following contents of the
> whole book are to be conceived of ultimately within the thematic frame-
> work of Daniel 2 (and probably its parallel apocalyptic chapters).[33]

## Assessment

Beale has shown that Daniel 7 has been a significant factor in the composition of Revelation but his overall position is open to criticism. For example, his attempt to show that Rev. 1, 4–5, 13, 17 are a midrash on

31. *Use of Daniel*, p. 183.
32. Charles lists Isa. 23.17; 49.26; Jer. 28.7,13; Ezek. 23.29; 40.1-2 (*Revelation*, I, pp. lxviii-lxxxi).
33. *Use of Daniel*, p. 277.

Daniel 7 is forced. This is particularly evident for Revelation 4–5. By showing that Daniel 7 has been an important influence on Revelation 5 and arguing that Revelation 4–5 must be taken together, he seeks to refute the consensus view that Revelation 4 is modelled on Ezekiel 1 by providing a list of parallels:[34]

| Revelation | Daniel | Parallel |
| --- | --- | --- |
| 4.1 | 7.9 | Introduction to vision |
| 4.2a | 7.9a | Throne(s) in heaven |
| 4.2b | 7.9b | God on the throne |
| 4.3a | 7.9c | God's appearance |
| 4.5 | 7.9d-10a | Fire before the throne |
| 4.4b, 6b-10 | 7.10b | Throne attendants |

However, this is really sleight of hand, for if the relevant descriptions are set out, they do not have much in common, apart from the fact that they are both throne visions:

> As I watched, thrones were set in place, and an Ancient One took his throne, his clothing was white as snow, and the hair of his head like pure wool; his throne was fiery flames, and its wheels were burning fire. A stream of fire issued and flowed out from his presence. A thousand thousands served him…(Dan. 7.9-10).

> At once I was in the spirit, and there in heaven stood a throne, with one seated on the throne! And the one seated there looks like jasper and carnelian, and around the throne is a rainbow that looks like an emerald. Around the throne are…twenty-four elders, dressed in white robes… Coming from the throne are flashes of lightning… (Rev. 4.2-5).

Secondly, it is a very big step to move from the observation that John employs the prophetic formula ἃ δεῖ γενέσθαι at 1.1, 19; 4.1; 22.6 (ἃ μέλλει γενέσθαι in 1.19) to the view that he wants the whole book to be understood within the thematic framework of Dan. 2. One can acknowledge that these are important markers in the book without declaring that they are the only ones. Just as important, for example, are the two books of Revelation 5 and 10 (which Bauckham considers to be the same book). The unsealing of the first book (βιβλίον) is accompanied by the judgments of Revelation 6–9. In Revelation 10, however, John is told to consume a little book (βιβλαρίδιον) and then 'must prophesy again about many peoples and nations and languages

---

34. *Use of Daniel*, pp. 181-82.

and kings' (Rev. 10.11). As a result, D.L. Barr suggests a threefold division of the book:[35]

Rev. 1–3       Jesus comes to his church in salvation and judgment.
Rev. 4–11      He enables the work of cosmic worship to persist.
Rev. 12–22     He overthrows the work of the evil one.

Fiorenza[36] goes for a more complicated analysis. She agrees that the two scrolls mark off sections of the book but sees a parallel between the beginning (inaugural vision and messages) and the end (vision of the Lamb and the fulfilment of the promises in the new Jerusalem). She thus offers a concentric structure:

| | | | |
|---|---|---|---|
| A | 1.1-8 | $C^1$ | 15.1, 5–19.10 |
| B | 1.9-3.22 | $B^1$ | 19.11–22.9 |
| C | 4.1–9.21; 11.15-19 | $A^1$ | 22.10–22.21 |
| D | 10.1–15.4 | | |

John has clearly used the phrase ἃ δεῖ γενέσθαι as a structural marker but it is by no means the only one. It is certainly going well beyond the evidence to conclude that the whole of Revelation is to be 'conceived of ultimately within the framework of Daniel 2'.[37] Further, I will show in the next chapter that a much better case can be made for the book of Ezekiel having influenced the structure of John's book. To his credit, Beale does hint at a more dialectical relationship when he deliberately modifies the words of Lindars:

> the place of the Old Testament in the formation of thought in the Apocalypse is both that of a servant and a guide: for John the Christ-event is *the* key to understanding the Old Testament, and yet reflection back on

35. D.L. Barr, 'The Apocalypse as a Symbolic Transformation of the World: A Literary Analysis', *Int* 38 (1984), pp. 39-50.

36. 'The Composition and Structure of Revelation', *Justice and Judgment*, pp. 159-80. See also J. Lambrecht, 'A Structuration of Revelation 4:1–22:5', in *L'Apocalypse johannique et l'apocalyptique dans le Nouveau Testament* (ed. J. Lambrecht; Leuven: Leuven University Press, 1980), pp. 77-104. The complexity is highlighted in Bauckham's study ('Structure and Composition', *Climax of Prophecy*, pp. 1-37), where he shows that John has used at least 3 compositional techniques: Linguistic markers to divide the text, repetition to bind sections together, numerical schemes which may or may not have structural significance (e.g. the 7 Beatitudes).

37. *Use of Daniel*, p. 277.

the Old Testament context <u>leads the way</u> to further comprehension of this event and provides the redemptive-historical background against which the apocalyptic visions are better understood.[38]

## *Conclusion*

In the previous chapter, the view that local conditions led John to particular scriptures was found to be untenable. It is possible that local knowledge affected John's expression (e.g. χαλκολίβανος), but such knowledge is totally inadequate as an explanation for the particular texts and combination of texts used by John. In this chapter I have shown that John is indebted to the book of Daniel, but Beale's view that Revelation is to be 'conceived of ultimately within the framework of Daniel 2' must also be set aside. Both views are one-sided, assuming that one context (local or Old Testament) is able to swallow up the other, instead of allowing an interaction between them. Beale is correct when he says that Old Testament texts are 'utilized as a lens through which past and present eschatological fulfilment is understood',[39] but his view needs to do justice to the other side of the interaction, namely, that Revelation is a fresh composition which has used Daniel as *one* of its significant sources. As Ruiz says,

> By qualifying Revelation's use of Daniel as midrashic, and in describing Daniel's influence as dominant, Beale fails to credit John with sufficient autonomy with respect to the sources from which he drew material... The sort of mechanical adherence to the Daniel model which Beale proposes denies John due mastery over his own work, and this is unacceptable.[40]

38. 'Revelation', *Scripture Citing Scripture*, p. 333 (underlining mine, italics his). Nevertheless, in his 1992 article ('The Interpretative Problem') there is the same quotation that Revelation is to be 'conceived of ultimately within the framework of Daniel 2'.

39. 'Revelation', *Scripture Citing Scripture*, p. 325.

40. *Ezekiel in the Apocalypse*, p. 121. Part of the problem is one of terminology. 'midrash' is properly a literary genre where 'the audience's attention is focussed on the prior text' and the 'new composition exists for the sake of the old text' (A. Wright, 'The Literary Genre Midrash', *CBQ* 28 [1966], p. 444). See also J. Neusner, *What is Midrash?* (Philadelphia: Fortress Press, 1987). Some scholars prefer the term 'Inner-Biblical Exegesis' (e.g. Fishbane), but this puts too much emphasis on what the new author does with the old text. A more neutral term would be 'Inner-Biblical Allusion', though I argue in Chapter 6 that 'Intertextuality' has the most to offer.

Chapter 4

JOHN'S USE OF EZEKIEL

One of the most controversial aspects of the book of Revelation in the early church was its teaching on the millenium.[1] After the series of devastating plagues that form the bulk of the visions, the book seems to come to a climax in chapter 19, where we read,

> Then I saw the beast and the kings of the earth with their armies gathered to make war against the rider on the horse and against his army. And the beast was captured, and with it the false prophet who had performed in its presence the signs by which he deceived those who had received the mark of the beast and those who worshipped its image. *These two were thrown alive into the lake of fire that burns with sulphur. And the rest were killed by the sword of the rider on the horse*, the sword that came from his mouth; and all the birds were gorged with their flesh (Rev. 19.19-21).

This accounts for two of the great adversaries, along with all the human kings and armies.[2] The third, the dragon, is dealt with in the verses that follow. First, he is bound (20.2). Then he is thrown into a bottomless pit (20.3a), which is shut and sealed (20.3b). This allows the people of God to be free of persecution and deception so that they can be 'priests of God and of Christ, and they will reign with him a thousand years' (Rev. 20.6b). However, it is at this point that John introduces something which is not present in any other New Testament writing—a resurgence of evil:

> When the thousand years are ended, Satan will be released from his prison and will come out to deceive the nations at the four corners of the earth, Gog and Magog, in order to gather them for battle; they are as numerous as the sands of the sea (Rev. 20.7-8).

1.  See Mealy, *After the Thousand Years*, pp. 11-58.
2.  'The sense of these words is as plain as it is consistent with the pattern leading up to them: no one on earth survives the confrontation with the returning Christ' (Mealy, *After the Thousand Years*, p. 91).

The peculiar thing about this is that it assumes the presence of rebellious nations at the four corners of the earth, whereas Rev. 19.21 reports that all such people have been destroyed. Where have they come from? One suggestion is that they are not human enemies (which have all been destroyed) but demonic.[3] In support of this, one could take the expression 'at the four corners of the earth' to be a picture of evil spirits coming up from the underworld. However, if this were the case, we would not expect John to refer to them as 'the nations', especially in the light of Rev. 21.26, where the 'glory and the honour of the nations' is brought into the new city. Nor would we expect Satan to have to go out and deceive them, since they would be in league with him anyway.

A different view is that the enemies are the disembodied spirits of those slain in Rev. 19.21.[4] We know that Rev. 19.21 is not the final word since Rev. 20.15 says that 'anyone whose name was not found written in the book of life was thrown into the lake of fire'. Having lost the battle in their earthly life, does John narrate a further battle as disembodied spirits, before being consigned to the lake of fire? If he does, the plot is becoming hopelessly confused, for, as Mealy[5] asks, 'If ordinary bodily death is presumably the "first death" to which resurrected experience of the lake of fire corresponds as the "second death" (v. 15), then what room is left for this third, supposedly intermediate ("ghostly death") experience?' His view is that the release of Satan in Rev. 20.7 coincides with the release and resurrection of those

3.    Mealy cites Fiorenza, Wikenhauser, Lohse, Kraft and Pohl as holding this view (*After the Thousand Years*, p. 42).

4.    'Satan entices the ghostly nations of the dead, and the demons, "innumerable as the sand of the sea", from the four corners of the earth where the underworld manifests itself, in order to make war on the resurrected ones' (M. Rissi, *The Future of the World: An Exegetical Study of Revelation* 19.11–22.5 [London: SCM Press, 1972], p. 35).

5.    *After the Thousand Years*, p. 123. His view is that by 'conspicuously plotting the release of Satan from the underworld and the resurrection of the unrepentant at the same time, John is encouraging his readers to expect for the release of the unrepentant from the prison of Hades to issue in their resurrection and punishment with Satan, after the pattern of Isa. 24.21-22: "They will be gathered together like prisoners in the dungeon, and will be confined in prison; and after many days they will be punished". In other words, just as Satan and the wicked were punished together at the parousia and imprisoned together for the duration of the millenium, so presumably they will be released and punished together "after the thousand years are completed"' (*After the Thousand Years*, pp. 124-25).

slain in 19.21. Satan's confinement 'that he would deceive the nations no more' (Rev. 20.3b) cannot mean that Satan is removed from the scene and 'the nations' are left, for Rev. 19.21 makes it clear that none of the unrepentant survives the parousia. He thus interprets Rev. 20.3b as meaning that Satan is imprisoned in the same place as the disembodied spirits and is thus seen to be as helpless as they are. When he is released after the millenium to make war on the (resurrected) saints, the disembodied spirits are resurrected but immediately fall into league with Satan:

> They marched up over the breadth of the earth and surrounded the camp of the saints and the beloved city. And fire came down from heaven and consumed them. And the devil who had deceived them was thrown into the lake of fire and sulphur, where the beast and the false prophet were, and they will be tormented day and night forever and ever (Rev. 20.9-10).

Those who took this sequence of events literally and looked forward to a millenial reign with Christ were branded heretics in 431 CE. The spiritual interpretation of Tyconius and championed by Augustine, according to which the millenium was a symbol of the church age, became the orthodox view and 'chiliasm' (the belief in a literal reign of 1000 years) was thereafter confined to sects and minority groups.[6] However, before this time, it seems that many Christians thought this view was perfectly orthodox. Thus Justin said,

> I and others, who are right-minded Christians at all points, are assured that there will be a resurrection of the dead, and a thousand years in Jerusalem, which will then be built adorned and enlarged as the prophets Ezekiel and Isaiah and others declare.[7]

The interesting thing about this quotation is that not only does he accept the millenial reign, which he places in Jerusalem, but he imagines it to be 'built adorned and enlarged' as the Old Testament prophets predicted. Thus in Ezekiel 37, the revival of the dry bones, the reunited kingdom and the messianic reign are all followed by a final battle with Gog of Magog (Ezek. 38–39). Only then do we find the description of the new Temple in the new City (Ezek. 40–48). Ezekiel's order is thus:

---

6.  See R.L. Wilken, 'Early Christian Chiliasm, Jewish Messianism and the Idea of the Holy Land', *HTR* 79 (1986), pp. 298-307.
7.  *Dial. Tryph.* 80, quoted by Barclay, *Revelation*, II, p. 189.

| Ezek. 37a | Revival of dry bones |
| Ezek. 37b | Reunited kingdom with Messianic king reigning |
| Ezek. 38–39 | Final battle against Gog of Magog |
| Ezek. 40–48 | Vision of the New Temple in the New City |

Ezekiel does not specifically say that the reunited kingdom was to last a thousand years, but he does envisage a resurgence of evil after the restoration of the dry bones. Indeed, as Kuhn[8] notes, the order of events in Revelation 20–22 is substantially modelled on Ezekiel 37–48. There are also a number of specific parallels. For example,

1. Both use the names Gog and Magog. In Ezek. 38.2, the Hebrew text speaks of 'Gog, of the land of Magog' but the LXX rendering (Γωγ καὶ τὴν γῆν τοῦ Μαγωγ) is indicative of a tendency that is found later in certain rabbinic works (e.g. Aqiba in *b. 'Ed.* 2.10; *b. Ber.* 7b) and the Targums (Exod. 40.11; Num. 11.26; Deut. 32.39) to treat these as the names of two heathen leaders.

2. In both, fire from heaven comes down and destroys Gog and his followers (Rev. 20.9; Ezek. 38.32).

3. Both describe a gorging by the birds (Rev. 19.17-18, 21; Ezek. 39.4, 17-20.). The birds are first summoned and then commanded to eat of the flesh of kings, of mighty men, of horses and their riders. In Ezekiel, this refers to Gog and his armies but John utilizes it in his description of the first battle. It is possible that this change in order may have been suggested by different text forms of Ezekiel, since in the earliest Greek MS (967) and in the Würzburg Codex of the Old Latin, ch. 37 follows chs. 38–39.[9]

---

8. K.G. Kuhn, 'Γὼγ καὶ Μαγώγ', *TDNT*, I, pp. 789-91.

9. So J. Lust, 'Ezekiel 36–40 in the Oldest Greek Manuscript', *CBQ* 43 (1981), pp. 517-33. Mealy finds this an unlikely solution: 'The integral setting for the battle of Ezekiel 38 is the peaceful age after the exile, and the dry bones and messianic kingdom section in Ezekiel 37 does not properly parallel the judgment of the non-elect in Rev. 20.11-15, but rather the resurrection of the saints for the messianic age in 20.4-6. To cut and paste Ezekiel to match Revelation, one would want to see something like chs. 36–39–37–38–40' (*After the Thousand Years*, p. 131 n. 1). However, Lust's point is not so much that John follows the order found in these early MSS but that they show that the order was fluid and hence open to various interpretations.

4.  Both John and Ezekiel are taken to a high place where they are shown a vision of a new city (Rev. 21.10; Ezek. 40.2).

5.  Both see a figure with a measuring rod (κάλαμος) who measures the dimensions of the city/temple (Rev. 21.15; Ezek. 40.5). There are walls, gates and foundations. It is square, with three gates on each side.

6.  Both state that the new City (Rev. 21.22) or Temple (Ezek. 43.2) is filled with the glory of God.

7.  Both describe the healing properties of the tree(s) of life, bearing its fruit each month (Rev. 22.2; Ezek. 47.12).

How is this to be understood? Is it a question of fulfilment, as Beale argued for Daniel? Is John telling his audience to keep faith with the ancient prophecies for their fulfilment is coming soon? Or is he trying to show how the new revelation fits in with the old? Vogelgesang thinks it is part of an overall strategy to 'democratize' Ezekiel's visions and make them accessible to all, a theory to be considered in due course. Before that, I want to move back to John's throne vision in Revelation 4, where John is invited to enter heaven and see 'what must take place after this' (Rev. 4.1). What he sees first is a throne:

> And the one seated there looks like jasper and carnelian, and around the throne is a rainbow that looks like an emerald…and in front of the throne there is something like a sea of glass, like crystal. Around the throne, and on each side of the throne, are four living creatures, full of eyes in front and behind: the first living creature like a lion, the second living creature like an ox, the third living creature with a face like a human face, and the fourth living creature like a flying eagle…Day and night without ceasing they sing, 'Holy, holy, holy, the Lord God the Almighty, who was and is and is to come' (Rev. 4.3-8).

There are a number of throne visions in the Old Testament (e.g. 1 Kgs 22; Isa. 6; Ezek. 1; Dan. 7) and John has probably drawn on all of them. In particular, the song of the creatures is undoubtedly taken from the song of the seraphim in Isaiah 6. However, the most striking parallels are with Ezekiel's vision, where the four creatures are also called 'living beings' (ζῷα) and have the faces of a man, a lion, an ox and an eagle:

> In the middle of it was something like four living creatures…As for the appearance of their faces: the four had the face of a human being, the face of a lion on the right side, the face of an ox on the left side, and the face of an eagle…(Ezek. 1.5, 10).

There is an interesting coincidence of language with respect to the location of the creatures. Ezekiel first describes a cloud from the north, bright and gleaming with 'fire flashing forth continually' (1.4). He then says, 'In the middle of it was something like four living creatures' (LXX: ἐν τῷ μέσῳ...τεσσάρων ζῴων). John's Greek is similar (ἐν μέσῳ τοῦ θρόνου...τέσσαρα ζῷα, Rev. 4.6), except that he is referring to the throne, not the cloud. We thus have the confusing picture of the living creatures being in the midst of the throne. A possible explanation is that if they are supporting the throne, part of them might be under it and part of them around it. However, John does not say that the creatures support the throne and 'underneath' is hardly more accurate a rendering of ἐν μέσῳ than the NRSV's 'on each side'. Sweet suggests it might be an Hebraism for 'between', whereas Brewer[10] explains it by reference to the Greek theatre, stating that it refers to the space between the stage (throne) and the chorus (elders).

Other parallels with Ezekiel's vision are the mention of a rainbow (Ezek. 1.28), the crystal sea (Ezek. 1.22) and the curious expression 'full of eyes' (Ezek. 1.18), which in Ezekiel's vision are associated with the wheels (*ôpannîm*). There are also a number of differences:[11]

1. John has four creatures, each with a different face. Ezekiel has four creatures, each of which has four faces. Further, the faces are given in a different order in Revelation.

2. John's creatures have six wings (as in Isa. 6), not four.

3. John's throne is not supported by the creatures and is stationary. There is no mention of wheels.

4. John's creatures sing God's praises (as in Isa. 6), whereas Ezekiel's are silent (though movement of the wings is like thunder and the 'sound of mighty waters'—a feature to be exploited in later merkabah mysticism).

5. John says the creatures are 'full of eyes'. In Ezekiel, it is the wheels that are 'full of eyes' (though in Ezek. 10.12 the cherubim are said to be full of eyes. This is probably a later corruption but could well have been available to John).

10. R.R. Brewer, 'Revelation 4.6 and Translations Thereof', *JBL* 71 (1952), pp. 227-31. See also R.G. Hall, 'Living Creatures in the Midst of the Throne. Another Look at Revelation 4:6', *NTS* 36 (1990), pp. 609-13.

11. See Charles, *Revelation*, I, pp. 121-27.

John's vision is much shorter than Ezekiel's and so some simplification (points 1, 3) is to be expected. This is the opposite of the Targum, which goes on to say that each of the faces had four faces, and each of these sixteen faces had four wings, making a total of 256 wings for the four creatures.[12] Points 2 and 4 show that John is combining Ezekiel's vision with Isaiah 6 (as in *Apoc. Abr.* 18 and possibly 4Q Second Ezekiel),[13] especially the song:

> Holy, holy, holy, the Lord God the Almighty, who was and is and is to come (Rev. 4.8b).

> Holy, holy, holy is the Lord of hosts; the whole earth is full of his glory (Isa. 6.3).

In 2 *En.* 21.1, the cherubim and seraphim also stand before the throne and sing, 'Holy, holy, holy is the Lord God of Sabaoth: heavens and earth are full of thy glory'. However, in *1 En.* 39.12, the 'Trisagion' is aimed at the 'Lord of spirits' and continues: 'He filleth the earth with spirits'. Charles comments, 'Here as in our text the writer has modified the trisagion to suit the main purpose of his Apocalypse'.[14]

Point 5 is interesting. John omits mention of the wheels but utilizes the description 'full of eyes' for his creatures. One cannot put this down to simplification since it has resulted in a rather confusing phrase (γέμοντα ὀφθαλμῶν ἔμπροσθεν καὶ ὄπισθεν). How a creature can have the face of a man (or any of the other animals) and have eyes 'all around and inside' is not clear. As Beasley-Murray says, the result is an 'impossible visual image, but comprehensible as a symbol'.[15] Thus in summary, John's use of Ezekiel's vision involves abbreviation, some recasting and some expansion, particularly under the influence of Isaiah 6.

---

12. The desire to have 256 wings may come from gematria, since that is the value of the consonants *rnw* (to sing). See S.H. Levey, *The Targum of Ezekiel Translated, with a Critical Introduction, Apparatus, and Notes* (The Aramaic Bible 13; Wilmington: Michael Glazier, 1987).

13. See G.J. Brooke, 'Ezekiel in some Qumran and New Testament Texts', *The Madrid Qumran Congress* (Proceedings of the International Congress on the Dead Sea Scrolls, Madrid 18–21 March, 1991; Leiden: Brill, 1992), pp. 317-37.

14. Charles, *Revelation*, I, p. 126. The second half of the verse ('the whole earth is full of his glory') is not simply discarded but reappears in Rev. 18.1 ('and the earth was made bright with his splendour').

15. Beasley-Murray, *Revelation*, p. 117.

*Three Further Parallels*

1. *Sealing of the Saints*
The sealing of the saints in Rev. 7.2-3 is almost certainly modelled on Ezek. 9.4-6:

> Go through the city, through Jerusalem, and *put a mark on the foreheads* of those who sigh and groan over all the abominations that are committed in it...Cut down old men, young men and young women, little children and women, *but touch no one who has the mark*...(Ezek. 9.4-6).

> I saw another angel ascending from the rising of the sun, having the seal of the living God, and he called with a loud voice to the four angels who had been given power to damage earth and sea, saying, *'Do not damage* the earth or the sea or the trees, *until we have marked the servants of our God with a seal on their foreheads* (Rev. 7.2-3).

Later tradition identified this sealing either with baptism, the laying on of hands or the marking of the cross, and perhaps Paul's use of σφραγίζειν (2 Cor. 1.22; Eph. 1.13; 4.30) made this inevitable. Nevertheless, it seems clear that John's meaning is closer to Ezekiel's, namely, that God's people are to be given a special mark to protect them from the approaching slaughter.[16] The two main questions that arise from John's use of this tradition concern the identity of those protected (the 144,000 and their relation to the great throng of Rev. 7.9), and what it is that they are protected from. In regards to identity, most commentators think that the 144,000 and the great throng refer to the same group of people, but opinions differ on whether this is a symbol of the whole church (Swete, Beasley-Murray, Sweet) or just the martyrs (Charles, Caird, Kiddle).[17] The opinion of Victorinus that the 144,000 represents Jewish Christians is not widely held today.

As to the danger, it does not appear to be protection against physical

---

16. Ford, *Revelation*, pp. 116-17, says that to the prophet's contemporaries, 'seal' would have connoted:

1. Branding of cattle or slaves to denote ownership
2. A mark denoting ownership by a god
3. A mark denoting a prophet (1 Kgs 20.41; Zech. 13.6; Isa. 44.5)
4. A phylactery denoting devotion to Yahweh
5. The seal of circumcision
6. The seal stamped on the human soul

17. The relationship between these two descriptions will be discussed in Chapter 6.

attacks, given that they have already had to endure the effects of the first six seals. Neither is it likely to be death, since Revelation consistently portrays martyrdom as the way to victory. Charles[18] thinks it is protection against the Satanic forces about to be unleashed (9.1ff.), though one might have expected it to come directly before this (instead of before the trumpets). One further point of interest is that the sealing episode is followed by an angel reaching into the altar and hurling fire onto the earth: 'Then the angel took the censer and filled it with fire from the altar and threw it on the earth' (Rev. 8.5). A similar thing follows Ezekiel's account of the sealing: 'He said to the man clothed in linen, "Go within the wheelwork underneath the cherubim; fill your hands with burning coals from among the cherubim, and scatter them over the city"' (10.2).

## 2. *The Great Harlot*

The second parallel in the middle section of the two books is the description of the great harlot in Revelation 17, which draws mainly on the description of Jerusalem in Ezekiel 16 and 23. Ford[19] cites this as evidence that John is referring to Jerusalem rather than Rome but few commentators have found this convincing. Some of the parallels are:

| | |
|---|---|
| Rev. 17.1 | The city is called a Harlot or Whore (Ezek. 16.15-16) |
| Rev. 17.2 | She was world-famous (Ezek. 16.15, 25, 29) |
| Rev. 17.4a | She wore jewels and fine linen (Ezek. 16.13) |
| Rev. 17.4b | She holds a cup of abominations (Ezek. 23.31-32) |
| Rev. 17.6 | She is guilty of shedding blood (Ezek. 16.38; 23.45) |

John interrupts this description by giving the interpretation of the heads and horns of the beast on which she sits. The seven heads are seven hills (17.9) and also seven kings (17.10), five of whom have fallen, one is presently reigning and one is to come. The ten horns also stand for kings (17.12) who will give their authority to the beast (17.13) and make war on the Lamb (17.14). Some commentators (e.g. Charles) have found this dual interpretation artificial and suggest that it is the work of a later redactor. Whether this is so or not, the book returns to the theme of the Harlot and describes her destruction in terms which are very similar to those of Ezek. 16.39 and 23.22-29:

18. Charles, *Revelation*, I, pp. 196-99.
19. Ford, *Revelation*, pp. 283-93.

And the ten horns that you saw, they and the beast will hate the whore; they will make her desolate and naked; they will devour her flesh and burn her up with fire (Rev. 17.16).

I will deliver you into their hands...they shall strip you of your clothes and take your beautiful objects and leave you naked and bare (Ezek. 16.39).

They shall seize your sons and your daughters, and your survivors shall be devoured by fire. They shall also strip you of your clothes and take away your fine jewels...and they shall deal with you in hatred...and leave you naked and bare (Ezek. 23.25-29).

## 3. *Fall of Babylon*

The third parallel in the middle sections of the two books is the lament over the fall of Babylon in Revelation 18, which is based on a similar lament for Tyre in Ezekiel 26–27. Charles[20] highlights four allusions from Ezekiel, but others[21] have added to this:

| *Revelation 18* | *Ezekiel 26–27* |
| --- | --- |
| And the merchants of the earth weep and mourn for her, since no one buys their cargo any-more, cargo of gold, silver, jewels and pearls, fine linen, purple...and human lives (ψυχὰς ἀνθρώπων) (vv. 11-13). | Tarshish did business with you out of the abundance of your great wealth; silver, iron, tin and lead...they exchanged human beings (ψυχαῖς ἀνθρώπων) Edom did business with you... purple, embroidered work, fine linen (27.12-16). |
| 'What city was like the great city?' (v. 18) | 'Who was ever destroyed like Tyre in the midst of the sea?...' (27.32) |
| And they threw dust on their heads, as they wept and mourned (v. 19). | wail aloud over you, and cry bitterly. They throw dust on their heads and wallow in ashes (27.30). |
| and the sound of harpists and minstrels and flutists and trumpeters will be heard in you no more (v. 22). | I will silence the music of your songs; the sound of your lyres shall be heard no more (26.13). |

The most obvious difference is that John's list is considerably shorter, omitting the long list of trading partners (Tarshish, Javan, Tubal, Meshech, Beth-togarmah, Rhodes, Edom, Judah etc.) and condensing the products

20. *Revelation*, I, p. lxxv, who believes they are all taken from the Hebrew text.
21. For example, Vanhoye, 'L'utilisation', pp. 475-76.

74   *The Old Testament in the Book of Revelation*

into two verses. There appears to be some attempt to systematize, with products listed under jewelry, clothes, building materials, tools, aromatics, food and livestock. However, John has not simply abbreviated, since under aromatics he has κιννάμωμον, ἄμωμον, θυμιάματα, μύρον and λίβανον, whereas Ezekiel only has μύρον. It is possible that John is trying to update Ezekiel and give a list of Rome's imports, though it is unclear how he would know such a thing.[22] Ruiz suggests that the main motivation is a literary one, rearranging the list so that it substantially coincides with the description of the harlot in 17.4. In this way, John 'binds the metaphors of Prostitute and Babylon together by mediating between 17,4 and 18,16, where Woman and City are decked out identically'.[23]

Five parallels have now been considered, to which Vanhoye[24] gives the name 'utilisations d'ensembles', that is, major sections of Revelation which derive their inspiration from major sections of Ezekiel. What is of particular interest is that these sections occur in the same order in both works, and so it looks as though Ezekiel rather than Daniel has had the greatest influence on the structure of John's book:

| Rev. 4 | Throne creatures/eyes/bow/crystal | Ezek. 1 |
| Rev. 7–8 | Marking/scattering of fire | Ezek. 9–10 |
| Rev. 17 | Punishment of the Harlot city | Ezek. 16, 23 |
| Rev. 18 | Lament over fallen city, trading list | Ezek. 26–27 |
| Rev. 20–22 | Revival, reign, battle, new Jerusalem | Ezek. 37–48 |

Goulder tries to take this further by offering a one-to-one correspondence between the two books. Rejecting a literary solution as 'rather bookish and implausible',[25] he suggests that John's inspiration has come from the weekly readings of Ezekiel in the context of worship.

22. See Bauckham, 'The Economic Critique of Rome in Revelation 18', *Climax of Prophecy*, pp. 338-83.

23. Ruiz, *Ezekiel in the Apocalypse*, p. 440. Bauckham says, 'No doubt it was Ezekiel's list which suggested the idea of a list of cargoes. It is true that a number of items of merchandise are common to both lists, but no more than would be practically inevitable in any two lengthy lists of items traded in the ancient world. Closer study of John's list will reveal that what he has done is to substitute for Ezekiel's, which is an accurate account of Tyre's trade in the sixth century BC, a list which is just as accurate in representing the imports of the city of Rome' (*Cimax of Prophecy*, pp. 350-51).

24. 'L'utilisation', p. 440.

25. M.D. Goulder, 'The Apocalypse as an Annual Cycle of Prophecies', *NTS* 27 (1981), p. 349.

He notes that John himself says his visions came to him 'on the Lord's day' (1.10) and that the work is intended to be read aloud (1.3). Using the two throne visions as his starting point (Rev. 4 = Ezek. 1), Goulder offers the following scheme of readings:[26]

THE APOCALYPSE, EZEKIEL, AND THE JEWISH CHRISTIAN YEAR

| Rev. | Theme | Ezek. | Calendar |
|------|-------|-------|----------|
| 1 | Risen Christ | 43a | PASSOVER |
| 2a | Ephesus | 43b | |
| 2b | Smyrna | 44 | |
| 2c | Pergamum | 45 | |
| 2d | Thyatira | 46 | |
| 3a | Sardis | 47 | |
| 3b | Philadelphia | 48 | |
| 3c | Laodicea | | |
| 4 | Throne-vision | 1 | PENTECOST |
| 5a | Scroll, Lion | 2 | |
| 5b | Lamb as slain | 3 | |
| 6a | 4 Seals | 5 | |
| 6b | Martyrs | 6 | |
| 6c | Earthquake | 7 | |
| 7a | 144,000 sealed | 8–9 | |
| 7b | Multitude | 10 | |
| 8a | Incense, altar | 11 | |
| 8b | 4 Trumpets | 12 | |
| 9a | Locust-scorpions | 13 | |
| 9b | Lion cavalry | 14 | |
| 10a | Angel of oath | 15 | |
| 10b | Little scroll | 16 | |
| 11a | 2 Witnesses | 16 | |
| 11b | 7th Trumpet | 17 | |
| 12a | Woman and Dragon | 18 | NEW YEAR |
| 12b | Michael and Dragon | 19 | ATONEMENT |
| 12c | Woman in wilderness | 20 | TABERNACLES |
| 13a | Beast from the Sea | 21 | |
| 13b | Beast from the land | 22 | |
| 14a | Lamb and 144,000 | 23 | |
| 14b | Cup of wrath | 23 | |
| 14c | Harvest and vintage | 24 | |
| 15a | Bowl angels | 25 | |
| 15b | Glory in Temple | 26 | |

26. 'Annual Cycle', pp. 353-54, given here without the exact chapter divisions.

| | | | |
|---|---|---|---|
| 16a | 3 Bowls | 27 | |
| 16b | 2 Bowls | 28 | |
| 16c | 7th bowl | 29 | DEDICATION |
| 17a | Babylon the Harlot | 30 | |
| 17b | Mystery Expounded | 31 | |
| 18a | Fallen is Babylon | 32 | |
| 18b | Lament over Babylon | 33 | |
| 19a | Lamb's Bride | 34 | |
| 19b | Rider on White Horse | 35 | |
| 19c | Armageddon | 36 | |
| 20a | Resurrection and Millenium | 37 | |
| 20b | Gog and Magog | 38 | |
| 20c | Last Judgment | 39 | |
| 21a | New Jerusalem | 40 | |
| 21b | City, walls, gates | 40 | |
| 22a | God's glory, River of Life | 41 | |
| 22b | Come! | 42 | |

Goulder acknowledges that such a scheme is purely hypothetical but finds it amazing that such a linear progression should correspond with the main Christian feasts (see chart). However, there are also enormous problems. For example, Goulder follows Boismard[27] and others in seeing Ezekiel 37–39 as the inspiration behind Revelation 20, and this parallel is easily arranged by dividing Revelation 20 into three sections (vv. 1-6, 7-10, 11-15). After this, it becomes more difficult. Boismard saw the whole of Ezekiel 40–48 as the inspiration behind Revelation 21–22 but Goulder has to utilize only Ezekiel 40–42, leaving the remaining chapters (43–48) to carry over (as it were) to the inaugural vision and messages to the seven churches (Rev. 1–3). To make this seem plausible, he notes that the phrase 'like the sound of many waters' occurs in Ezek. 43.2 and Rev. 1.15 (though its occurrence in Rev. 14.2; 19.6 makes this less significant), and reference to the name of the city in Ezek. 48.35 would fit the promise to the church at Philadelphia (3.12), whose inhabitants were to have the name of God and the name of the city inscribed on them (the most likely understanding of the αὐτόν). Unfortunately, this expediency means losing two of the most prominent parallels between Ezekiel and Revelation 21–22, namely, the river of life (Rev. 22.2; Ezek. 47.12) and the twelve gates with the names of the twelve tribes (Rev. 21.12; Ezek. 48.30-35).

27. M.E. Boismard, '"L'Apocalypse" ou "Les Apocalypses" de St Jean', *RB* 56 (1949), pp. 507-41.

Secondly, whilst the sealing/marking of the saints falls approximately in the right position (taking Ezek. 8 and 9 together), the same is not true of either the Harlot chapters (Ezek. 16, 23 = Rev. 17) or the Tyre/Babylon lament (Ezek. 26–27 = Rev. 18). On Goulder's arrangement, these two chapters of Revelation were inspired by Ezekiel 30–33, whereas Ezekiel 16, 23, 26, 27 correspond to Revelation 11a, 14ab, 15b and 16a respectively.

A further factor against such a linear scheme of readings is the observation of Vanhoye[28] that John sometimes uses a passage more than once ('double utilisation'). For example, Ezekiel's throne-vision is followed by the command to eat a scroll:

> I looked, and a hand was stretched out to me, and a written scroll was in it...it had writing on the front and on the back...He said to me, Mortal, eat this scroll that I give you and fill your stomach with it. Then I ate it; and in my mouth it was as sweet as honey (Ezek. 2.9–3.2).

As Goulder notes, John's throne-vision is also followed by the mention of a scroll and there is a correspondence in that John's scroll is also written 'on the inside and on the back' (Rev. 5.1). However, John's main use of this incident is in Revelation 10, where 'another mighty angel' says,

> Take it, and eat; it will be bitter to your stomach, but sweet as honey in your mouth (Rev. 10.9).

The majority of scholars have assumed that this is a different scroll from that of Revelation 5 because John calls it a βιβλαρίδιον. However, this is probably not to be pressed (cf. ἀρνίον, θηρίον). The sealed scroll of Revelation 5 has been opened (Rev. 6–8) and is now given to John to digest. Thus it seems clear that Ezekiel's scroll is the main inspiration behind Revelation 5 and Revelation 10.

Another example cited by Vanhoye[29] is John's use of the measuring incident in Ezekiel 40–43. In Ezekiel, this is a literary device, both to add realism to the vision and to record the various dimensions of the Temple and its environs. In Rev. 11.11, the function is much closer to the sealing episode:

> Then I was given a measuring rod like a staff, and I was told, 'Come and measure the temple of God and the altar and those who worship there, but

---

28. 'L'utilisation', p. 462.
29. 'L'utilisation', pp. 463ff.

> do not measure the court outside the temple; leave that out, for it is given
> over to the nations, and they will trample over the holy city for forty-two
> months...' (Rev. 11.1-2).

Here, John is told to do the measuring himself and what he measures
is promised safety. The function is thus quite different from Ezek. 40-43,
though its focus is similar, namely, the temple and its environs.
However, the incident is given a second hearing in Rev. 21.15-17, where
this time it is the angel who does the measuring and its function is very
close to that found in Ezekiel, namely, to add realism to the vision and
record the dimensions of the new city. The major difference is that the
measuring does not concern the temple because John's city does not
have one.

For these reasons, Goulder's theory of a linear correspondence
between Revelation and Ezekiel is untenable. John has used Ezekiel to a
remarkable degree and in something like the same order, but his method
is much more complicated than a lectionary theory allows. Nevertheless,
the agreements do call for an explanation. John's readers are addressed
by someone who reports a throne vision like Ezekiel's and is
commissioned to prophesy by eating a scroll. In his visions of
destruction, he speaks of God's people being protected by a seal whilst
the persecuting power is called Babylon. Its destruction is described
under the themes of 'whore' and 'exploiting city' with a dirge-like
lament from all who profited by her. He then describes a battle where
God's enemies are destroyed, the birds gorge on the remains and the
saints come back to life. Then comes the final battle against Gog and
Magog, who are destroyed by fire, making way for the final vision, the
new Jerusalem. The city is measured, the gates contain the names of the
twelve tribes and the tree of life provides healing for the nations. If a
lectionary theory is inadequate, what else can be suggested?

The most obvious explanation is that John has taken on the 'persona'
of Ezekiel. Through meditation and study (of which there are ample
precedents), John has absorbed something of the character and mind of
the prophet. This is why he can make so many allusions to the book
without ever actually quoting it. Fiorenza[30] uses this fact to draw a
distinction between using its 'words, images, phrases and patterns' for
his own compositions and treating the book as authoritative Scripture. In
part, this is correct, though it should be noted that this does not imply

---

30. 'Apokalypsis and Propheteia', *Justice and Judgment*, p. 135.

that John is any more distant from Ezekiel than those who do quote it. It is possible that he does not quote it as Scripture because he does not see it as an external source. He has taken on the mind of Ezekiel and writes 'in the spirit' (ἐν πνεύματι).

Further support for such a hypothesis might come from the following. First, adopting the part of an ancient worthy is standard practice for those who wrote apocalypses. Such works are invariably pseudonymous and claim, quite explicitly, to come from the said person (e.g. Enoch). Most commentators have pointed out that Revelation differs from this tradition by specifically declaring its authorship, and this is quite correct. Attempts to see 'John' as a pseudonym for the apostle have not gained much support.[31] Nevertheless, it is possible that John's ἐν πνεύματι makes a similar claim, though in a somewhat different way. Not only are many of John's visions modelled on Ezekiel, but he himself seems to see a similarity between his experiences and those of the prophet:

> And in the spirit he carried me away to a great, high mountain and showed me the holy city... (Rev. 21.10).

> He brought me, in visions of God, to the land of Israel, and set me down upon a very high mountain, on which was a structure like a city to the south (Ezek. 40.2).

Secondly, meditating on the book of Ezekiel for the purpose of achieving ecstatic visions is also well documented. Although it was forbidden in some circles, there existed in Judaism a form of mystic practice known as 'merkabah' mysticism, from the Hebrew word for chariot. Ezekiel's description of God's throne speaks of wheels and moving across the heavens. In merkabah mysticism,[32] these descriptions were used to achieve trance-like visions and heavenly transportation. John is much more restrained but Revelation 4 bears some resemblance to such visions:

---

31. See F.D. Mazzaferri, *The Genre of the Book of Revelation from a Source-Critical Perspective* (BZNW 54; Berlin: de Gruyter, 1989), pp. 3-4, who cites R. Dunkerley, 'The Five Johns', *London Quarterly and Holborn Review* 30 (1961), pp. 292-98, as one of the few scholars who holds this position. Mazzaferri does not find it convincing.

32. The classic study is G. Scholem, *Major Trends in Jewish Mysticism* (New York: Schocken, 1961). For a brief introduction, see J. Dan, 'The Religious Experience of the Merkavah', in *Jewish Spirituality: From the Bible through the Middle Ages* (ed. A. Green; London: SCM Press, 1989), pp. 289-307.

> After this I looked, and there in heaven a door stood open! And the first
> voice, which I had heard speaking to me like a trumpet, said, '*Come up
> here*, and *I will show you* what must take place after this'. At once *I was in
> the spirit*, and there in heaven stood a throne...

Thirdly, John's teaching of a resurgence of evil under the leadership
of Gog and Magog is not found in any other New Testament writing but
appears to be taken from Ezekiel or traditions based on it. What is the
explanation of this? Farrer says that the 'chief moral significance of the
millenium in St John's book, is the special promise it makes to the
martyr'.[33] Caird agrees, though he adds that this does not sufficiently
explain why John chose to use it. There were a great variety of traditions which he could have drawn from, including the direct translation of
the martyrs to heaven. The fact that he speaks of a millenium must be
because it was an 'indispensable element in his vision of the future'.[34]
That is probably true, though according to Farrer it was also because
John is following Ezekiel.

Thus the claim that John has taken on the 'persona' of Ezekiel has
something to be said for it. However, its weaknesses must now be
considered. First, how can it be reconciled with his extensive use of
Daniel and other books like Isaiah? Has he taken on their 'persona' as
well? There would perhaps be an answer to this if we could accept
Beale's view that one text acts as the *Vorbild* while others are brought
in by association, but neither Daniel nor Ezekiel can be said to act in this
way throughout Revelation. Indeed, it is possible that parts of Revelation
are based on sequences of the minor prophets:[35]

| Rev. | Theme | Parallel | Old Testament |
|---|---|---|---|
| 8.6-13 | 4 Trumpets | Fire, sun, moon | Joel 2 |
| 9.1-12 | Locust-scorpions | Smoke, locusts | Joel 3 |
| 9.13-21 | Lion cavalry | Lions, fire (horses) | Amos 1–2 |
| 10.1-7 | Angel of oath | Mystery revealed to the prophets | Amos 3 |

The presence of so many Old Testament traditions in Revelation
undoubtedly weakens the argument that he has particularly adopted the
'persona' of any one of them. Indeed, Vanhoye thinks that John is rarely
dependent on a single source. His explanation for this is instructive:

33. *Revelation*, p. 206.
34. *Revelation*, p. 251.
35. Goulder, 'Annual Cycle', p. 362.

Jean excelle à trouver les textes qui se complètent ou se corrigent mutuellement de façon à exprimer avec plus de fidélité l'accomplissement chrétien.[36]

As an example of this, he cites Rev. 19.17-21, which is unquestionably based on the 'gorging' of Ezekiel 39. In Ezekiel, the meal is explicitly called a 'sacrifice' (39.17), but Vanhoye says that John does not wish to follow this for the idea is repugnant to him. He thus sets the incident in the context of the 'feast provided by God', as found in passages like Isa. 25.6. Thus by alluding to more than one scripture, he is able to arrive at the meaning which he wishes to impart.

Moreover, while Revelation 20–22 is substantially modelled on Ezekiel 37–48, there are also significant differences. For example, while Ezekiel 40–48 focuses on the temple and its ordinances, John denies that his city has such a thing, 'for its temple is the Lord God the Almighty and the Lamb' (Rev. 21.22). The glory that belongs to Ezekiel's temple belongs to John's city:

As the glory of the Lord *entered the temple* by the gate facing east, the spirit lifted me up, and brought me into the inner court; and the glory of the Lord *filled the temple* (Ezek. 43.4-5).

And *the city* has no need of sun or moon to shine on it, for the glory of God is its light, and its lamp is the Lamb (Rev. 21.23).

There also appears to be a conscious expanding of Ezekiel's horizons.[37] Thus while Ezek. 47.12 promises trees whose leaves are for healing, John says that 'the leaves of the tree are for the healing *of the nations*' (Rev. 22.2). Ezekiel looks forward to a time when the tribes will be united under a Davidic king (37.24), will dwell in the land of their fathers (37.25) and God will make his dwelling with them:

My dwelling place shall be with them; and I will be their God, and they shall be my people. Then the nations shall know that I the Lord sanctify Israel, when my sanctuary is among them forevermore (Ezek. 37.27-28).

John uses much of this but with significant changes. First, when alluding to the first part in Rev. 21.3 ('He will dwell with them as their God; they will be his peoples'), John probably uses the plural λαοί (so א

36. 'L'utilisation', p. 468.
37. Vogelgesang calls it 'democratization' (*The Interpretation of Ezekiel*, pp. 128-32). See also D. Georgi, 'Who is the True Prophet', *HTR* 79 (1986), pp. 100-26.

A and accepted by NA$^{26}$) instead of the singular λαός. Secondly, John makes it quite clear that the nations are not just spectators but are fully part of the city:

> The nations will walk by its light, and the kings of the earth will bring their glory into it. Its gates will never be shut by day—and there will be no night there. People will bring into it the glory and the honour of the nations (Rev. 21.24-26).

Thus despite the impressive similarities between Revelation and Ezekiel, the differences are no less significant. By firmly making the reader think of Ezekiel's visions and then confronting him or her with drastic changes, the reader is forced to stop and ask what is going on. Ruiz thinks that the Greek itself has this function:

> The idiosyncratic Greek of Revelation often serves precisely this function: it stops the reader in mid-course with a signal that the familiar conventions of ordinary discourse are suspended. It is not simply a matter of inelegant composition or incompetence in Greek on the author's part, but of conscious and intentional difficulties placed before the reader as obstacles to confound an ordinary reading of the text.[38]

On the side of the hearers/readers, they are invited to 'reappropriate biblical metaphors through the lens of Revelation itself'.[39] This is the opposite of Beale's view that the Old Testament texts are 'utilized as a lens through which past and present eschatological fulfilment is understood'.[40] The reader is confronted with two contexts and each

---

38. *Ezekiel in the Apocalypse*, p. 220. Ruiz is not the first to suggest that John's solecisms are deliberate. A.Y. Collins put forward the view that they are part of John's protest against the establishment (*Crisis and Catharsis*, p. 47). Beale says that John was trying to produce a 'biblical effect' ('Revelation', in *Scripture Citing Scripture*, p. 332). Other scholars follow Charles, who claims that while 'John writes in Greek, he thinks in Hebrew', *Revelation*, I, p. cxliii. See also S. Thomson, *The Apocalypse and Semitic Syntax* (SNTSMS 52; Cambridge: Cambridge University Press, 1985), and for a critique, S.E. Porter, 'The Language of the Apocalypse in Recent Discussion', *NTS* 35 (1989), pp. 582-603. Ruiz seems to imply that the purpose of the solecisms is to cause the reader to 'suspend' an ordinary reading of the text. However, it would be difficult to maintain that the major solecisms (e.g. 1.5, 10, 15, 20; 2.27; 4.4 etc.) all act in this way. Indeed, one might question whether 'solecisms' is really the right way of speaking about such grammatical features. John's handling of Greek may occasionally be casual (or poetic—e.g. 1.4), but it is in no sense incompetent.

39. *Ezekiel in the Apocalypse*, p. 223.

40. 'Revelation', *Scripture Citing Scripture*, p. 325.

affects the other. The context in Ezekiel has chronological priority for it will have already affected the minds of his readers. This corresponds to Caird's 'permanent furniture of his well-stocked mind',[41] which presumably applies to at least some of his readers. Into this situation comes John's work, a work closely modelled on parts of Ezekiel but with some surprising differences. The reader is caught in a dilemma. Much of the book sounds familiar, yet he or she is constantly having to wrestle with the 'literary landmines' buried in the text. As Vogelgesang says,

> John made detailed use of Ezekiel 40–48 in constructing the new Jerusalem vision. Yet a greater contrast with that vision, where seven of nine chapters describe this temple, its ordinances and its priests, and the glory of God dwelling therein, cannot be imagined.[42]

John has not offered an interpretation of Ezekiel as a finished product. This is the truth of Fiorenza's comment that John is not offering the reader an interpretation of Scripture. Rather, by utilizing much of its structure and language, he has bound the two works together to form a complex set of interactions. As John Collins says,

> Mythological allusions, like biblical allusions, are not simple copies of the original source. Rather they transfer motifs from one context to another. By so doing they build associations and analogies and so enrich the communicative power of the language.[43]

Some of the incidents might come under the category of typology— God seals the saints against the Satanic forces, just as he sealed/marked the faithful in Jerusalem before sending in the destroyer. However, the vision of the new city is a complex mixture of similarities and differences which have to be thought out. The reader is not expected to create a synthesis and then retire from the exegetical task. The specific declaration, 'This calls for a mind that has wisdom' (17.9), does not end when one has deduced that the beast is Rome. That is perfectly obvious (in the opinion of most scholars), and the symbolism of the seven hills is hardly meant to hide it, should the book fall into the wrong hands. What is required of the reader is to think out the implications of calling Rome a Beast and to be ready to act upon it. In other words, John's use of Ezekiel involves the reader in a hermeneutical challenge.

41. *Revelation*, p. 74.
42. *Interpretation of Ezekiel*, p. 77.
43. J.J. Collins, *The Apocalyptic Imagination: An Introduction to the Jewish Matrix of Christianity* (New York: Crossroad, 1984), p. 16.

The nature of this challenge can be explored by using the literary concept of intertextuality. However, in order to avoid the possibility of anachronism, the next chapter will consider the various uses of Scripture at Qumran. Some of these uses offer close parallels to Revelation, but the main point of the chapter is to show that the need for an interactive model is not confined to the book of Revelation. Understanding the use of Scripture at Qumran requires a similar level of sophistication.

## Chapter 5

## THE USE OF SCRIPTURE AT QUMRAN

The texts discovered in the caves of Qumran are both numerous and varied. Vermes groups the non-biblical scrolls under four headings. First, there are the rules, including the Community rule (1QS), the Damascus rule (CD), the War Scroll (1QM, 4QM) and the Temple Scroll (11QT). Second, there are Hymns, Liturgies and Wisdom Poetry, for example the Thanksgiving Hymns (1QH), the Apocryphal Psalms (11QPsᵃ) and the Songs for the Holocaust of the Sabbath (4Q400-407, 11Q5-6). His third category is Biblical Interpretation, including the Genesis Apocryphon (1QapGen), commentaries on Isaiah (4Q161-64), Hosea (4Q166-67), Micah (1Q14), Nahum (4Q169), Habakkuk (1QpHab) and the Psalms (4Q171, 4Q173), a Midrash on the Last Days (4Q174 or 4QFlor), a Testimonia (4Q175 or 4QTest) and a work about the Heavenly Prince Melchizedek (11QMelch). Lastly, Vermes prints a few horoscopes (4Q186, 4QMessAr) under the heading Miscellanea. For this study, eight texts have been chosen in order to illustrate the variety of uses of Scripture at Qumran, some of which offer close parallels to the book of Revelation. The first is known as the 'Amos–Numbers Midrash', found in the A-text of the Damascus Document.

### *CD 7.14-21*[1]

*I will exile the tabernacle of your king and the bases of your statues from my tent to Damascus* (Amos v. 26-27). The Books of the Law are the *tabernacle* of the king; as God said, *I will raise up the tabernacle of David which is fallen* (Amos ix,11). The *king* is the congregation; and the *bases of the statues* are the Books of the Prophets whose sayings Israel despised. The *star* is the Interpreter of the Law who shall come to

1. Text in C. Rabin, *The Zadokite Documents* (Oxford: Clarendon Press, 1954). The relationship between Text A and Text B is complex. For a brief summary of views, see G.J. Brooke, *Exegesis at Qumran*, pp. 302-304.

> Damascus; as it is written, *A star shall come forth out of Jacob and a*
> *sceptre shall rise out of Israel* (Num. xxiv,17). The *sceptre* is the Prince
> of the whole congregation, and when he comes *he shall smite all the*
> *children of Seth* (Num. xxiv,17).

In this passage, two texts from Amos (both concerning the 'tabernacle', as our author reads it) are linked with the 'star' or 'sceptre' of Num. 24.17. The explanation of 'star' seems abrupt since it precedes rather than follows the quotation from Numbers. The link might be the fact that the first part of Amos 5.26 speaks of 'Kaiwan your star-god', which is both explained (star = Interpreter of the Law) and then clarified by the quotation from Numbers. The bulk of the midrash consists of various identifications:

| | | |
|---|---|---|
| Tabernacle | = | Books of the Law |
| King | = | Congregation |
| Bases of the statues | = | Books of the Prophets |
| Star | = | Interpreter of the Law |
| Sceptre | = | Prince of congregation |

John's use of Scripture in Revelation 17 offers a parallel to this. The chapter begins with a series of descriptions ('the great whore who is seated on many waters'; 'a scarlet beast that was full of blasphemous names'; 'it had seven heads and ten horns'; 'in her hand a golden cup full of abominations' etc.). These are not explicit quotations as in CD 7, but they certainly echo key passages (e.g. Ezek. 16 and 23; Jer. 28; Dan. 7). John then proceeds to make a number of identifications:

| | | |
|---|---|---|
| The seven heads | = | Seven mountains and also Seven kings |
| The beast | = | Eighth king (and one of the seven) |
| Ten horns | = | Ten kings |
| The waters | = | Peoples, multitudes… |
| The woman | = | Great city |

It could be argued that these are less arbitrary than the identifications in CD 7, but that might be because we are more familiar with the imagery of Revelation. Thus Brooke[2] suggests that the final letter of 'Sakkuth' (which our author reads as 'sukkuth' = tabernacle) might have suggested the Law (תורה), while the final letter of 'Kaiwan' (which the author expounds as 'kannē')[3] might have suggested prophets (נביאים).

---

2.   *Exegesis at Qumran*, p. 307.
3.   See F.F. Bruce, *Biblical Exegesis in the Qumran Texts* (London: Tyndale Press, 1960), pp. 37-38, and his article, 'Biblical Exposition at Qumran', in Gospel

Alternatively, the use of anagram might have led צלמים to be read as
מליצים, which can mean 'interpreters' (and hence prophets). How
'arbitrary' or 'artificial' this will seem depends on the mindset of the
reader. F.F. Bruce concludes that 'by reason of coincidence in wording
or similarity in subject-matter, a whole catena of biblical texts is viewed
as presenting the origin, history and prospects of the community'.[4]
Could the same be said for Revelation 17?

*1QH Col 3 Lines 6-10 (Vermes Hymn 4)*

| | |
|---|---|
| 6 | They caused [me] to be<br>like a ship on the deeps of the [sea], |
| 7 | and like a fortified city<br>before [the aggressor],<br>[and] like a woman in travail<br>with her first-born child,<br>upon whose belly pangs have come |
| 8 | and grievous pains,<br>filling with anguish her child-bearing crucible.<br>For the children have come to the throes of Death, |
| 9 | and she labours in her pains who bears a man.<br>For amid the throes of Death<br>she shall bring forth a man-child,<br>and amid the pains of Hell |
| 10 | there shall spring from her child-bearing crucible a Marvellous<br>Mighty Counsellor;<br>and a man shall be delivered from out of the throes. |

Because of the state of the scroll, it is difficult to tell where one hymn
ends and another begins. Vermes calls this Hymn 4, but on Holm-
Nielsen's[5] reckoning it is Hymn 5. Modelled (it would appear) on the
biblical psalms, these hymns contain a wealth of allusions to both the
Psalms (about 150 according to Holm-Nielsen) and Isaiah (about 120).
There is a much smaller number from the Pentateuch (about 40) and
about 20 each from Jeremiah, Ezekiel, Job and Proverbs.[6] Thus the

*Perspectives* , III (ed. R.T. France and D. Wenham; Sheffield: JSOT Press, 1983),
p. 90.
    4.   'Biblical Exposition at Qumran', p. 91.
    5.   S. Holm-Nielsen, *Hodayot: Psalms from Qumran* (Universitetsforlaget 1;
Aarhus, 1960).
    6.   *Hodayot*, pp. 354-59.

general distribution is closer to Revelation than Matthew, Romans or Hebrews. This particular passage draws on a number of the 'travail' (NRSV 'labour') texts in the Old Testament, such as:

| Isa. 13.8 | *Pangs* and agony will seize them;<br>they will be in *anguish like a woman in labour.* |
|---|---|
| Jer. 4.31 | For I heard a cry as of a *woman in labour*,<br>*anguish* as of one bringing forth her *first child.* |
| Isa. 37.3 | *children have come to the birth*,<br>and there is no strength to bring them forth. |
| Isa. 66.7 | Before she was in labour she gave birth;<br>before her pain came upon her she *delivered a son.* |
| Isa. 9.6 | For a child has been born for us, a son given to us;<br>authority rests upon his shoulders;<br>and he is named *Wonderful Counsellor . . .* |

In the first part of the hymn, birth-pangs appears to be one of a number of metaphors for suffering ('ship in a storm', 'city under siege'), but as the psalm progresses the messianic overtones become more pronounced ('Marvellous Mighty Counsellor') and invite comparison with Revelation 12:

> A great portent appeared in heaven: a woman clothed with the sun . . . She was pregnant and was crying out in birthpangs, in the agony of giving birth . . . And she gave birth to a son, a male child, who is to rule all the nations . . . Then the dragon was angry with the woman, and went off to make war on the rest of her children, those who keep the commandments of God and hold the testimony of Jesus (Rev. 12.1, 2, 5, 17).

If the hymn is talking about the 'nativity of the Wonderful Counsellor', as Brownlee[7] calls it, then the author appears to be identifying with the 'pregnant mother'. Brownlee says he 'may have felt that in a peculiar way it would be through his sufferings (though not without reference to the Community) that the Messiah would be born'.[8] The parenthesis indicates Brownlee's awareness that the more natural understanding of the 'virgin mother' is the community (as in Rev. 12) rather than an individual (as in Mt. 1.23). Further, Holm-Nielsen points out that the parallel between the children coming to the throes of death

7. W.H. Brownlee, 'Messianic Motifs of Qumran and the New Testament', *NTS* 3 (1956–57), p. 25.
8. 'Messianic Motifs', p. 25.

and the mother giving birth 'amid the throes of death' shows that we are dealing with a plurality of persons. Thus in his view, the psalm represents 'the sufferings sustained at that time by the community, and in particular by their leader, the "Teacher of Righteousness", with the idea that these sufferings were warnings of the dawn of the Messianic era. Thus the psalm is interpreted eschatologically, but not directly of the Messiah.'[9]

### 4Q405 20 ii 21-22[10]

> The [cheru]bim prostrate themselves before him and bless. As they rise, a whispered divine voice [is heard], and there is a roar of praise. When they drop their wings, there is a [whispere]d divine voice. The cherubim bless the image of the throne-chariot above the firmament, [and] they praise [the majes]ty of the luminous firmament beneath his seat of glory. When the wheels advance, angels of holiness come and go. From between his glorious wheels there is as it were a fiery vision of most holy spirits. About them, the appearance of rivulets of fire in the likeness of gleaming brass, and a work of...radiance in many-coloured glory, marvellous pigments, clearly mingled. The spirits of the living 'gods' move perpetually with the glory of the marvellous chariot(s). The whispered voice of blessing accompanies the roar of their advance, and they praise the Holy One on their way of return.

Like John's throne vision in Revelation 4, this passage relies heavily on Ezek. 1, 10. The movable throne is now specifically called a throne-chariot ('merkabah') and is attended by cherubim (cf. Ezek. 10.3). There seems to be a particular interest in the praise offered by the cherubim and the sound made by their wings (cf. Ezek. 1.24). There is mention of a firmament (Ezek. 1.23), moving wheels (Ezek. 1.15-16 ôpannîm) and rims (Ezek. 10.2 galgilîm). In amidst the wheels is fire (Ezek. 1.4), the appearance of which is like 'gleaming brass' (ḥašmal). Carol Newsom says,

9. Holm-Nielsen, *Hodayot*, p. 63. See further R.D. Aus, 'The Relevance of Isaiah 66:7 to Revelation 12 and 2 Thessalonians 1', *ZNW* 67 (1976), pp. 252-68.
10. Text first published by J. Strugnell, 'The Angelic Liturgy at Qumran', in *Congress Volume, Oxford 1959* (VTSup 7; Leiden: Brill, 1960), pp. 318-45. Now available in a critical edition by C. Newsom, *Songs of the Sabbath Sacrifice: A Critical Edition* (Harvard Semitic Studies 27; Atlanta: Scholars Press, 1985).

the text of Ezekiel's vision has been transformed in the twelfth Sabbath Shirot in the interest of describing celestial praise. More specifically, the passage in question uses and exegetically transforms the text of Ezekiel in order to answer the implicit question, 'How does the chariot throne itself praise God?'[11]

Newsom believes that the point of departure for this exegesis was Ezek. 3.12-13, where according to Halperin, the original reading רום כבוד was changed to ברוך כבוד not by copyist error but deliberate exegesis.[12] If this is correct, then it was an early change, for it is supported by the LXX and MT. Newsom thinks that our author shows knowledge of both readings, for the text says that the cherubim 'bless as they lift themselves up' (her translation). With respect to the sound generated by the wings, Ezekiel says it is

a.  like the sound of mighty waters, like the thunder of the Almighty, a sound of tumult like the sound of an army (1.24)
b.  the sound of loud rumbling (קול רעש גדול) (3.12)
c.  like the voice of God Almighty when he speaks (10.5)

However, our author calls it a 'whispered divine voice' (קול דממת אלוהים) or 'sound of divine stillness' (Newsom), which seems to be derived from 1 Kgs 19.11-12, where God is not in the earthquake but the 'still small voice' (קול דממה דקה). It is the use of 'earthquake' (NRSV 'rumbling') in Ezek. 3.12 that provides the link with 1 Kings 19 (*gᵉzērâ šāwâ*) and Newsom thinks our author is consciously 'correcting' the statement of Ezek. 3.12.

There is an interesting parallel here with John's use of these traditions. In the inaugural vision, John appears to be following (and augmenting) Dan. 10.5-6, but when he comes to the description of the voice 'like the roar of a multitude', he substitutes 'like the sound of

---

11. 'Merkabah Exegesis in the Qumran Sabbath Shirot', *JJS* 38 (1987), p. 19. Already in the LXX there appears to be speculation about this praise. So the LXX of Ezek. 1.23 speaks of the 'fluttering' of their wings (αἱ πτέρυγες αὐτῶν ἐκτεταμέναι πτερυσσόμεναι) and the coming of the glory of God in Ezek. 43.2 is like the 'sound of many repeating' (φωνὴ διπλασιαζόντων πολλῶν) instead of the MT's 'sound of many waters'. See D.J. Halperin, 'Merkabah Midrash in the Septuagint', *JBL* 101 (1982), pp. 351-63. The Targum, as well as expanding the number of wings of the four creatures to 256, also glosses Ezek. 1.24: 'as they went, the sound of their words were as though they were thanking and blessing their Master, the everliving King of the worlds'. In Rev. 4, the creatures specifically sing the trisagion of Isa. 6.

12. 'Merkabah Midrash in the Septuagint', p. 356.

many waters'. Swete suggests this was because of John's sojourn on Patmos, but a more likely solution is his desire to link up with these texts in Ezekiel (and thus to the description of God's glory in Ezek. 43.2). This is indicated by his further use of these metaphors in Rev. 14.2 and 19.6. In Rev. 14.2, there is a voice from heaven which is 'like the sound of many waters and like the sound of loud thunder'. It is also like the sound of 'harpists playing on their harps', though it is not clear what element of the playing is in mind. Then in 19.6, Daniel's expression comes first (ὡς φωνὴν ὄχλου), followed by the other two expressions:

> Then I heard what seemed to be the voice of a great multitude, like the sound of many waters and like the sound of mighty thunderpeals...

After speaking of the sound of the wings, Ezek. 3.12-13 mentions the sound of the 'wheels beside them'. Newsom believes that the author of the Shirot now attempts to elucidate how the wheels (*ôpannîm*) produce their sound. This is done by declaring that the movement of the wheels is accompanied by a corresponding movement of 'holy angels'. Drawing on the language of Ezekiel 10, where the man 'clothed in linen' was told to go 'within the wheelwork', Newsom says,

> The novel picture thus generated by the exegetical activity of the author of the Shirot is that of fiery angelic beings who habitually move back and forth with the movement of the ophannim.[13]

There then follows a description of these fiery spirits, mostly drawn from Ezek. 1, 10, though 'rivulets of fire' probably comes from Dan. 7.9-10. John also draws on both of these texts, where hair as 'white as white wool' (Rev. 1.14) is a clear reference to Dan. 7.9 but the use of ποδήρης (1.13) probably points to Ezek. 10.2 (LXX).[14] Finally, after a further reference to the movement of the spirits, our author is now able to draw the required conclusion: 'The whispered voice of blessing accompanies the roar of their advance, and they praise the Holy One on their way of return'.

### *4QFlor10-13*[15]

> *The Lord declares to you that He will build you a House* (2 Sam. vii,11c).
> *I will raise up your seed after you* (2 Sam. vii,12). *I will establish the throne of his kingdom [for ever]* (2 Sam. vii,13). *I [will be] his father and*

---

13. 'Merkabah Exegesis in the Qumran Sabbath Shirot', p. 26.
14. So Hanson, *Utterances*, p. 167.
15. Text in J.M. Allegro, *DJD*, V (Oxford: Clarendon Press, 1968), pp. 53-57.

*he shall be my son* (2 Sam. vii,14). He is the Branch of David who shall arise with the Interpreter of the Law [to rule] in Zion [at the end] of time. As it is written, *I will raise up the tent of David that is fallen* (Amos ix,11). That is to say, the fallen *tent of David* is he who shall arise to save Israel.

In this part of the florilegium, we have an abbreviated quotation of 2 Sam. 7.11-14, which is then linked to the fallen tent of Amos 9.11. It is probably a coincidence that homoeoteleuton could explain the author's omissions, for they do not seem to be accidental:

Moreover *the LORD declares to you that* the LORD *will make you a house.* When your days are fulfilled and you lie down with your ancestors, *I will raise up your offspring after you*, who shall come forth from your body, and *I will establish* his kingdom. He shall build a house for my name, and I will establish *the throne of his kingdom forever. I will be a father to him, and he shall be a son to me* (2 Sam. 7.11c-14a).

Brooke[16] offers a reason for each of the omissions. The first omission is 'When your days are fulfilled and you lie down with your ancestors', which ties the text to its original temporal context. Loosing its moorings in this way helps to facilitate its application to the new situation. The second phrase, 'come forth from your body', speculates on the origins of the Messiah, which is generally avoided at Qumran. Lastly, the phrase 'he shall build a house for my name', is probably omitted since it clashes with the document's claim that the house will not be built by human hands.

I have already shown how John uses abbreviation in connection with the throne vision (Rev. 4) and the list of merchandise in Revelation 18. Another example is the use of Ezek. 39.17-20 in Rev. 19.17-18:

As for you, mortal, thus says the Lord God: *Speak to the birds* of every kind and to all the wild animals: *Assemble and come, gather* from all around to the sacrificial feast that I am preparing for you, a *great* sacrificial *feast* on the mountains of Israel, and you shall eat flesh and drink blood. You shall *eat the flesh of the mighty*, and drink the blood of the princes of the earth—of rams, of lambs, and of goats, of bulls, all of them fatlings of Bashan. You shall eat fat until you are filled, and drink blood until you are drunk, at the sacrificial feast that I am preparing for you. And you shall be filled at my table with *horses and charioteers, with warriors and all kinds of soldiers*, says the Lord God (Ezek. 39.17-20).

Also in Brooke, *Exegesis at Qumran*, pp. 86-97, with restorations and translation.
    16. *Exegesis at Qumran*, p. 112.

> Then I saw an angel standing in the sun, and with a loud voice he *called to all the birds* that fly in midheaven, '*Come, gather* for the *great* supper of God, *to eat the flesh of kings*, the *flesh* of captains, the *flesh of the mighty*, the *flesh* of *horses and their riders—flesh* of all, both free and slave, both small and great' (Rev. 19.17-18).

Judging by what he retains, John's chief interest in the passage appears to be the classes of people involved in the slaughter. This is confirmed by his own expansion, 'free and slave, both small and great'. As to what he omits, he does not call it a 'sacrificial feast', he does not mention drinking blood, and, apart from the horses, he does not include the animals. This is probably due to his desire to concentrate on the human participants of the battle. The omission of blood might be because he has already made use of the 'spilt blood' image in the harvesting of Revelation 14 and Vanhoye thinks the reason for omitting 'sacrifice' is because '*Jean répugnait sans doute à conserver le nom de sacrifice pour désigner l'exécution des jugements divins contre le monde pécheur*'.[17]

Abbreviation can perform a number of functions. If the passage is familiar, it may simply be a device for being less wordy. The reader already know the substance of the passage and merely needs to be directed towards it. Long quotations of familiar passages might only challenge the reader's patience. On the other hand, if the passage is familiar, the omissions will almost certainly be noticed and this may have the effect of drawing attention to them. This will be considered more fully in the next chapter. A third function, particularly if the passage is less familiar, might be to change the emphasis, as Vanhoye suggests. Concerning the Dead Sea Scrolls, Fishbane says that on occasions, the author's purpose was to produce a composition in which the reader 'confronts the text as a new Torah, even while perceiving the biblical base around which the sources and innovations were integrated. One may confidently surmise that this was the very hope and intent of the author.'[18] Thus in skilled hands, abbreviation can act as a genuine mode of exegesis and interpretation.

17. 'L'utilisation', p. 469.
18. M. Fishbane, 'Use, Authority and Interpretation of Mikra at Qumran', in *MIKRA: Text, Translation, Reading and Interpretation of the Hebrew Bible in Ancient Judaism and Early Christianity* (ed. M.J. Mulder; Philadelphia: Fortress Press, 1988), p. 351.

*11QMelch 2-10*[19]

And concerning that which He said, *In [this] year of Jubilee [each of you shall return to his property* (Lev. xxv,13); and likewise, *And this is the manner of release:] every creditor shall release that which he has lent [to his neighbour. He shall not exact it of his neighbour and his brother], for God's release [has been proclaimed]* (Deut. xv,2). [And it will be proclaimed at] the end of days concerning the captives as [He said, *To proclaim liberty to the captives* (Isa. lxi,1). Its interpretation is that He] will assign them to the Sons of Heaven and to the inheritance of Melchizedek; f[or He will cast] their [lot] amid the po[rtions of Melchize]dek, who will return them there and will proclaim to them liberty, forgiving them [the wrong-doings] of all their iniquities.

And this thing will [occur] in the first week of the Jubilee that follows the nine Jubilees. And the Day of Atonement is the e[nd of the] tenth [Ju]bilee, when all the Sons of [Light] and the men of the lot of Mel[chi]zedek will be atoned for. [And] a statute concerns them [to prov]ide them with their rewards. For this is the moment of the Year of Grace for Melchizedek. [And h]e will, by his strength, judge the holy ones of God, executing judgement as it is written concerning him in the Songs of David, who said, ELOHIM *has taken his place in the divine council; in the midst of the gods he holds judgement* (Pss. lxxxii,1).

The words of the opening source text, 'In this year of Jubilee', could come from either Lev. 25.13 or 27.24, but in view of the use made of Leviticus 25 in the rest of the text, the former is preferable. This is then linked with the Sabbatical year of Deut. 15.2, probably through the common use of ἄφεσις in the LXX.[20] An explanation is then introduced, which Fitzmyer restores: 'Its meaning [is] for the end of days' (cf. Vermes, 'it will be proclaimed at the end of days') and concerns 'the captives'. The supporting text is missing, but from the lines that follow it

19. Text is conveniently found in the article by M. de Jonge and A.S. van der Woude, '11Q Melchizedek and the New Testament', *NTS* 12 (1965–66), pp. 301-26. Also with restorations and commentary, J.A. Fitzmyer, 'Further Light on Melchizedek from Qumran Cave 11', *JBL* 86 (1967), pp. 25-42. The connected text offered by Vermes (despite the use of brackets) disguises the fact that we are dealing with the restoration of 13 fragments, resulting in many lacunae. On average, about one half of each line has to be restored, though lines 9-10 are quite well preserved.

20. So Fitzmyer, 'Further Light', p. 33, and de Jonge and van der Woude, '11Q Melchizedek', p. 304. The Hebrew text of Lev. 25.13 says, 'In this year of Jubilee', but the LXX rendering ἐν τῷ ἔτει τῆς ἀφέσεως σημασίᾳ shares the word ἀφέσεως with Deut. 15.2 (καὶ οὕτως τὸ πρόσταγμα τῆς ἀφέσεως).

appears to have been Isa. 61.1, facilitated, according to Fitzmyer,[21] by the common use of *d*ᵉ*rôr* ('release') in Leviticus 25 and Isaiah 61.

The interpretation that follows is difficult to understand because of the fragmentary nature of the text. It is clear that it concerns Melchizedek (written here as two words), but is he the intended subject of 'proclaim to them liberty, forgiving them [the wrong-doings] of all their iniquities'? The first expression picks up Isa. 61.1, though Fitzmyer also cites Jer. 34.8 and Lev. 25.10 as possibilities. In view of its use later in the passage, the second expression probably comes from Dan. 9.24 ('Seventy weeks are decreed for your people and your holy city: to finish the transgression, to put an end to sin, and to atone for iniquity'). M. de Jonge and A.S. van der Woude admit the possibility that Melchizedek might be the intended subject of these words but declare that certainty is impossible. In the second paragraph, however, Melchizedek's exalted status is affirmed through the application of Ps. 82.1. The original appears to mean that God (ELOHIM) presides over the 'gods' in the divine council, but here, ELOHIM applies to Melchizedek. Fitzmyer thus translates: 'Elohim has taken his stand in the assembly of El, in the midst of gods he gives judgment'.

The book of Revelation also applies texts that were originally associated with God to another figure. For example, in the inaugural vision (Rev. 1.14) the description of God in Dan. 7.9 ('hair of his head like pure wool') is applied to Jesus. In Rev. 1.17, the words of Isa. 44.6 ('I am the first and I am the last') are put into his mouth and the rider of the white horse is called 'King of kings and Lord of lords' (see Deut. 10.17, Dan. 2.47 and the LXX text of Dan. 4.37). According to Newman,[22] John was aided in this process by the way that Daniel 7 had already used Ezekiel 1 to describe two figures, namely, the 'Ancient One' of 7.9 and the 'one like a human being' in 7.13. Newman[23] thinks that the reason this did not constitute a breach with monotheism was that it did not involve worship of such figures. If this is true, then it is

---

21. 'Further Light', p. 34. Likewise, de Jonge and van der Woude, '11Q Melchizedek', p. 306.

22. C.C. Newman, *Paul's Glory-Christology* (NovTSup 69; Leiden: Brill, 1992), pp. 92-99.

23. 'Jews were quite willing to clothe God's vice-regents with divinity; what Jews were unwilling to do, however, was to give worship to these special agents as God' (*Paul's Glory-Christology* p. 98). See further L.W. Hurtado, *One God, One Lord: Early Christian Devotion and Ancient Jewish Monotheism* (London: SCM Press, 1988); R. Bauckham, 'The Worship of Jesus', *Climax of Prophecy*, pp. 118-49.

significant that Revelation not only applies such attributes to Jesus but also portrays him as sharing in the adoration and praise of God:

> 'To the one seated on the throne and to the Lamb be blessing and honour and glory and might forever and ever!' And the four living creatures said, 'Amen!' And the elders fell down and worshiped (Rev. 5.13b-14).

## 1QpHab 6.12–7.5[24]

*I will take my stand to watch and will station myself upon my fortress. I will watch to see what He will say to me and how [He will answer] my complaint. And the Lord answered [and said to me, 'Write down the vision and make it plain] upon the tablets, that [he who reads] may read it speedily* (ii,1-2)…and God told Habakkuk to write down that which would happen to the final generation, but He did not make known to him when time would come to an end. And as for that which He said, *That he who reads may read it speedily*: interpreted this concerns the Teacher of Righteousness, to whom God made known all the mysteries of the words of His servants the Prophets.

The commentary on Habakkuk was one of the first discoveries at Qumran and offers interpretations (*pesharim*) on the first two chapters of the biblical book. The omission of the third chapter might be because the first two chapters circulated independently or simply that it did not serve the author's purpose.[25] According to Knibb, it is the 'best preserved and in many ways the most important of the Qumran biblical commentaries…primarily…for the very full illustration it provides of methods of biblical exegesis employed by the Qumran community'.[26] It

---

24. Text in M. Burrows, *The Dead Sea Scrolls of St Mark's Monastery. I. The Isaiah Manuscript and the Habakkuk Commentary* (New Haven: American Schools of Oriental Research, 1950). For commentary, see W.H. Brownlee, *The Midrash Pesher of Habakkuk* (SBLMS 24; Missoula: Scholars Press, 1979); M.P. Horgan, *Pesharim: Qumran Interpretations of Biblical Books* (CBQMS 8; Washington: Catholic Biblical Association of America, 1979).

25. The final column of the scroll only consists of four lines so it is not a case of the last chapter being lost. Some scholars had already argued that the third chapter of Habakkuk was a later addition and the evidence of 1QpHab could be used to support this. In support of the unity of the book, Haak points to the presence of Hab. 3 in the Greek minor prophets scroll found at Naḥal Ḥever. He also points out that none of the extant pesharim are of complete books. See R.D. Haak, *Habakkuk* (VTSup 44; Leiden: Brill, 1992), pp. 1-10.

26. M.A. Knibb, *The Qumran Community* (Cambridge: Cambridge University Press, 1987), p. 221.

is for this reason that two examples have been taken from this text.

In the above passage, the biblical text occurs at the bottom of column 6 and has to be restored in three places. The final restoration is helped by the repetition of the words in the pesher ('he who reads it may read it speedily'), though not without ambiguity, since the verb 'to run' (taken figuratively by Vermes to mean 'speedily') appears above the line in a different hand. There is also dispute as to its meaning. Vermes takes it figuratively but Brownlee claims that such a use is unattested. He prefers to take it literally of a herald who runs to proclaim his message.[27] Haak agrees but insists on a more specific meaning: 'The emphasis is not on the fact that the reader may run, but rather that the message of judgment is to be so clear that the reader *will* run in terror'.[28]

The first part of the pesher (presumably on Hab. 2.1) is lost at the bottom of column 6 but what remains at the top of column 7 is well preserved and gives a number of clues as to the community's understanding of prophecy. First, the words of Habakkuk are said to apply to the 'final generation', even though Habakkuk was told by God to make them plain. The verb here (*bā'ēr*) can mean 'engrave' and this would fit with what follows ('upon the tablets'). However, most scholars take it in the sense of Deut. 1.5 ('Moses undertook to expound this law') and render it something like 'make it plain on tablets' (NRSV). Nevertheless, our author believes that there was something incomplete about this and adds, 'but He did not make known to him when time would come to an end'. Brownlee translates, 'but the fulness of that time He did not make known to him', since it 'was not mere chronological knowledge which Habakkuk lacked, such as when the consummation would come or how long the period of the last days would last...but it was an understanding of the specific events to which his words made veiled and enigmatic allusions'.[29]

In the light of the next line about God making known the mysteries to the Teacher, this is no doubt correct. However, it may also be the case that the community was very concerned about the time of the end and so Vermes's translation could be right. As for making known 'all the mysteries of the words of His servants the Prophets', John makes a similar claim in Rev. 1.1-3 and 10.5-7. In the first, the allusion to Amos 3.7 ('Surely the Lord God does nothing, without revealing his secret to

27. *Midrash Pesher*, p. 108.
28. *Habakkuk*, p. 56 (italics his).
29. *Midrash Pesher*, p. 110.

his servants the prophets') is combined with an allusion to Dan. 2.28 ('there is a God in heaven who reveals mysteries, and he has disclosed to King Nebuchadnezzar what will happen at the end of days'). The notion of 'mystery' is picked up in the explanation of Rev. 1.20 and subsequently echoed in Rev. 10.7 (the use of μυστήριον in Rev. 17.5, 7 is somewhat different). In Rev. 10.5-7, the Amos 3 + Daniel 2 combination is elaborated by drawing in the 'swearing angel' of Dan. 12.7:

> Then the angel whom I saw standing on the sea and the land raised his right hand to heaven and swore by him who lives forever and ever... 'There will be no more delay, but in the days when the seventh angel is to blow his trumpet, the mystery of God will be fulfilled (ἐτελέσθη), as he announced to his servants the prophets'.

The parallel between John and the Teacher of Righteousness is denied by Fiorenza: 'Rev. does not attribute to John the same prophetic authority. John's task is not exposition and interpretation of the Old Testament prophets but prophetic proclamation.'[30] There is some truth in this in that John is careful to claim only a derived authority (God—Jesus—Angel—John) and it is clearly not a systematic exposition of Scripture like the *pesharim*. Nevertheless, this is not the whole story. John may claim a derived authority but he appears to be in little doubt about the authority of his finished work:

> I warn everyone who hears the words of the prophecy of this book: if anyone adds to them, God will add to that person the plagues described in this book; if anyone takes away from the words of the book of this prophecy, God will take away that person's share in the tree of life and in the holy city, which are described in this book (Rev. 22.18-19).

Further, since there is a huge variety of literary forms (and hence uses of Scripture) among the documents of Qumran, it is a mistake to read too much into the difference between Revelation and the *pesharim*. There are other documents, such as the *Shirot* and the hymns, which are much closer to the allusive style of Revelation. Bauckham[31] has a brief

---

30. 'Apokalypsis and Propheteia', *Justice and Judgment*, p. 136.

31. 'John's relation to the Old Testament prophets is not unlike that of the Teacher of Righteousness. This is denied by Schüssler Fiorenza (1985), p. 136, because she entirely misunderstands and misrepresents Revelation's use of the Old Testament. Certainly, John sees himself as a prophet in the Old Testament tradition of prophecy and receives a revelation given to him as a prophet. But just as late Old Testament prophecy already takes up, interprets and develops the authoritative oracles of its predecessors, so John's prophecy gathers up and interprets all the prophecies

discussion of the parallel between John and the Teacher of Righteousness, but it really warrants a detailed study.

### 1. *'did not make known to him when time would come to an end'*
However this phrase is translated, it goes against the emphasis in Hab. 2.2 that God was going to make his reply clear. Such an interpretation, Brownlee says, 'would contradict the presuppositions of Qumrân; for if the meaning had been written with full clarity, the ingenious interpretations of Qumrân would be an imposition. Consequently, the text had to be made to say just the opposite.'[32] In answer to this, he mentions the possibility that our author might have read (or deliberately punned) *bā'ēr* ('make empty') for *bā'ēr* ('make plain'), a suggestion also found in Knibb.[33]

### 2. *'he who reads may read it speedily/run'*
The original copyist omitted the verb *yārûṣ*, giving the meaning 'for the sake of one who reads it', which might have been taken to mean the 'Teacher of Righteousness'. Silberman[34] offers further possibilities. First, he notes that in the Babylonian Talmud (*b. San.* 34 a), Jer. 23.29 is interpreted by taking *pṣṣ* ('shatter') to mean 'interpret', on the basis that 'just as the rock is split into many splinters, so also may one biblical verse convey many teachings'. If our verb is taken from *rṣṣ* ('crush') rather than *rûṣ* ('run'), there may be an analogous usage here. Secondly, Silbermann notes that auditory word plays abound in this commentary, so that our author may have been influenced by the Aramaic *trṣ*, which can mean 'interpret'. Brownlee[35] adds a further suggestion that our author may have read *yārîṣ*) instead of *yārûṣ* (the two letters are almost indistinguishable in the scrolls), which in the hiphil can mean 'to arrange subjects for debate'.

of the Old Testament prophets which he regarded as relating to the eschatological coming of God's kingdom. Because the Old Testament prophecies are authoritative for him, his fresh revelation cannot be discontinuous with them, but must be closely related to interpretation of them, thereby providing the culmination of the whole prophetic tradition'(*Climax of Prophecy*, p. 262 n. 32). See also D. Hill, 'Prophecy and Prophets in the Revelation of Saint John', *NTS* 18 (1971–72), pp. 401-18.

32. *Midrash Pesher*, p. 109.

33. *The Qumran Community*, p. 233.

34. L.H. Silberman, 'Unriddling the Riddle: A Study in the Structure and Language of the Habakkuk Pesher (1QpHab.)', *RevQ* 3 (1961–62), pp. 344-45.

35. *Midrash Pesher*, p. 111

3. *'to whom God made known all the mysteries'*
It has already been suggested that this is an allusion to Amos 3.7 and
probably Dan. 2.28-29 as well. Brownlee[36] thinks there is a connection
between *rûṣ* ('run') and *rāz* ('mystery') and illustrates the use of *rāz* by
quoting from the Thanksgiving hymns:

> Through me Thou hast illumined the face of the Congregation and hast
> shown Thine infinite power. For Thou hast given me knowledge through
> Thy marvellous mysteries, and hast shown Thyself mighty within me in
> the midst of Thy marvellous Council (1QH 4.27-29).

### *1QpHab 8.3-10*

*Moreover, the arrogant man seizes wealth without halting. He widens his
gullet like Hell and like Death he has never enough. All the nations are
gathered to him and all the peoples are assembled to him. Will they not
all of them taunt him and jeer at him saying, 'Woe to him who amasses
that which is not his! How long will he load himself up with pledges?'*
(ii,5-6) Interpreted, this concerns the Wicked Priest who was called by the
name of truth when he first arose. But when he ruled over Israel his heart
became proud, and he forsook God and betrayed the precepts for the sake
of riches.

### 1. *Relation of Habakkuk 2.5-6 (MT) and Text Quoted*
The text quoted by our author differs from the MT in several respects.
The most important is the reading *hōn* ('wealth') instead of the MT's
*hayyayin* ('wine'). As wealth forms one of the main themes of the
interpretation ('for the sake of riches'), it is easy to think that our author
deliberately made the change, especially as the following word appears
to have gained a *'yod'*. However, it is commonly recognized that 'wine'
is a difficult reading and it may be that the original did read 'wealth' (so
Jerusalem Bible). Haak suggests an original of *hywn ybgd* ('mire') to
account for the MT's *hyyn bwgd* and the scroll's *hwn ybgwd*.[37] It is
therefore unclear whether our author is exploiting a variant, changing
the text or indeed preserving an ancient reading.

### 2. *Relation between Text and Interpretation*
Whatever stood in the author's *Vorlage*, the quotation in the scroll
speaks of 'wealth' and that, according to our author, is the reason why

36. *Midrash Pesher*, pp. 111-112.
37. *Habakkuk*, p. 61. Brownlee suggests an original of *hawwān* (presumptious)
to account for the various readings, *Midrash Pesher*, p. 132.

the Wicked Priest 'forsook God and betrayed the precepts'. It is possible
that our author is trying to show that the Wicked Priest has failed the
criteria for taking office found in Exod. 18.21 ('You should also look for
able men among all the people, men who fear God, are trustworthy, and
hate dishonest gain').[38] There also appears to be a link between 'taunt
him' (*māšāl*) and 'ruled over Israel' (*māšal bᵉ-yiśrā'ēl*) and Brownlee
notes that even modern lexicographers are unsure whether we are
talking about different meanings of the same word or different roots.[39]

Perhaps the most significant relation between text and interpretation is
how our author took this to be about the 'Wicked Priest'. This is the
first mention of this character since 1.13, where the title is probably to
be inferred. Commenting on Hab. 1.4 ('The wicked surround the
righteous'), the only words of the pesher which have survived are '...is
the Teacher of Righteousness'. Vermes restores: 'The wicked is the
Wicked Priest, and the righteous is the Teacher of Righteousness'.
However, the next verse of Habakkuk starts: 'Look at the nations', and
this signals the beginning of a long treatment of the author's political
foes, the 'Kittim'. It is therefore understandable that the 'Wicked Priest'
fades into the background and so the question is, what was it about Hab.
2.5-6 that led to his reintroduction? According to Haak,[40] Hab. 2.5
marks the beginning of five woe oracles:

| | | |
|---|---|---|
| 1. | 2.5-7 | The insatiable appetite and its results |
| 2. | 2.8-10 | The plunder of nations/peoples |
| 3. | 2.11-13 | The one building by wickedness |
| 4. | 2.14-17 | Covering and uncovering |
| 5. | 2.18-20 | The ineffectiveness of the idols |

The 'Wicked Priest' is made the subject of the first four but does not
appear in the fifth. This might be because 2.18-20 specifically mentions
idols and our author could not resist a jibe at the 'nations which serve
stone and wood' (13.1-2). On the other hand, one might have expected
the description 'teacher of lies' to be applied to the 'Wicked Priest'.
Nevertheless, it is worth pointing out that there is an interesting division

---

38. So Brownlee, *Midrash Pesher*, p. 135.

39. *Midrash Pesher*, pp. 143-44. It is unclear in BDB (p. 605) whether it is
listing 3 roots or 3 categories of the same root.

40. *Habakkuk*, pp. 20-22. These divisions do not coincide with the occurrence of
*hôy* (v. 6, 9, 12, 15, 19). Haak argues that these divisions make better sense of the
material and hence the author of Habakkuk must have broken with the usual tradition
to begin a woe oracle with *hôy*.

in the author's interpretation of Habakkuk, with the Kittim being the subject of the 'Chaldean oracles' (exception at 2.8) and the 'Wicked Priest' the subject of the 'woe oracles' (exception at 1.4). Despite the strangeness of some of the author's exegesis (to the modern reader), this at least shows some contextual awareness. Finally, Slomovic[41] thinks that 'Priest' was suggested by reading כי הון as one word with *yod* and *waw* transposed.

John's use of Scripture often entails weaving various texts together to form a new compositional unit. Vos[42] concludes from this that John has little regard for the original context (as many have said about the DSS),[43] but this judgment is too simplistic. For example, though the inaugural vision alludes to as many as fourteen different texts, the core is based on the visions of Daniel 7 and 10. The description of the beast in Revelation 13 is modelled on the beasts of Daniel 7. The five major uses of Ezekiel (throne, sealing, harlot, lament, new Jerusalem) are used to construct a throne vision, a sealing incident, a description of 'the great city that rules over the kings of the earth', a lament over its downfall and a description of the new Jerusalem. The judgments set loose by the trumpets (Rev. 8–9) and bowls (Rev. 16) are largely modelled on the Exodus plagues. The fact that he often combines these basic models with other texts will be the focus of the next chapter, but it is clear from the above that John does show considerable contextual awareness.[44]

41. E. Slomovic, 'Toward an Understanding of the Exegesis in the Dead Sea Scrolls', *RevQ* 7 (1969), pp. 14-15.

42. L.A. Vos, *The Synoptic Traditions in the Apocalypse* (Kampen: Kok, 1965), pp. 21-37.

43. Thus Brownlee says that the interpretations are often 'ascertained through a *forced, or abnormal construction of the Biblical text*' ('Biblical Interpretation among the Sectaries of the Dead Sea Scrolls', *BA* 14 [1951], pp. 60-62 [italics his]). R. Eisenman and M. Wise declare, 'Such interpretations often had nothing to do with the underlying Biblical text, often playing on but a few words or an isolated allusion in it to produce the desired commentary. Sometimes words in the underlying were deliberately changed to produce the desired exegesis having to do with contemporary events and almost nothing to do with the original prophecy, except casually' (*The Dead Sea Scrolls Uncovered*, p. 77). For a critique of such views, see Brooke, *Exegesis at Qumran*, ch. 3.

44. Fekkes says, 'when John wants to emphasize his own prophetic status and authority or illustrate his throne-room vision, he draws on the well-known experiences and examples of earlier prophets. And when he comes to describe the New Jerusalem, he builds on a biblical substructure of OT prophecies relating to the future glorified Jerusalem. Political oracles correspond to political oracles; prophecies of judgment to

## 3. *Relation between Interpretation and Historical Events*

The discussion of CD 7.14-21 above ended with a quotation by Bruce to the effect that the author found in the biblical texts the 'origin, history and prospects of the community'. This will now be considered in more detail with respect to the 'Wicked Priest'. The question might be put in this way: Where does the portrait of the 'Wicked Priest' derive from? the biblical text, an actual person or persons, or a combination of both? With respect to the former, I have already shown how the author might have derived 'wealth', 'rule', 'wicked' and 'Priest' from the biblical text. Slomovic[45] suggests that the rest of the pesher can be derived from? the text via passages such as Isa. 48.8 ('For I knew that you would deal very treacherously'), Isa. 5.14 ('Sheol has enlarged its appetite and opened its mouth beyond measure') and Prov. 30.15-16 ('Three things are never satisfied...Sheol').

On the other hand, the expression 'called by the name of truth when he first arose'[46] has been taken as primary evidence for the identity of the Priest. Van der Woude says, 'we must look for a priest who was acceptable to the Pious of Qumran as far as the earlier part of his life is concerned, which must therefore by necessity have antedated the rift between the Hasmonean dynasty and the Qumran community'.[47] According to van der Woude, the only person who fits the bill is Judas Maccabaeus. As son of Mattathias, he was highly regarded for his part in the revolt and for the purification of the Temple in 164 BCE. However,

prophecies of judgment; and promises of salvation serve as the basis for promises of salvation' (*Isaiah and Prophetic Traditions*, p. 102).

45. 'Towards an Understanding', pp. 14-15. As Brooke notes, some of his other suggestions (1 Chron. 5.2; Exod. 15.2) seem a bit far-fetched but he endorses his general approach with the words, 'the overall presentation of material by Slomovic would seem to provide sufficient evidence in support of an understanding of 1QpHab 8.3-13 such as he outlines' (*Exegesis at Qumran*, p. 290).

46. The phrase is not without its difficulties and Brownlee, *Midrash Pesher*, pp. 134-38, cites 9 different proposals for translating the first part, of which the first is his own: Called by the NAME of Truth/Had a name for being true/Was considered a member of the Truth party/Summoned against the name of truth/Called in the cause of truth/Called by the right title/Called by the true title/Called by his real name/Called by a trustworthy name. Brownlee renders the second phrase, 'At the beginning of his rule', but notes other proposals: at the beginning of his ministry/*au commencement de son office*/when he first took office as chief priest.

47. A.S. van der Woude, 'Wicked Priest or Wicked Priests? Reflections on the Identification of the Wicked Priest in the Habakkuk Commentary', *JJS* 33 (1982), p. 353.

1 Maccabees goes on to narrate his plundering of foreign nations, and van der Woude thinks that the description in 1 Macc. 6.18-27 corresponds so closely with the pesher that the identification is almost certain.[48]

Vermes,[49] on the other hand, thinks the allusions point to a High Priest and suggests Jason, Menelaus, Alcimus, Jonathan or Simon as possibilities (given his chronological framework). The first three, however, were Hellenizers and can therefore be dismissed. Of the remaining two, he thinks Jonathan is to be preferred because Simon was murdered by his son-in-law rather than at the hands of the army. Other scholars suggest Menelaus, Jannaeus or Hyrcanus II. The variety of solutions could be because of the paucity of the evidence, but it might be that we are not so much dealing with historical allusions as with biblical stereotypes. Or more likely, perhaps, a combination of the two.

### 4Q Second Ezekiel—Fragment 2, 1-9[50]

[that I am Yahweh] who redeem My people, giving unto them the covenant...[And I said: "Yahweh.] I have seen many men from Israel who have loved Thy Name and have walked in the ways of [righteousness; And th]ese (things) when will they *be*, and how will they be recompensed for their loyalty?" And Yahweh said to me: "I will cause the children of Israel to *see, and* they shall know that I am Yahweh...[And He said:] "Son of Man, prophesy *over* the bones and say: be ye joined bone to its bone and joint [to its joint". And it wa]s so. And He said a second time: "Prophesy and let sinews come upon them and let them be covered with skin [above". And it wa]s s[o]. And He said again: "Prophesy *concerning* the four *winds* of heaven and let the win[ds of heaven] blow [*upon them and they shall revive,*] and a great crowd of people shall stand up, and they shall bless Yahweh Sabaoth wh[o has given them life again"]....I said: "O Yahweh, when shall these things be?" And Yahweh said to m[e]...

---

48. 'we may confidently accept' (p. 355). It should be noted that van der Woude does not believe that all the references to the Wicked Priest refer to Judas. Indeed, his theory is that they refer to a succession of people, beginning with Judas and ending with Alexander Jannaeus.

49. *The Dead Sea Scrolls in English*, pp. 23-35.

50. Text in J. Strugnell and D. Dimant, '4Q Second Ezekiel', *RevQ* 13 (1988), pp. 45-58, and Eisenman and Wise, *The Dead Sea Scrolls Uncovered*, pp. 60-64. See also D. Dimant and J. Strugnell, 'The Merkabah Vision in Second Ezekiel (4Q385 4)', *RevQ* 14 (1990), pp. 331-48, and G.J. Brooke, 'Ezekiel in some Qumran and New Testament Texts', pp. 321-26.

This fragmentary text is extant in a number of copies[51] and has some interesting parallels with the book of Revelation. It is clear that Ezekiel's vision of the dry bones (37.1-14) lies at the heart of the passage but the setting is a dialogue between God and the prophet, a strategy usually associated with apocalypses (e.g. 4 *Ezra*). Strugnell and Dimant comment:

> It is significant that all this new material deals with topics with which we are familiar from Apocalyptic literature: the history of Israel, the problem of retribution and recompense, and the question of resurrection...Second-Ezekiel presents us, for the first time, with Hebrew formulations of some typical apocalyptic ideas.[52]

It is perhaps for this reason that the author introduces the vision with a number of evocative phrases which produce a 'tableau of interlocking allusions'.[53] For example, Yahweh is the one who redeems his people (Exod. 6.6) and gives them the covenant (Gen. 17.2; Num. 25.12). The remnant are those who have loved his name (Ps. 5.11) and walked in his ways (Deut. 8.6). The reference to the 'many men from Israel' might be related to Dan. 12.2 ('Many of those who sleep in the dust of the earth shall awake'). Lastly, in keeping with a number of writings (Ps. 89.46; Dan. 12.6; Rev. 6.10), the author wants to know 'when shall these things be?'

John alludes to the 'dry bones' passage when he says of the two witnesses that a 'breath of life from God entered them, and they stood on their feet' (Rev. 11.11).[54] John provides it with a different setting (Ezekiel's measuring of the temple) and surrounds it with a cluster of scriptural echoes (Daniel's 42 months, Zechariah's two olive trees, Elijah's drought, Moses' rivers of blood and Daniel's conquering beast).[55] It cannot claim to be more significant to John than any of these

51. The exact number is unclear. Strugnell and Dimant originally thought it was five but that has had to be revised. See Brooke, 'Ezekiel in some Qumran and New Testament Texts', p. 322.

52. '4Q Second Ezekiel', p. 55.

53. The phrase comes from Fishbane, 'Use, Authority and Interpretation of Mikra at Qumran', p. 356.

54. John differs from the MT by telescoping 'and breath came into them, and they lived' to the genitival 'breath of life from God entered them', as also in the LXX.

55. This seems to be an example of a passage that does not rely on one base text but deliberately draws on a variety of texts. Charles, I, pp. lxviii-lxxxii, cites 1 Sam. 4.8; 2 Sam. 22.9; Ezek. 37.10; Jer. 5.14; Dan. 7.3, 21, 25; 12.7; Zech. 4.2ff. as allusions and Est. 9.19; Isa. 1.10; Ezek. 40.3, 41.13; Dan. 9.24; Zech. 12.3 as

other passages, though it is possible that its use here prefigures its use in Rev. 20.4 (καὶ ἔζησαν καὶ ἐβασίλευσαν μετὰ τοῦ Χριστοῦ). Indeed, if it is correct that John's answer to the elder's question in Rev. 7.13-14 (κύριέ μου, σὺ οἶδας) echoes Ezek. 37.3 ('O Lord God, you know'),[56] then it could be argued that John's use of Ezek. 37.3, 5, 10 in Rev. 7.14, 11.11 and 20.4 all build to a climax with his use of 37.27 ('My dwelling place shall be with them; and I will be their God, and they shall be my people') in Rev. 21.3. As Mealy says, John builds an 'extensive network of cross-references and allusions that affects the interpretation of virtually every passage in Revelation'.[57]

### *Summary: Qumran and Revelation*

A major difference between the Qumran texts and the book of Revelation concerns the manner in which Scripture is quoted. Nothing in Revelation corresponds to the formal technique of citation and exposition found in the Habakkuk commentary. However, one must be careful what conclusions are drawn from this for Revelation has very little in common with Matthew's formula quotations either (even though they share the idea of fulfilment in Christ). What is clear is that many of the techniques used by John do have parallels in the Qumran writings:

1.  *Identifications.* Texts or imagery based on texts are systematically explained by making a number of identifications ('The star is the interpreter of the law'; 'The woman you saw is the great city').

2.  *Catchwords.* Moving from text to text is often facilitated by a common word or phrase (*gᵉzērâ šāwâ*). Newsom suggests that the word 'earthquake' led the author of the *Shirot* from Ezekiel 3 to 1 Kings 19. The use of 'like the sound of' in Ezek. 1.24, 43.2 allows the link with Dan. 10.6 in John's inaugural vision. As Fekkes notes, this often leads to *conflation* of two or more texts.[58]

echoes. See further C.H. Giblin, 'Revelation 11.1-13: Its Form, Function, and Contextual Integration', *NTS* 30 (1984), pp. 433-59; Bauckham, *Climax of Prophecy*, pp. 266-83.

56. So Vanhoye, 'L'utilisation', p. 449.
57. Mealy, *After the Thousand years*, p. 13.
58. See Fekkes, *Isaiah and Prophetic Traditions*, pp. 283-84.

3. *Abbreviation.* This might be for the sake of brevity or it may have a more theological purpose, namely, to exclude views that are contrary to the author's position ('He shall build a house for my name'; 'a great sacrificial feast').

4. *Applying attributes to a new subject.* In the inaugural vision of Revelation 1, attributes drawn from an angel (Dan. 10), the servant of the Lord (Isa. 42) and God (Dan. 7) are used to describe the 'one like the Son of Man'. 11QMelch appears to apply Ps. 82.1 ('Elohim has taken his place in the divine council') to Melchizedek.

5. *Correcting one text by means of another.* Newsom thinks that 1 Kings 19 ('still small voice') is used to correct Ezek. 3.12 ('loud rumbling'). Vanhoye thinks John employs the 'feast of God' idea in passages like Isa. 25.6 to correct the sacrificial idea in Ezekiel 39.

6. *Interpretative handling of Hebrew roots.* We have seen many examples of this in the DSS. It is more difficult to assess with John because his work is in Greek. However, a number of commentators think his use of 'Amen' in Rev. 3.14 stems from a particular vocalization of Isa. 65.16.[59]

It can be seen from this that the task of exploring how texts interact with their subtexts is as important for the Qumran literature as it is for the book of Revelation. Drawing on ancient sources, whether by quotation or allusion, sets up a correspondence between the two works. The author may wish to guide the reader into specific interpretations or proposals, but ultimately the reader must actively engage in a 'dialogue with the text and with the texts within the text'.[60] Chapter 6 will now explore this further.

---

59. The wording of this category comes from Fekkes, *Isaiah and Prophetic Traditions*, p. 284, who also suggests Rev. 21.21 (= Isa. 54.12) as another example.
60. Ruiz, *Ezekiel in the Apocalypse*, p. 520.

Chapter 6

## REVELATION AND INTERTEXTUALITY

Biblical critics are not the only people interested in studying the effect of allusions in a piece of literature. T.S. Eliot said of the poet that

> not only the best, but the most individual parts of his work may be those in which the dead poets, his ancestors, assert their immortality most vigorously.[1]

He complains that poets have become obsessed with originality and tend to 'dwell with satisfaction upon the poet's difference from his predecessors'.[2] Originality is not the only or even the best criteria for art. Brower says of Pope,

> Through allusion, often in combination with subdued metaphors and exquisite images, Pope gets his purchase on larger meanings and evokes the finer resonances by which poetry (in Johnson's phrase) 'penetrates the recesses of the mind'.[3]

This getting a 'purchase on larger meanings', evoking 'finer resonances' and penetrating 'the recesses of the mind' is a good description of the allusive use of Scripture found in the book of Revelation and some of the Qumran writings. Since the article by Julia Kristeva, it is often discussed under the rubric of 'intertextuality'.[4] Hollander says,

---

1. T.S. Eliot, *Selected Essays* (London: Faber, 3rd edn, 1951), p. 14.
2. *Selected Essays*, p. 14.
3. R. Brower, *Alexander Pope: The Poetry of Allusion* (Oxford: Clarendon Press, 1959), p. viii; quoted in Hays, *Echoes of Scripture*, p. 18.
4. For a useful introduction to Intertextuality, see *Intertextuality: Theories and Practices* (ed. M. Worten and J. Still; Manchester: Manchester University Press, 1990).

> The reader of texts, in order to overhear echoes, must have some kind of access to an earlier voice, and to its cave of resonant signification, analogous to that of the author of the later text.[5]

He notes that this 'cave of resonant signification' can be lost to a community so that the allusion or echo is no longer heard. As an example, he cites the words of Lincoln: 'Fourscore and seven years ago, our fathers brought forth on this continent a new nation, conceived in liberty'. This is not usually considered to be an allusive text but to one who is attuned to the resonances of the Bible, the two phrases 'brought forth' and 'conceived in' will bring to mind the creation story and its exegetical developments. Hollander sketches the implied contrasts:

> *'Whereas in the beginning, at Our Father's command, the earth brought forth grass*...a mere fourscore and seven years ago our forefathers brought forth on this piece of earth a new nation'...and 'Whereas man is *conceived in* sin, this nation was conceived in liberty'.[6]

As Hollander notes, most people would not have recognized these echoes for themselves, but once pointed out they greatly enhance one's appreciation of the speech. The difficulty in detecting such echoes is that the actual evidence can be extremely slight, for the 'fragmentations and breakings-off of intertextual echo can result in pieces of voice as small as single words, and as elusive as particular cadences'.[7] As an example, he cites two lines drawn from Empson ('Missing Dates') and Tennyson ('Tithonus'):[8]

> The waste remains, the waste remains and kills
> *The woods decay, the woods decay and fall*

Here is an example where none of the significant words are echoed but there appears to be a sort of tuneful correspondence:

> This rebound gives back neither word nor phrase, but instead a kind of cadence, involving phonemic and semantic elements, locked in a syntactic and metrical pattern.[9]

5.    J. Hollander, *Figure of Echo*, p. 65.
6.    *Figure of Echo*, p. 66. He adds, 'The rhythm of "fourscore...forth" makes us notice the ellipsis of "fore (-fathers)", but that ellipsis itself makes the forebears into secular forms of *pater noster*'.
7.    *Figure of Echo*, p. 88.
8.    *Figure of Echo*, p. 96.
9.    *Figure of Echo*, p. 96.

Thus one aspect of a criticism attuned to allusions and echoes is to point out the 'cave of resonant signification' so that others are enabled to 'listen in'. With reference to the book of Revelation, there is no shortage of books and articles that point out the wealth of Old Testament material contained in its pages. Swete[10] lists some 278 verses or phrases which contain an allusion to a particular Old Testament text. Charles[11] goes further and tries to categorize them according to their affinity to the Greek or Hebrew text. Since then, other scholars have not only listed such allusions but have attempted to class them according to the 'volume' of the echo.[12]

However, a criticism attuned to such allusions and echoes must do more than simply point out their presence, for an allusion is not simply a footnote to a previous work. By absorbing words used in one context into a new context or configuration, a metaphorical relationship is established. In the words of Davidson, 'The work alluded to reflects upon the present context even as the present context absorbs and changes the allusion'.[13] At one level, of course, all language is allusive. Each word has a history and that history is expanded when it is used again in a new work. The meaning of a word depends on its previous contexts and yet each new use adds a context to its range of possibilities.[14] However, this study is not so much concerned with the general allusiveness of all language but the effect of alluding to particular texts. Hays says,

> The twofold task of a criticism attuned to such echoes, then, is (a) to call attention to them so that others might be enabled to hear; and (b) to give an account of the distortions and new figuration that they generate.[15]

At the end of Chapter 4, it was suggested that John's use of Ezekiel involves both continuity and discontinuity. The reader 'hears' the Old

10.   Swete, *Revelation*, pp. cxl-cliii.
11.   Charles, *Revelation*, I, pp. lxviii-lxxxii.
12.   See Chapter 1 n. 19.
13.   H. Davidson, *T.S. Eliot and Hermeneutics: Absence and Interpretation in the Waste Land* (Baton Rouge: Louisiana State University Press, 1985), p. 117.
14.   It is this aspect that A.C. Thiselton has in mind when he writes, 'What is problematic about current notions of intertextuality is not the huge scope of the boundaries which have been enlarged, but the transposing of horizons of understanding into matrices which generate an infinite chain of semiotic effects' (*New Horizons in Hermeneutics* [London: HarperCollins, 1992], p. 506).
15.   *Echoes of Scripture*, p. 19.

Testament text but its meaning is affected by the new context or configuration. For Fiorenza, the new context speaks so loudly that despite modelling whole sections of his work on parts of the Old Testament, she insists that John 'does not interpret the Old Testament but uses its words, images, phrases, and patterns as a language arsenal in order to make his own theological statement or express his own prophetic vision'.[16] However, the very act of referring to another text automatically puts it in some sort of correspondence or relationship with the new material.[17] The task of intertextuality is to explore how the source text continues to speak through the new work and how the new work forces new meanings from the source text. Hays, in describing Hollander's use of the term 'metalepsis', says that

> Allusive echo functions to suggest to the reader that text B should be understood in light of a broad interplay with text A, encompassing aspects of A beyond those explicitly echoed…(it)…places the reader within a field of whispered or unstated correspondences.[18]

In his seminal work on the place of the Old Testament in the development of New Testament theology, C.H. Dodd argues that Paul's references to Scripture are not limited to the actual words quoted but bring in the whole context of that part of Scripture. It was this that led him to his grand claim that these passages, together with their application to the 'gospel facts', form the 'substructure of all Christian theology…[which] contains already its chief regulative ideas'.[19] Hays agrees that the significance of Paul's allusions extends beyond the actual words quoted, but he is searching for a more sophisticated way of describing this:

> the most significant elements of intertextual correspondence between old context and new can be implicit rather than voiced, perceptible only within the silent space framed by the juncture of two texts.[20]

16.   'Apokalypsis and Propheteia', *Justice and Judgment*, p. 135.
17.   Beale says, 'the very act of referring to an Old Testament text is to place it in some comparative relationship to something in the New Testament' ('Revelation', *Scripture Citing Scripture*, p. 326). However, in practice, he puts most of the emphasis on reading Revelation in the light of the book of Daniel.
18.   *Echoes of Scripture*, p. 20.
19.   C.H. Dodd, *According to the Scriptures: The Substructure of New Testament Theology* (London: Collins, 1952), p. 127.
20.   *Echoes of Scripture*, p. 155.

For example, in his discussion of Rom. 1.16-17, Hays says that despite great differences of interpretation, all parties assume that Paul employs Hab. 2.4 as a proof-text with complete disregard for its original setting. However, when it is remembered that Habakkuk is concerned about the apparent injustice of God's ways (theodicy), it may be that Paul has listened to Habakkuk more than the critics have:

> By showcasing this text—virtually as an epigraph—at the beginning of the letter to the Romans, Paul links his gospel to the Old Testament prophetic affirmation of God's justice and righteousness.[21]

Of course, the contexts are very different. Habakkuk is worried about the military domination of the Chaldeans, whereas Paul's concern is the 'apparent usurpation of Israel's favored covenant status by congregations of uncircumcised Gentile Christians'.[22] The analogy, he says, is off-centre and hence metaphorical:

> When a literary echo links the text in which it occurs to an earlier text, the figurative effect of the echo can lie in the unstated or suppressed (transumed) points of resonance between the two texts.[23]

Previous studies of Paul's use of Scripture have concentrated on his explicit quotations and have therefore been of limited use for students of Revelation. Hays, however, while taking his cue from the quotations, seeks to unearth the 'unstated or repressed points of resonance' contained in the text. For Hays, Paul's faith 'is one whose articulation is inevitably intertextual in character, and Israel's Scripture is the "determinate subtext that plays a constitutive role" in shaping his literary production'.[24] This is in contrast to the comment of Sanders[25] that what Paul says in his own words is a more reliable guide than what he says by way of allusion. If our purpose in reading Paul's letters is to extract information or doctrine, then the presence of Old Testament allusions is no doubt a complicating factor. As has already been noted, 'every quotation distorts and redefines the "primary" utterance by relocating it within another linguistic and cultural context'.[26] However,

21. *Echoes of Scripture*, p. 40.
22. *Echoes of Scripture*, p. 40.
23. *Echoes of Scripture*, p. 20.
24. *Echoes of Scripture*, p. 16.
25. E.P. Sanders, *Paul, the Law and the Jewish People* (London: SCM Press, 1983), p. 22.
26. M. Worten and J. Still, 'Introduction', *Intertextuality: Theories and Practices*,

for Hays, the presence of allusions is precisely what draws the reader into Paul's letters:

> Echoes linger in the air and lure the reader of Paul's letters back into the symbolic world of Scripture. Paul's allusions gesture toward precursors whose words are already heavy with tacit implication.[27]

It is not that Paul is being deliberately obstructive by interlocking his words with a distinguished predecessor; it is that his message requires it. As Hays says, Paul's articulation is 'inevitably intertextual in character' for it is vital to involve the reader in the source text if he is to make himself understood. From the point of view of this study of Revelation, his discussion of 2 Corinthians 3 is particularly illuminating. Paul introduces the figure of Moses, Hays says, as a 'foil against which to commend the candor and boldness of his own ministry'.[28] The reader is led to expect a completely negative verdict of religion under the old covenant, but v. 16 introduces a turn as dramatic as the one mentioned in that verse ('but when one turns to the Lord, the veil is removed').

Initially, the implication seems clear. The generation of Moses was unable to see clearly but those who have responded to Paul's preaching have had the veil removed. However, the mention of 'veil' reminds Paul that Moses did in fact remove his veil when he entered God's presence. Thus Moses is both a contrast to ministry under the new covenant and a witness to it:

> The rhetorical effect of this ambiguous presentation is an unsettling one, because it simultaneously posits and undercuts the glory of Moses' ministry...Since Paul is arguing that the ministry of the new covenant outshines the ministry of the old in glory, it serves his purpose to exalt the glory of Moses; at the same time, the grand claims that he wants to make for his own ministry require that the old be denigrated.[29]

p. 11. They continue, 'Therefore, despite any intentional quest on the part of the quoting author to engage in an intersubjective activity, the quotation itself generates a tension between belief both in original and originating integrity and in the possibility of (re)integration and an awareness of infinite deferral and dissemination of meaning'. H. Davidson says, 'The work's meaning is in the tension between its previous contextual definition and its present context' (*T.S. Eliot and Hermeneutics*, p. 117).

27. *Echoes of Scripture*, p. 155.

28. *Echoes of Scripture*, p. 147.

29. *Echoes of Scripture*, pp. 132-33. Similarly, C.K. Stockhausen says, 'Paul is both like Moses and not like Moses. Paul is not like Moses because he may be bold and does not need to veil himself in either shame or humility. Paul is like Moses because he also has a share in the glory given to the minister of God's covenant with

Hays calls this a dissimile. Paul begins by saying what his ministry is not like but then uses the negated material to add further dimensions to his main claim. Heb. 12.18-25 is another example:

> You have not come to something that can be touched, a blazing fire, and darkness, and gloom, and a tempest, and the sound of a trumpet, and a voice whose words made the hearers beg that not another word be spoken to them (Heb. 12.18-19).

Since the writer declares that Christians have not come to things like this, we might wonder why we are being given so much detail about it. However, with these descriptions still ringing in our ears, the author warns in v. 25,

> See that you do not refuse the one who is speaking; for if they did not escape when they refused the one who warned them on earth, how much less will we escape if we reject the one who warns from heaven!

Thus it turns out that the fearsome images have a positive function after all, even though the passage began with a negation. Hays notes that the same thing has been observed of Milton:

> Milton repeatedly denies the beauty of countless pagan paradises in comparison with Eden, while tacitly employing their strong legendary associations to enhance and embellish its incomparable perfections.[30]

The relevance of this to Chapter 4 should now be apparent. John draws extensively on Ezekiel and in something like the same order, but his use of the material is sometimes to place it in direct antithesis to what he himself wants to say. For example, John draws extensively on the temple chapters of Ezekiel 40–48, while denying the existence of the very thing that these chapters are about. As Vogelgesang says,

> John made detailed use of Ezekiel 40–48 in constructing the new Jerusalem vision. Yet a greater contrast with that vision, where seven of nine chapters describe this temple, its ordinances and its priests, and the glory of God dwelling therein, cannot be imagined.[31]

---

Israel. Like Moses, who received visions on the mountain and in the tent, Paul's glorification in 2 Cor. 3:18 is also visionary' ('2 Corinthians 3 and the Principles of Pauline Exegesis', in *Paul and the Scriptures of Israel* [ed. C.A. Evans and J.A. Sanders; JSNTSup 83; Sheffield: JSOT Press, 1993], p. 147).

30.    *Echoes of Scripture*, p. 142. The quotation is by G. Lord, *Classical Presences in Seventeenth-Century English Poetry* (New Haven: Yale University Press, 1987), pp. 40-41.

31.    *Interpretation of Ezekiel*, p. 77.

Vogelgesang's conclusion was that this is part of a consistent strategy by John to 'democratize' Ezekiel's vision and to combat the esotericism of the traditions based on it. What is particular, local and ethnic is to be given universal expression and what is esoteric and the possession of a privileged few is to be made available to all who have 'ears to hear'. This position is certainly open to criticism but it does provide a strong challenge to those who dwell mainly on the similarities between the two works. The differences are just as notable. Thus whilst much of the book sounds familiar, the reader is constantly being challenged to think again. John does not offer an interpretation of Ezekiel as a finished product. Rather, by utilizing much of its structure and language, he has forced the two works into mutual interaction. This can be compared with the description of Paul's use of Exodus by Hays:

> the dissimile in 2 Cor. 3.12–4.4 allows Paul to appropriate some of the mythical grandeur associated with the Sinai covenant—particularly the images of glory and transformation—even while he repudiates the linkage of his ministry to that covenant.[32]

In a similar way, John 'appropriates some of the mythical grandeur' of Ezekiel's temple, 'particularly the images of glory and transformation', 'even while he repudiates' the existence of a temple in the new Jerusalem. Hays describes the effect of Paul using dissimile in these words:

> Rhetorically, the act of positing a dissimile and then lavishly developing it has a backlash effect: by distancing his ministry from Moses, Paul paradoxically appropriates attributes similar to those that he most insistently rejects; connotations bleed over from the denied images to the entity with which they are discompared.[33]

The phrase 'connotations bleed over' is a useful one even when we are not specifically dealing with dissimile. By incorporating allusions into his work, John has created a new figuration whereby the old words are given a new context and principally derive their meaning from that. This is why Fiorenza is so insistent that John 'does not interpret the Old Testament but uses its words, images phrases...to express his own prophetic vision'.[34] Nevertheless, we must ask whether the old context is so easily silenced. Is it not true, at least for some of the allusions, that 'connotations bleed over' and affect John's meaning? As Davidson says,

---

32. *Echoes of Scripture*, p. 142.
33. *Echoes of Scripture*, p. 142.
34. 'Apokalypsis and Propheteia', *Justice and Judgment*, p. 135.

'the work alluded to reflects upon the present context even as the present context absorbs and changes the allusion'.[35] In order to explore this further, a text will now be considered that offers very different meanings depending on the weight given to the Old Testament context. The text is Rev. 1.5a, where grace and peace are said to come

> from Jesus Christ, the faithful witness (ὁ μάρτυς ὁ πιστός), the firstborn of the dead (ὁ πρωτότοκος τῶν νεκρῶν), and the ruler of the kings of the earth (ὁ ἄρχων τῶν βασιλέων τῆς γῆς).

Charles offers Ps. 89.27, 37 (LXX: 88.28, 38) as the source of the allusion and declares that 'our author appears to have had the LXX before him'.[36] The phrase 'faithful witness' is found in Prov. 14.5 ('A faithful witness does not lie') while in Isa. 55.4, David is said to have been made a 'witness to the peoples, a leader and commander'.[37] However, it is the occurrence of both 'firstborn' and 'kings of the earth' in Ps. 88.28 (LXX) that convinced Charles that 'faithful witness' (ὁ μάρτυς ὁ πιστός) most likely comes from the LXX of Ps. 88.38 (ὁ μάρτυς ἐν οὐρανῷ πιστός). Verse 28 (NRSV 89.27) reads,

> I will make him the firstborn (πρωτότοκον), the highest of the kings of the earth (βασιλεῦσιν τῆς γῆς).

Thus the psalm appears to be the inspiration for all three titles in Rev. 1.5a, and as a consequence of this both Swete and Charles take John's words to be references to power. Charles says we must take πρωτότοκος in its secondary sense of 'sovereignty' and notes that there is evidence that God himself was called 'first-born of the world'. He thus paraphrases Rev. 1.5a: 'the true witness of God, the *sovereign* of the dead, the ruler of the living'.[38] Swete says the words ὁ ἄρχων τῶν βασιλέων 'stand appropriately at the head of a book which represents the glorified Christ as presiding over the destinies of nations'.[39] As for the threefold title μάρτυς...πρωτότοκος... ἄρχων, this 'answers to the threefold purpose of the Apocalypse, which is at once a Divine testimony, a revelation of the Risen Lord, and a forecast of the issues of history'.[40]

35. *T.S. Eliot and Hermeneutics*, p. 117, and hence the meaning of an allusive text 'is in the tension between its previous contextual definition and its present context'.
36. Charles, *Revelation*, I, p. 14.
37. Both of these are cited by Swete, *Revelation*, p. 6.
38. Charles, *Revelation*, I, p. 14.
39. Swete, *Revelation*, p. 7.
40. Swete, *Revelation*, p. 7.

Caird, however, sees it quite differently. He agrees that the source text is Psalm 89, but claims that 'By two small adjustments he has given a profoundly Christian application to the words of scripture'.[41] Christ is indeed 'king' but that kingship is not based on the exercise of royal power but must be understood in the light of his earthly suffering. This is clearly indicated by John's addition τῶν νεκρῶν, which makes it certain that πρωτότοκος is a reference to the resurrection. Christ is king but it is a kingship won by passing through suffering and death, so that for Caird '**firstborn**, instead of being an honorific title, is the guarantee that others will pass with him through death to kingship'.[42] The titles were chosen because they express the pastoral aims of the book, not out of any desire to apply Psalm 89 to Christ:

> His friends are called to bear the costly witness of martyrdom, trusting that in his death Christ has been a **faithful witness** to God's way of over-coming evil; to look into the open jaws of death, remembering that he has risen as **the firstborn** of many brothers; to defy the authority of Imperial Rome in the name of a **ruler** to whom Caesar himself must bow.[43]

Two things can be said of this. First, it is not at all clear that con-notations of royal power (v. 27) and cosmic stability (v. 37) are quite as out of place as Caird imagines. The psalm speaks of God's anointed (v. 20; cf. Rev. 1.1, 2, 4 etc.), whose throne will be established forever (v. 29; cf. Rev. 3.21). It promises that his horn will be exalted (v. 24; cf. Rev. 5.6) and that God's faithfulness and steadfast love (vv. 1, 2, 5, 8, 14, 24, 33, 49) shall be with him (v. 24; cf. Rev. 1.5; 3.14). Finally, the psalm ends with the cry, 'How long, O Lord?' (v. 46; cf. Rev. 6.10). In view of these parallels (it is not being suggested that they are more than this), it would be precarious to argue that connotations of power and stability from vv. 27, 37 would be entirely unwelcome to John. It would also be precarious to argue that these would not meet the needs of the recipients. To those facing death (the background assumed by Caird), the assertion that Christ is 'Sovereign of the dead' would be extremely relevant, albeit in a different way from what Caird suggests.

Secondly, even if it is agreed that John's meaning is quite different from the psalm, this does not mean that the psalm has been silenced. As

---

41. Caird, *Revelation*, p. 16. The same point is made by J. Casey, 'Exodus Typology in the Book of Revelation' (PhD Dissertation, Southern Baptist Theological Seminary, 1981), pp. 138-39.

42. Caird, *Revelation*, p. 17.

43. Caird, *Revelation*, p. 16.

Hays puts it, 'connotations bleed over from the denied images to the entity with which they are discompared'.[44] There is no denying that a Christian will read into words like 'firstborn' and 'faithful witness' connotations that were not present in the psalm. This is to be expected for words 'gather more meanings over time'.[45] Nevertheless, providing the reader has access to the 'cave of resonant signification'[46] (in this case Ps. 89), the words will continue to evoke the messianic descriptions and these will affect a reading of the text. Further, since John makes it clear that he has Psalm 89 in mind, it is reasonable to suppose that this is not entirely unwelcome to him. That is not to say that discussion of the effect of intertextual echo must be limited to John's conscious intention. There is no reason to assume that John thought out all the possibilities of bringing Psalm 89 into a relationship with the living Christ. Nevertheless, the fact that he did so means that

> The twofold task of a criticism attuned to such echoes, then, is (a) to call attention to them so that others might be enabled to hear; and (b) to give an account of the distortions and new figuration that they generate.[47]

### Forms of Imitation

In his study of Renaissance poetry, Thomas Greene[48] offers a typology of 'forms of imitation'. He calls these reproductive, eclectic, heuristic and dialectic, and describes them thus:

### Reproductive
This is when a poet imitates a previous work with such precision that it is virtually a copy. The original is treated as a sacred object, 'beyond alteration and beyond criticism, a sacred original whose greatness can never be adequately reproduced'.[49] The author perceives the subtext as

---

44. *Echoes of Scripture*, p. 142.
45. Ruiz, *Ezekiel in the Apocalypse*, p. 223.
46. Hollander, *Figure of Echo*, p. 65.
47. Hays, *Echoes of Scripture*, p. 19.
48. *Light in Troy*, pp. 16-53. The rationale for this is that 'each literary work contains by definition what might be called a revivalist initiative, a gesture that signals the intent of reanimating an earlier text or texts situated on the far side of a rupture...it would seem useful to distinguish four types of strategies of humanist imitation, each of which involves a distinct response to anachronism and each an implicit perspective on history' (pp. 37-38).
49. *Light in Troy*, p. 38.

coming from a golden age which is now over. All that can be done is to rewrite the subtext 'as though no other form of celebration could be worthy of its dignity'.[50]

### Eclectic

Eclectic imitation is where the author draws on a wide range of sources, seemingly at random, without laying special emphasis on any one of them. At its weakest, this can be mere plagiarism, but in skilled hands the author has access to a 'vocabulary of a second and higher power, a second keyboard of richer harmonies'.[51] Thus the 'art of poetry finds its materials everywhere, materials bearing with them the aura of their original contexts, charged with an evocative power implanted by the poet or the convention from which they are taken'.[52]

### Heuristic

This is where the new work seeks to define itself through the rewriting or modernizing of a past text. In so doing, the poem becomes a sort of '*rite de passage* between a specified past and an emergent present'.[53] It establishes a distance between new and old, not to leave the reader in a hermeneutical chasm but to make way for an act of resolution. The new is not a pale imitation of the old but its true successor. 'Heuristic imitations come to us advertising their derivation from the subtexts they carry with them, but having done that, they proceed to *distance themselves* from the subtexts and force us to recognize the poetic distance traversed'.[54]

---

50. *Light in Troy*, p. 38. Although this form of imitation corresponded to a 'new and appealing impulse, it could not in itself produce a large body of successful poetry...Rather it condemned the reproductive poet to a very elementary form of anachronism, since any reproduction must be made in a vocabulary that is unbecoming the original and whose violations remain out of artistic control.'

51. *Light in Troy*, p. 39.

52. *Light in Troy*, p. 39. 'This very simple type of imitation was termed *contaminatio* by Renaissance rhetoricians and it is by no means to be despised...It could reconcile within its own frame momentary conflicts of heterogeneous motifs; it could tolerate the counterpoint of the voices it brought together; but it could not find out the drama of that counterpoint at a deeper pitch of conflict' (pp. 39-40).

53. *Light in Troy*, p. 41.

54. *Light in Troy*, p. 40. 'Thus the imitative poem sketches, far more explicitly and plainly than most historically conscious texts, its own etiological derivation; it acts out its own coming into being. And since its subtext is by definition drawn from an

*Dialectic*

Lastly, Greene speaks of 'dialectical imitation'. This is when the poem engages the precursor in such a way that neither is able to absorb or master the other. In exposing the vulnerability of the subtext, it exposes itself to 'potential agression'.[55] As an example, he quotes the *Praise of Folly* by Erasmus, which draws repeatedly on Lucian but in the last hymn 'introduces values totally incompatible with Lucian and ancient comedy'.[56] The effect is to create 'a kind of struggle between texts and between eras which cannot easily be resolved'.[57] In other words, 'anachronism becomes a dynamic source of artistic power'.[58]

## Revelation and Imitation

There is nothing in the book of Revelation that could fairly be described as reproductive. Boismard speaks of John's use of Ezekiel in the words *'elle dénote une imitation, un démarquage si serviles'*,[59] but few would agree with that judgment. Beale believes that key chapters of Revelation are a midrash on Daniel 7 and that the whole book is to be 'conceived of ultimately within the thematic framework of Daniel 2', but it is unlikely that he would agree that this dependence on Daniel is because 'no other form of celebration could be worthy of its dignity'. The

alien culture, the imitative poem creates a bridge from one *mundus significans* to another. The passage of this rite moves not only from text to text but from an earlier semiotic matrix to a modern one. Thus the poem could be read as an attempt to heal that estrangement which humanism had constantly to face. Imitation of this type is heuristic because it can come about only through a double process of discovery: on the one hand through a tentative and experimental groping for the subtext in its specificity and otherness, and on the other hand through a groping for the modern poet's own appropriate voice and idiom.'

55.    *Light in Troy*, p. 45.

56.    *Light in Troy*, p. 45. 'The text makes a kind of implicit criticism of its subtexts, its authenticating models, but it also leaves itself open to criticism from the irreverent Lucianic spirit that it had begun by invoking.'

57.    *Light in Troy*, p. 45. 'The text is the locus of a struggle between two rhetorical or semiotic systems that are vulnerable to one another and whose conflict cannot easily be resolved' (p. 46).

58.    *Light in Troy*, p. 46. Greene sketches the contrast between heuristic and dia-lectical imitation: 'heuristic imitation involves a passage from one semiotic universe to another...dialectical imitation, when it truly engages two eras or two civilizations at a profound level, involves a conflict between two *mundi significantes*' (p. 46).

59.    '"L'Apocalypse" ou "Les Apocalypses"', p. 532.

consciousness of the New Testament writers that they have received something new forbids them from regarding even the Torah in this light. Many passages might be considered to belong to Greene's second category, 'eclectic' imitation. For example, the seventh bowl in Rev. 16.17-21 appears to allude to a number of texts 'without laying special emphasis on any one of them'. The passage reads,

> The seventh angel poured his bowl into the air, and a loud voice came out of the temple, from the throne, saying, 'It is done!' And there came flashes of lightning, rumblings, peals of thunder, and a violent earthquake, such as had not occurred since people were upon the earth, so violent was that earthquake. The great city was split into three parts, and the cities of the nations fell. God remembered great Babylon and gave her the wine-cup of the fury of his wrath. And every island fled away, and no mountains were to be found; and huge hailstones, each weighing about a hundred pounds, dropped from heaven on people, until they cursed God for the plague of the hail, so fearful was that plague.

The passage can certainly be read in its own right, but it is clear that many of its phrases come 'charged with an evocative power'. For example, consider the following phrases:

*a loud voice came out of the temple*
Ruiz thinks this is an allusion to Isa. 66.6 ('Listen, an uproar from the city! A voice from the temple! The voice of the Lord, dealing retribution to his enemies!'). The effect, he says, is to 'suggest that what follows will concern retributive judgment'.[60]

*flashes of lightening, rumblings, peals of thunder,*
*and a violent earthquake*
Descriptions like this have already occurred at Rev. 4.5, 8.5 and 11.19 and appear to echo the Sinai theophany. Bauckham[61] has shown how they build to a climax in 16.18-21, with the mention of a *great* earthquake and *great* hailstones:

| | |
|---|---|
| 4.5 | ἀστραπαὶ καὶ φωναὶ καὶ βρονταί |
| 8.5 | βρονταὶ καὶ φωναὶ καὶ ἀστραπαὶ καὶ σεισμός |
| 11.19 | ἀστραπαὶ καὶ φωναὶ καὶ βρονταὶ καὶ σεισμὸς καὶ χάλαζα μεγάλη |
| 16.18-21 | ἀστραπαὶ καὶ φωναὶ καὶ βρονταὶ καὶ σεισμός...μέγας...καὶ χάλαζα μεγάλη |

---

60. *Ezekiel in the Apocalypse*, p. 259.
61. *Climax of Prophecy*, p. 202.

The earthquake is not prominent in the Sinai theophany (it is entirely absent from the account in Deut. 6) but occurs in a number of other texts (Judg. 5.4-5; Ezek. 38.19-20; Joel 2.10; Mic. 1.3-4). Pride of place should probably be given to Ezekiel 38 in view of its use in Revelation 20 ('Gog and Magog'). It has a number of parallels with the seventh bowl. For example, both speak of the manifestation of God's wrath (Ezek. 38.19; Rev. 16.19), both speak of mountains falling (Ezek. 38.20; Rev. 16.20) and both mention hail (Ezek. 38.22; Rev. 16.21).[62]

*as had not occurred since people were upon the earth*
This phrase is used to emphasize the severity of the Egyptian plagues (Exod. 9.18; 10.6; 11.6) and is picked up in Dan. 12.1 ('a time of anguish, such as has never occurred since nations first came into existence') to describe eschatological judgment. Perhaps we are supposed to recognize a sequence here. In Exodus, it is the worst calamity since the founding of Egypt. In Daniel, it is the worst since the founding of any nation. In Revelation, it is the worst since there was a human being on the earth.

*The great city was split into three parts,*
*and the cities of the nations fell*
Not all commentators agree that there is an allusion here. Ford and Sweet cite Zech. 14.4-15, where the Lord stands on the Mount of Olives and it splits in two 'so that one half of the Mount shall withdraw northward, and the other half southward'. The parallel is 'off-centre' but at least bears witness to the fact that in some quarters, the day of the Lord was associated with a splitting of the great city (in this case Jerusalem). On the other hand, mention of cities falling might well have invoked the 'walls of Jericho' story.[63]

*God remembered great Babylon*
The title 'great Babylon' comes from Nebuchadnezzar's boastful words in Dan. 4.27 and may call to mind the irony of that passage. The NRSV uses an active verb here but the Greek is ἐμνήσθη ἐνώπιον τοῦ θεοῦ. The passive verb is found in Ezek. 3.20; 18.22, 24; 33.16 (A) and Ruiz says that these texts 'bring to light one of the several dimensions of this

---

62. As pointed out by Ruiz, *Ezekiel in the Apocalypse*, p. 281.
63. So Bauckham, *Climax of Prophecy*, p. 205.

verb, namely, the presence of human conduct (both righteous and sinful) before God'.[64]

*gave her the wine-cup of the fury of his wrath*
The Greek simply speaks of the 'cup', but the NRSV is carrying over the metaphor from Rev. 14.10, which says 'they will also drink the wine of God's wrath, poured unmixed into the cup of his anger'.[65] The image of the 'cup of wrath' is a common one in the Old Testament (Ps. 75.9; Jer. 25.15; Hab. 2.15-16; Ezek. 23, 31, 33; Isa. 51.17; Zech. 12.2), but two of these passages are particularly interesting. In Jer. 25.15 (= LXX 32.15) and Ps. 75.9 (= LXX 74.9) the MT reads 'wine of wrath', but the LXX has 'unmixed wine', as in Rev. 14.10. This could be evidence for John's use of the LXX, though some scholars suggest an earlier form of the Hebrew text.[66]

*every island fled away*
This is a commonplace in apocalyptic (*Ass. Mos.* 10.4; *1 En.* 1.6) and can be found in Isa. 41.5 and Ezek. 26.18, and is perhaps implied in Ezek. 38.20. It has already occurred in the description of the sixth seal (Rev. 6.14).

*until they cursed God for the plague of the hail*
This alludes both to the Sinai theophany (Exod. 19.16-18) and the seventh Egyptian plague (Exod. 9.18-26). Bauckham suggests that the reason John ends the bowl series with 'hail' is so as to conclude the series with an allusion to Sinai. This is part of an *Endzeit als Urzeit* theme whereby 'God's redemptive acts in the future are portrayed on the model of his past acts'.[67]

## Revelation and the Old Testament in Dialogue

It is debatable whether John has used a variety of texts 'seemingly at random, without laying special emphasis on any one of them'. A good

---

64.   *Ezekiel in the Apocalypse*, p. 272.

65.   The NRSV translation represents an interesting attempt to help the reader to take these two passages together.

66.   See Charles, *Revelation*, II, p. 16 and Ruiz, *Ezekiel in the Apocalypse*, pp. 275-79.

67.   Bauckham, *Climax of Prophecy*, p. 201.

case can be made for the dominance of the Sinai story (including the plague sequence), probably combined with Ezekiel 38. However, if the above analysis is sound, he also alludes to at least four other prophets (Isaiah, Jeremiah, Daniel and Zechariah) and possibly the fall of Jericho. Fekkes would certainly take issue with the word 'random', for there is clearly a common theme of judgment running through all these passages.[68] Nevertheless, it is probably true to say that other texts are included because of their 'evocative power' rather than in an attempt to delineate the nature of the judgment more accurately.

What of the second task mentioned by Hays? What effect does it have on the reader to recognize some (or all) of these possible allusions? What distortions or new figurations do they produce? The answer will obviously vary from reader to reader but may include:

1.   Isa. 66.6 suggests the calamity concerns retributive judgment and prompts the reader to take the phrase 'God remembered great Babylon' in the sense of 'remembered her evil deeds'. The title 'great Babylon' echoes Dan. 4.27 and drops a hint that one of these deeds was pride.

2.   Dan. 12.1 suggests this is eschatological judgment. The allusion to Zecheriah 14, if present, implies that it is God intervening on behalf of his people.[69]

3.   The allusions to Sinai and the seventh plague suggests that the end is to be like the beginning. People will not repent, but like Pharaoh, they will harden their hearts and bring more destruction upon themselves.

4.   The fall of cities and mention of earthquakes would be particularly poignant for readers of the time. Sardis and Philadelphia suffered from an earthquake in 17 CE and Laodicea in 60 CE, and the destruction of Pompeii in 79 CE left a deep unease amongst the populace.[70]

5.   Previous passages in Revelation are recalled, along with their contexts and associations. For example, the first use of the 'flashes of lightning' theme is in the throne vision of

68.   *Isaiah and Prophetic Traditions*, pp. 281-90.
69.   So Ruiz, *Ezekiel in the Apocalypse*, p. 269.
70.   See Hemer, *Local Setting*, pp. 129-77.

Revelation 4, which is primarily about praise and adoration. The plague sequence is clearly connected with the seals and trumpets. Babylon and the cup or wine of fury have already occurred in Rev. 14.8.

The first three of these relate to how the source text continues to speak to the reader, and this operates in a number of ways. First, Old Testament intertexts bring with them certain connotations, such as retribution or pride, which are not otherwise present (or explicit). Secondly, these connotations actually influence the way other parts of the narrative are read. For example, 'God remembered great Babylon' could mean no more than the fact that while God was busy demolishing the cities, he did not forget to include Babylon. However, with the connotations of retribution from Isa. 66.6 and pride from Dan. 4.27, not to mention the biblical background of μιμνήσκομαι (= Heb. זכר), the reader is more inclined to see this as Babylon getting her just deserts (at last). Indeed, the greatest intertextual echo in this passage is probably the name 'Babylon', with its long history of pride (tower of Babel), exile and oppression. Brueggemann claims that in the Old Testament, 'the theological struggle concerning public power and divine purpose remains focused on the reality, memory, experience, and symbolization of Babylon'.[71] He speaks of 'spillover' to describe this ability of a text to move 'beyond its intended or ostensive meaning to other meanings', and claims that this is not just a matter of 'wilful, imaginative interpreters'. It is also 'rooted in the metaphors and images themselves, which reach out in relentless sense making'.[72]

Thirdly, as well as adding 'ambience' to the reading, the allusions to Sinai and the plagues may be pointing to a particular view of God and history. John is not explicit about this but his presentation may be acting as the vehicle for a particular understanding of salvation history.

The fourth point broadens the range of intertextual echo to include contemporary experiences. As well as playing on the 'evocative power' of texts, John may well be playing on the 'evocative power' of shared experiences. It was noted in Chapter 2 that local allusions were not sufficient to generate all the texts that are used for the inaugural vision. That does not mean, however, that John was unaware of the effect of

71. W. Brueggemann, 'At the Mercy of Babylon: A Subversive Rereading of the Empire', *JBL* 110 (1991), p. 13.
72. 'At the Mercy of Babylon', p. 20.

'earthquake' language on the people of Asia. It may be no coincidence that the promises given in the message to Philadelphia are about stability ('pillar in the temple', 'never go out of it'). This highlights an element of intertextuality which Hays does not pursue. The reader brings a range of experiences and expectations to the text and these also interact with the voices of the text and the texts within the text. More will be said about this in Chapter 7.

The fifth point is made a particular feature of Mealy's work. Thus 'context in Revelation consists of a system of references that progressively build up hermeneutical precedents in the text, precedents that precondition the meaning of each new passage in highly significant ways'.[73] We might call this 'intratextuality',[74] the way that the various parts of a text interact with one another as the reader progresses from beginning to end. Readers arriving at this passage are becoming familiar with a pattern of judgment that includes mention of the throne (6.16; 11.19), thunder and lightning (8.5; 11.19), earthquake (6.12; 8.5; 11.19), destruction of mountains and islands (6.14) and hail (11.19). This naturally affects the way the reader approaches this text.

'Heuristic' imitation is a good description of Caird's discussion of Rev. 1.5a. Caird thinks that by fastening on a given text (Ps. 89) and then changing it, John makes it clear that his understanding of messianic power is different from that of the Psalmist. The Psalm becomes, in Greene's words, a 'kind of *rite de passage* between a specified past and an emergent present'.[75] The clash between the Psalmist's view of the Messiah and one based on knowledge of Christ's earthly suffering allows the reader to perceive the 'poetic distance traversed'.[76] In short, Caird says that John offers us a 'profoundly Christian application' of Scripture and not a mere reproduction. However, it is by no means certain that such expressions of messianic power would be as unwelcome to John as Caird suggests. As Hays says,

---

73.   *After the Thousand Years*, p. 13.

74.   In his discussion of the prologue in the Fourth Gospel, M.W.G. Stibbe speaks of its interactional function (involving the reader), its intertextual function (relation to other texts) and its intratextual function (relation to other parts of the book). *John* (Readings: A New Biblical Commentary; Sheffield: JSOT Press, 1993), pp. 22-31.

75.   Greene, *Light in Troy*, p. 41.

76.   Greene, *Light in Troy*, p. 40.

> The word of Scripture is not played off as a foil for the gospel, not patron-
> ized as a primitive stage of religious development, not regarded merely as a
> shadow of the good things to come.[77]

This leads on to Greene's fourth category, 'dialectical imitation', where the 'text is the locus of a struggle between two rhetorical or semiotic systems that are vulnerable to one another and whose conflict cannot easily be resolved'.[78] The author avoids bringing the interaction to premature closure but leaves the contexts in tension. In Chapter 2, I concluded that the inaugural vision is a scriptural construct, modelled on Dan. 10.5-6 and supplemented by descriptions of his hair (Dan. 7.9), face (Judg. 5.31), mouth (Isa. 11.4 + 49.2) and voice (Ezek. 1.24). However, it must now be acknowledged that the person being described was not unknown to the readers. They already had a conception of who Jesus was (and is) and what attributes he possesses. This was derived from whatever traditions had come down to them and their own personal and corporate experience. The vision would not, therefore, have been read in a vacuum but would be interpreted in the light of present knowledge. For example, the shining face and bright clothes might have been read in the light of the transfiguration tradition, in which Jesus 'was transfigured...and his face shone like the sun, and his clothes became dazzling white' (Mt. 17.2).

Nevertheless, it is doubtful if John's evocative descriptions would simply be absorbed into an already existing conception of Christ. The images are too strong to be silenced and retain the power to contend against such a simple reading.[79] Indeed, there is evidence that John wishes to promote this dialectical state of affairs. For example, in Rev. 1.17-18, the visionary figure says, 'I am the first and the last, and the living one. I was dead, and see, I am alive forever and ever.' Here a title of eternal existence ('first and the last') is combined with the statement: 'I was dead'. As Hays says, 'two symbolic worlds are brought into collision so that each is vulnerable to criticism and interpretation by the other'.[80] How can the sovereign being who is addressed as the 'first and

77. *Echoes of Scripture*, p. 176.
78. *Light in Troy*, p. 46.
79. 'We need to get out from under the model of methodical solipsism that pictures a solitary reader exercising strategic power over a text' (G.L. Bruns, 'The Hermeneutics of Midrash', in *The Book and the Text* [ed. R. Schwartz; Cambridge, MA: Basil Blackwell, 1990], p. 192).
80. *Echoes of Scripture*, p. 174.

the last' die? Or how can the martyr, who dies so that others might live, live forever? John does not resolve these, but by placing them side by side he encourages the mutual interpretation of one by the other. In the words of Boyarin (talking about midrash), it cannot be 'decided which signifier is the interpreter and which the interpreted'.[81]

This is further illustrated in Revelation 4–5, where praise and adoration are offered first to God and then to the Lamb:

> You are worthy, our Lord and God, to receive glory and honour and power, for you created all things, and by your will they existed and were created (Rev. 4.11).

> You are worthy to take the scroll and to open its seals, for you were slaughtered and by your blood you ransomed for God saints from every tribe and language and people and nation…(Rev. 5.9).

In the first, God is offered praise for being the creator and sustainer of all the universe, while in the second, such praise goes to the Lamb for being slaughtered (and hence ransoming people from every tribe, language, people and nation). John does not explain how these two fit together and avoid polytheism. He simply leaves them side by side. A similar tension exists in John's presentation of the Messiah. In Rev. 5.5, he calls him the 'Lion of the tribe of Judah' and the 'Root of David', traditional titles stemming from Gen. 49.9 and Isa. 11.10 respectively.[82] However, he then goes on to speak of a Lamb 'standing as if it had been slaughtered':

> 'Do not weep. See, the Lion of the tribe of Judah, the Root of David, has conquered, so that he can open the scroll and its seven seals.' Then I saw between the throne and the four living creatures and among the elders a Lamb standing as if it had been slaughtered…(Rev. 5.5-6).

Now apart from the obvious clash that Jesus is described both as a Lion and a Lamb, we would appear to have two quite different conceptions of the Messiah side by side. John Sweet says,

> the Lion of Judah, the traditional messianic expectation, is reinterpreted by the slain Lamb: God's power and victory lie in self-sacrifice.[83]

---

81.   D. Boyarin, 'The Song of Songs: Lock or Key? Intertextuality, Allegory and Midrash', in *The Book and the Text* (ed. R. Schwartz; Cambridge, MA: Basil Blackwell, 1990), p. 223.

82.   The messianic application is attested in such texts as Sir. 47.22, 4 *Ezra* 12.32 and 4QpIsa[a] 8–10.

83.   Sweet, *Revelation*, p. 125.

This gives one direction of influence. The traditional expectation is reinterpreted by the slain Lamb. Caird goes further, stating that this verse is the key to John's use of the Old Testament, as if he were saying to us,

> 'Wherever the Old Testament says "**Lion**", read "**Lamb**".' Wherever the Old Testament speaks of the victory of the Messiah or the overthrow of the enemies of God, we are to remember that the gospel recognizes no other way of achieving these ends than the way of the Cross.[84]

Here is a more explicit description of Caird's understanding of John's use of Scripture. It was suggested in the discussion of Rev. 1.5a that he was using a sort of hermeneutic of replacement. Now it is stated unambiguously. When the Old Testament reads 'Lion', we are to read 'Lamb', and when it speaks of the 'overthrow of the enemies of God, we are to remember that the gospel recognizes no other way of achieving these ends than the way of the Cross'. What is this if not a hermeneutic of replacement? The reader is not asked to wrestle with the tension of how the Messiah can be both Lion and Lamb but simply has to substitute one idea for the other. By alluding to the Lion of Gen. 49.9, John distances himself from such views and reminds his readers that the Christian knows no other Messiah than the slain Lamb.

On the other hand, J.M. Ford claims that in the animal symbolism of the apocalypses, the Messiah was represented both by a Lion and a Lamb. They are not contrasting figures, as if one represented 'raw power' while the other stood for more subtle ways of achieving its ends. Neither is the Lamb necessarily associated with sacrifice. She quotes *T. Jos.* 19.8:

---

84. Caird, *Revelation*, p. 75, and quoted with approval by Sweet, *Revelation*, p. 125, Boring, *Revelation*, p. 110, and Bauckham, *Climax of Prophecy*, p. 179. Boring says,'It is as though John had adopted the familiar synagogue practice of "perpetual Kethib/Qere", whereby a word or phrase that appears in the traditional text is read as another word or phrase: "wherever the tradition says 'lion', read 'Lamb'...Every event of apocalyptic violence in chapters 6–19 must be seen as derived from the scene of chapters 4–5' (pp. 110, 118). Bauckham is more nuanced, recognizing that the 'hopes embodied in the messianic titles of Revelation 5.5 are not dismissed by the vision of the Lamb' (*Climax of Prophecy*, p. 183). Nevertheless, he concludes that 'by juxtaposing these contrasting images, John forges a symbol of conquest by sacrificial death, which is essentially a new symbol'.

> And I saw that a virgin was born from Judah, wearing a linen stole; and from her was born a spotless lamb. At his left there was something like a lion, and all the wild animals rushed against him, but the lamb conquered them, and destroyed them, trampling them underfoot.[85]

Ford maintains that there is nothing in the book of Revelation which compels us to depart from this picture. The Lamb of Revelation 5 has seven horns, indicating power, and seven eyes, a symbol of omniscience. In the next chapter, those who suffer the calamities set loose by the Lamb cry out, 'Fall on us and hide us from the face of the one seated on the throne and from the wrath of the Lamb; for the great day of their wrath has come, and who is able to stand?' (Rev. 6.16-17). The picture does not change when the confederacy of kings in Rev. 17.14 confront the Lamb: 'they will make war on the Lamb, and the Lamb will conquer them, for he is Lord of lords and King of kings, and those with him are called and chosen and faithful'.

Ford thus concludes that John's use of the title 'Lamb' is thoroughly consonant with the apocalyptic destroying lamb known to tradition.[86] Few scholars have agreed with this, but it does show how 'loudly' the old context continues to speak if one has 'ears to hear'. On the one hand, we have Caird and others who see the slain Lamb in Revelation 5 as the interpretative key to the whole book (and the whole of the Old Testament!). On this view, Revelation becomes one of the most profoundly Christian works in the New Testament, reinterpreting the divine glory in the light of the cross of Christ. On the other hand, there has always been a suspicion (and in some cases, more than a suspicion) that Revelation is little more than a thinly disguised Jewish work.[87] Thus Ford believes that the bulk of Revelation comes from the followers of John the Baptist (cf. the title 'Lamb of God' in Jn 1.29) which has been given a Christian framework by the addition of Revelation 1–3 and the concluding verses (22.16-17a, 20-21). This can be detected, she says, because these additions 'display a higher Christology than chs. 4–22 and promise unheard of rewards to those who are faithful to Christ—even a place with him beside his Father'.[88]

---

85. Ford, *Revelation*, pp. 30-31. However, it may be that this verse is a Christian interpolation.

86. See Ford, *Revelation*, pp. 87-95.

87. E.g. R. Bultmann, *Theology of the New Testament*, II (London: SCM Press, 1955), p. 175.

88. Ford, *Revelation*, p. 56.

Rowland claims that the throne vision of Revelation 4 'shows no evidence at all of Christian influence and treated in isolation, it is evident that it is entirely Jewish in its inspiration'.[89] However, he believes this is a deliberate strategy, for 'the author obviously intends a deliberate contrast between the description of the divine court in Revelation 4 and the transformation which has taken place as the result of the exaltation of the Lamb'.[90] Hurtado[91] has contested the view that Revelation 4 shows no signs of Christian influence, but the point remains. The general impression that these two chapters give is undoubtedly one of contrast. In regard to Greene's categories, one can ask two questions of this:

1.  Does John intend a resolution of the tension so that Rev. 5 represents the 'true' picture (i.e. heuristic imitation)?

2.  Irrespective of what John may or may not have intended, does the text offer such a resolution to readers today?

The fact that Revelation can be taken as profoundly Christian or essentially Jewish (depending on what is thought to be its hermeneutical key) strongly suggests that the answer to the second question is that the tension is unresolved. Readers will differ as to how 'loudly' they will hear the old and what effect it has on their reading of the text. In Ford's case, she thinks that there is nothing that compels us to depart from the apocalyptic destroying lamb found in tradition.[92] Caird, on the other hand, says that wherever we read of the 'overthrow of God's enemies', we are to remember that the 'gospel recognizes no other way of achieving these ends than the way of the Cross'.[93] Both of these are overstatements, assuming that one side of the tension is able to 'swallow-up' the other without remainder. Ford does not consider the impact (on the original reader or on the modern reader) of the finished work but gives a theology of the sources, as she understands them. Caird goes to the other extreme, explaining how the different parts of the book can all be understood as deeply Christian, providing one starts with the right hermeneutical key. However, as much as the modern

89.  C. Rowland, *The Open Heaven: A Study of Apocalypticism in Judaism and Christianity* (London: SPCK, 1982), p. 222.

90.  *The Open Heaven*, p. 222.

91.  L.W. Hurtado, 'Revelation 4–5 in the Light of Jewish Apocalyptic Analogies', *JSNT* 25 (1985), pp. 105-24.

92.  Ford, *Revelation*, pp. 87-95.

93.  Caird, p. 75.

Christian might wish to see all the calamities described in the seals, trumpets and bowls as symbolic for Christ's non-coercive self-sacrifice, it has to be said that this is not how it reads to most people. Bloom is extreme but most people will understand why he says that Revelation is

> Lurid and inhumane, its influence has been pernicious, yet inescapable... Resentment and not love is the teaching of the Revelation of St. John the Divine. It is a book without wisdom, goodness, kindness, or affection of any kind. Perhaps it is appopriate that a celebration of the end of the world should be not only barbaric but scarcely literate. Where the substance is so inhumane, who would wish the rhetoric to be more persuasive, or the vision to be more vividly realized.[94]

Thus the answer to the second question is that the text, as we have it, preserves the tension rather than resolving it, at least for some readers. He who is called 'first and the last' has died and the slaughtered Lamb is none other than the Lion of Judah. John does not explain how these can be true without involving contradiction.

What of the first question? Is there evidence that John intended a resolution that some people, such as Bloom, have missed? Before commenting on this, it is worth pointing out that much of today's literary criticism no longer views authorial intention as decisive for the meaning of a text. We have no access to the author's mind, and even if we did, how he or she intended the text to 'work' is not the same thing as how the actual text does work with particular readers (cf. Ford and Caird). If the conclusion is that the text as we have it cannot easily be read as 'heuristic imitation' but leaves certain tensions unresolved, this conclusion is not affected by knowing what John's intentions were (even if we had some access to them outside of the text).

Nevertheless, to say that the meaning of a text is not dictated by authorial intention is not to say that John's purposes are of no interest to readers. Any reader is bound to show some interest in whether the interpretations being offered could possibly have been intended by John, even if the question cannot be fully answered. In this regard, I assume that the author implied by the text bears some relationship to the real author, even though it must be acknowledged that they are not identical. The question remains, then, as to whether the evidence suggests that the author intended to leave the reader with a dialogical tension, or did he intend a resolution? The evidence, as I see it, is as follows.

94. H. Bloom, *The Revelation of St John the Divine* (Modern Critical Interpretations; New York: Chelsea House, 1988), pp. 4-5.

*Evidence That John Intended a Dialogical Tension*
First, we have seen that John places images or titles side by side without offering any help as to which is the signifier and which the signified. He could presumably have done so had he wished. The fact that he did not suggests that this was not his intention. Further, there are other examples of this technique. For example, in the vision of Revelation 7, John *hears* that those who are to be sealed number 144,000 and that this number is made up of 12,000 from each of the twelve tribes of Israel. However, what he *sees* is a 'great multitude that no one could count, from every nation, from all tribes and peoples and languages' (7.9). Once again, John offers no help to the reader as to how these fit together, and some commentators have assumed that they refer to different groups (e.g. Jews and Gentiles or martyrs and ordinary Christians).[95]

Secondly, if John's intention is to reinterpret the language of the Davidic Messiah, it is strange that he continues to use it in the rest of the book. Thus at the parousia of Christ, he will 'smite the nations' (Isa. 11.4) and 'rule them with a rod of iron' (Ps. 2.9). Further, the book closes with the self-declaration, 'I am the root and the descendant of David, the bright morning star' (22.16). There is no mention of Lamb here with which to reinterpret this language. The reader is left with a messianic image (Isa. 11), just as the book opened with one ('ruler of the kings of the earth').

Thirdly, if John's intention is to reinterpret the military imagery, it is odd that he continues to use it profusely (as Ford points out). Few scholars would agree with the judgment of Bloom cited above, but they will understand where he gets it from. Revelation is full of military images. If John's aim is to reinterpret them in the light of Christ's sacrificial death, he sails pretty close to the wind.

Fourthly, it was noted at the end of Chapter 4 that Ruiz claimed that the abnormal Greek of the Apocalypse was intended to put conscious difficulties in front of the reader so as to confound an ordinary reading of the text. In support of such a view, he draws attention to those occasions in Revelation when the reader is called upon to exercise wisdom: 'This calls for wisdom: let anyone with understanding calculate the number of the beast' (13.18), and 'This calls for a mind that has wisdom' (17.9). Regardless of whether his explanation for John's Greek is accepted, these two verses suggest that the author was not seeking to

95. See on pp. 71-72.

provide easy answers but wishes to force the reader to stop and think. It is possible that his use of the Old Testament is also meant to do the same.

*Evidence That John Intended a Resolution*

Perhaps the main reason for assuming that John intended a resolution is that his book is now part of the canon of Scripture. It may be true that it can be read as a thinly disguised Jewish work, but its presence in the New Testament implies that it should be read as a Christian work. This seems to be the motivation behind Caird's words, though many will now find them embarrassingly supersessionist. What is required is a description of a resolution that does justice to the points mentioned above. In Chapter 8 of *The Climax of Prophecy*, Bauckham attempts to do this. In an earlier chapter, he quotes the words of Caird with approval but he also recognizes the need to provide an explanation for why there is so much military language in the book. Noting the way that Revelation 7 offers a parallel to Revelation 5 and how the 144,000 reappear in Revelation 14, he says,

> The fact that the latter are here called the 144,000 may seem surprising after their reinterpretation as the innumerable host in 7.9. But the usage is parallel to John's continued use of 'Root of David' as a messianic title for Jesus in 22.16, even after its reinterpretation by the vision of the Lamb in 5.5-6. By reinterpreting the militant Messiah and his army John does not mean simply to set aside Israel's hopes for eschatological triumph: in the Lamb and his followers these hopes are both fulfilled and transformed. The Lamb really does conquer, though not by force of arms, and his followers really do share his victory, though not by violence. The combination of the Lamb and the 144,000 conveys the sense that there is a holy war to be fought, but to be fought and won by sacrificial death.[96]

In the terminology of this chapter, Bauckham acknowledges that John does not wish to silence the military language because it does have something important to say. There really is a battle for Christians to face, just as there really was a battle for Christ. However, by juxtaposing this language with Christian images (Lamb, martyrdom, innumerable multitude), John forces a reinterpretation. It is not to be read as a military victory for it is juxtaposed with Christian imagery. Thus according to Bauckham, the

96.   *Climax of Prophecy*, pp. 229-30.

distinctive feature of Revelation seems to be, not its repudiation of apocalyptic militarism, but its lavish use of militaristic *language* in a non-militaristic *sense*. In the eschatological destruction of evil in Revelation there is no place for real armed violence, but there is ample space of the imagery of armed violence.[97]

## Conclusion

Previous studies on John's use of the Old Testament have concentrated on what John has done to the text in order to meet the needs of his readers. They have concentrated on what they believed to be John's purposes rather than asking what effect an allusion has on a reading of the text. At the end of Chapter 4, I concluded that John's use of Ezekiel involved both continuity and discontinuity. The similarities led Goulder to his lectionary hypothesis, whereas Vogelgesang interpreted the differences to be a deliberate contrast on John's part. Ruiz says, 'To the extent that the "interpreting subject" engages in an active reading of John's book, he or she engages in a dialogue with the text and with the texts within the text'.[98]

The contribution of this study has been to show how the literary concept of 'intertextuality' can be used to illuminate this 'dialogue with the text and the texts within the text'. It is not so much applying a method as asking certain types of questions and pondering particularly evocative phrases (like 'connotations bleed over'). Its premise is a very simple one, namely, that if an allusion points the reader to something outside of the text, it inevitably sets up a relationship between the two contexts which is in some sense unpredictable (and out of the hands of the author). The task of the interpreter is to give an account of how these two contexts potentially affect one another, or, as Hays puts it, 'the distortions and new figuration that they generate'.[99] In this respect, Fiorenza's claim that John 'does not interpret the Old Testament but uses its words, images, phrases and patterns...to express his own prophetic vision'[100] may be questioned. I would agree that John does not set out to offer a particular interpretation of the Old Testament (in the manner of the *pesharim*), and in this sense she is correct. On the other hand, the reader of John's book will look at the Old Testament in

97. *Climax of Prophecy*, p. 233.
98. *Ezekiel in the Apocalypse*, p. 520.
99. *Echoes of Scripture*, p. 19.
100. 'Apokalypsis and Propheteia', *Justice and Judgment*, p. 135.

quite a different light from one who has not read it (and vice versa), so Revelation does have an interpretative function after all. For example, who can doubt that the reader of Revelation would view Ezekiel 40–48 in a different light from one who has not read John's book. If he or she is attending carefully to Ezekiel's text this will not necessarily be intrusive, but it will nevertheless be present. By modelling much of his work on Ezekiel, both works travel through history together (unless a community emerges that has no contact with one or the other). Indeed, it can even happen that the later text becomes so well known that the earlier text appears to be based on it. Thus Bloom says of 'Paradise Lost':

> In Milton's grand metaleptic reversal, the account of Creation in Genesis has become a Midrash upon Milton.[101]

This is of course nonsense in term of conventional source criticism, but not in terms of reader-orientated methods of interpretation. Revelation is the only New Testament book that significantly alludes to the book of Ezekiel. For many Christian readers, this is the main reason that chapter after chapter of measurements and ordinances (Ezek. 40–48) still retains any interest. However, for some readers of Revelation, seemingly sub-Christian ideas such as the millenium and a resurgence of evil have somehow become acceptable on the basis that John was following Ezekiel. As Justin said,

> I and others, who are right-minded Christians at all points, are assured that there will be a resurrection of the dead, and a thousand years in Jerusalem, which will then be built adorned and enlarged as the prophets Ezekiel and Isaiah and others declare.[102]

This is an indication of the bond that exists between the two works. Both might have been destined for obscurity but each has helped the other in its fight for survival. Bloom observes of the Priestly writer,

> The Priestly Author has swept away by his own breath the enormous wars against the abyss and its creatures that God fights and wins, victories celebrated throughout the Psalms, the Prophets, Job and other biblical

101. H. Bloom, *The Breaking of the Vessels* (Chicago & London: University of Chicago Press, 1982), p. 84. Worten and Still say, 'Every literary imitation is a supplement which seeks to complete and supplant the original and which functions at times for later readers as the pre-text of the "original"', 'Introduction', *Intertextuality: Theories and Practice*, p. 7).

102. Quoted in Barclay, *Revelation*, II, p. 189.

texts. By a magnificent ellipsis of tradition, the Priestly Author has
strengthened the creative force of the divine by making that force transcend
its traditional opponents to the point where they have vanished wholly.[103]

On the other hand, now that science proposes quite different theories
about the creation of the world, many have found the significance of
Genesis 1 to lie precisely in its use of the older creation stories. Though
lost to generations of readers, archaeology has brought to light the
transumed material and given new significance to a narrative which was
itself being threatened with extinction.

The book of Revelation contains over 200 allusions to the Old
Testament. It can profitably be studied by asking how John weaves
these allusions into his composition in order to meet the needs of his
readers. However, one of the ways that he does this is apparently to
force his readers to enter into a 'dialogue with the text and with the
texts within the text'.[104] Bauckham acknowledges that John makes
'lavish use of militaristic *language*' but insists that this is to be taken in a
'non-militaristic *sense*'. There is clearly some truth in this in that victory
for the Christian comes through maryrdom rather than armed violence.
However, the 'lavish use of militaristic *language*' has a greater effect on
(most) readers than Bauckham is willing to acknowledge. As Eliot said
of the poet,

> not only the best, but the most individual parts of his work may be those in
> which the dead poets, his ancestors, assert their immortality most
> vigorously.[105]

The power of John's work is not that he replaces military imagery
with Christian imagery but that he forces an interaction between them.
As Davidson says,

> The work's meaning is in the tension between its previous contextual
> definition and its present context.[106]

This is achieved in a particulary subtle way in John's work since he
does not advertise the past context through explicit quotation. Rather,
by incorporating the words and images of the Old Testament into his
own composition, the reader is unsure whether he or she is reading
John's words or words from another context. This can be resolved by

103. *Breaking of the Vessels*, pp. 16-17.
104. Ruiz, *Ezekiel in the Apocalypse*, p. 520.
105. *Selected Essays*, p. 14.
106. *T.S. Eliot and Hermeneutics*, p. 117.

allowing one context to swallow up the other without remainder, but this misses the true dynamics of the work. Meaning in Revelation 'is in the tension between its previous contextual definition and its present context'. Or in the form of a diagram, the genius of Revelation is not that it borrows Old Testament language or that it has created something completely new—but in the dynamic intersection of shared language, imagery and style. My aim in this study has been to show that co-reading Revelation with the Old Testament in order to bring out these dynamics is not an imposition on the text but an important way of doing justice to its complexity. If it prompts others to produce 'intertextual readings' of other passages in Revelation then it will have served its purpose.

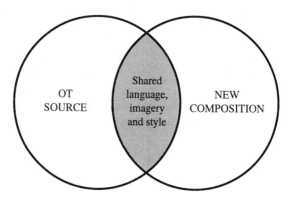

Chapter 7

EPILOGUE

The development of an interactive model in this study came as a
response to the nature of the book of Revelation. Its allusive use of
Scripture is not easily contained within traditional source criticism but
demands a broader approach. As Collins[1] says about 'mythological
allusions', they are not simply 'copies of the orginal source' but serve to
'transfer motifs from one context to another.' This study has shown
some of the ways that this can happen in a reading of John's text. It also
has implications for books other than Revelation, and I would like to
close by highlighting three areas.

*Respect for Context*

I said in the introduction that 'respect for context' was one of the keenly
debated issues in 'Use of the Old Testament' studies. Grollenberg takes
the view that the NT authors had little interest in what the text meant to
the original author. Rather, they read the Old Testament in the light of
the 'events brought about by God in which they themselves were
involved'.[2] Bruce says a similar thing about the Dead Sea Scrolls.[3] On
the other hand, others have emphasized the view that the authors were
serious exegetes, using prescribed methods to get at the 'true' meaning
of the text.[4] However, the quotation from Worten and Still puts the
matter in a different light:

> every quotation distorts and redefines the 'primary' utterance by relocating
> it within another linguistic and cultural context.[5]

1. *Apocalyptic Imagination*, p. 16.
2. *Unexpected Messiah*, p. 7.
3. *Biblical Exegesis*, pp. 9-18.
4. Brooke, *Exegesis at Qumran*, p. 44.
5. 'Introduction', *Intertextuality: Theories and Practices*, p. 11.

If this is taken as the starting point, it can be seen that the either/or option is misconceived. Every quotation is out of context because it has been relocated. It cannot possibly mean the same thing as it did in its old context, because most of the factors that affect interpretation have changed. A more constructive approach would be to consider how the two contexts might be related, and what effects might be produced by creating a bridge between them. For example, consider the catena of Rom. 3.10-18.[6] To an earlier generation of commentators, Paul cites these verses because they demonstrate the universality of sin.[7] This is what he says he is going to demonstrate in 3.9, and what he believes he has demonstrated in 3.19-20. It was therefore assumed that Paul respects the context of these quotations. However, in 1962, Edgar wrote in a New Testament Studies article,

> The verses Paul adduces in Rom 3 to prove the universality of sin do not,
> in their original contexts, refer to all men, but in most cases to the wicked,
> the enemies of Israel.[8]

This leads in two directions. First, there are those like Grollenberg who believe that the ancient authors had no interest in the original context. Käsemann, for example, describes the catena as a florilegium and then says that florilegiums are all about

> taking a sentence out of context, weaving together passages with different
> thrusts, and inserting an interpretation into a particular citation.[9]

Secondly, there are those that acknowledge that the verses are taken out of context but argue that this is part of Paul's hermeneutical strategy. Dunn says,

---

6.   See my article, 'The Catena of Rom 3:10-18', *ExpTim* (forthcoming).

7.   C.K. Barrett says, 'Paul has already (i.18–ii.29) brought the charge against Jews and Greeks; but he would not have it regarded as merely an intellectual analysis of the moral life of the first century. Far more important than any such analysis is the fact that **this is the verdict of Scripture**' (*The Epistle to the Romans* [BNTC; London: A. & C. Black, 1962], p. 69).

8.   S.L. Edgar, 'Respect for Context in Quotations from the Old.Testament.', *NTS* 9 (1962–63), p. 56.

9.   E. Käsemann, *Commentary on Romans* (London: SCM Press, 1980), p. 86. Stanley says, 'a line that attributes the behaviour of the people under discussion to their "foolishness" is left out...presumably because it conflicts with Paul's emphasis on the moral culpability of those who act in the manner described' (*Paul and the Language of Scripture*, pp. 97-98).

it needs to be stressed that the point of the catena is not simply to demonstrate that scripture condemns all humankind, but more precisely to demonstrate that scriptures which had been read from the presupposition of a clear distinction between the righteous and the unrighteous...in fact condemned all humankind as soon as that clear distinction was undermined.[10]

However, it is worth asking whether the dominant theme of the citations, namely, that God makes a distinction between the righteous and the wicked, is quite so unwelcome to Paul as these approaches suggest. It is clear that he wants to undermine the equation that righteousness means Jews and wickedness means Gentiles, but that does not mean that God no longer distinguishes between righteousness and wickedness (cf. Rom. 6.13). Indeed, the twin themes that God blesses the righteous (1.17; 2.7; 2.10) and punishes the wicked (1.18-32; 2.8; 3.10-20) are central to these early chapters. In the language of this study, Paul activates and reactivates these 'voices' (blessing and punishment) until he is ready to bring them into dialogue with the 'voice' of the gospel (3.21-26). He is not aiming to 'silence' them, since it is imperative that the gospel is seen in the light of God's righteousness (and vice versa). Thus rather than debating whether Paul respects the Old Testament context or not, a more fruitful approach would be to trace the effects of this interaction through the rest of the book.

In the book of Revelation, the promise to the church at Philadelphia that the Jews will 'come and bow down before your feet' (Rev. 3.9) seems like an obvious case of lack of respect for the Old Testament context, for what Isaiah actually says is that

The descendants of those who oppressed you shall come bending low to you, and all who despised you shall bow down at your feet; they shall call you the City of the Lord, the Zion of the Holy One of Israel (Isa. 60.14).

It is clear, however, that this is not simply carelessness on John's part. He could have expressed such a thought in his own words, but by alluding to Isaiah in this way (also 45.14; 49.23) John accesses a 'vocabularly of a second and higher power'.[11] The words come to him highly charged and hence ready to interact with the new context. As Beale says, 'This reversal of Isaiah's language is most likely attributable to a conscious attempt to express the irony that the submission which

10. J.D.G. Dunn, *Romans 1–8* (WBC; Dallas: Word Books, 1988), p. 151.
11. Greene, *Light of Troy*, p. 39.

unbelieving ethnic Jews hoped to receive from Gentiles, they themselves would be forced to render to the church'.[12] Nevertheless, this is not the end of the matter. The most fundamental thing is that John has built a bridge between two contexts, thereby setting in motion an interaction that continues to reverberate throughout the whole book. Finding ways of describing this is far more significant than sterile debates about whether John respects the context of his allusions.

### The Role of the Reader

Most 'Use of the Old Testament' studies belong to Source and Redaction criticism. They are interested in how a particular author has used the Old Testament in order to meet the needs of the recipients. For example, deviations from MT or LXX (unless alternative text-forms can be proved) are usually explained in terms of the 'intention' of the author. However, this emphasis on the author's 'intention' has been largely abandoned in New Testament study and replaced by a focus either on the text itself or on the role of the reader. This has been for both practical (we have no access to the author's 'intention') and theoretical reasons (meaning is not a 'given' but has to be 'created' by the reader). This study has shown that there is no reason why 'Use of the Old Testament' studies should be limited to the historical-critical paradigm. By utilizing past texts, the author has produced a fresh composition which invites the reader to participate and create meaning. As Ellen van Wolde says,

> The writer assigns meaning to his own context and in interaction with other texts he shapes and forms his own text. The reader, in much the same way, assigns meaning to the generated text in interaction with other texts he knows…A writer does not weave a web of meanings that the reader merely has to follow, but…presents them to the reader as a text. The reader reacts to the offer and enters into a dialogue with the possibilities the text has to offer him.[13]

In the same volume of essays, Vorster compares a 'Redaktions-geschichte' approach to 'Use of the Old Testament' with one based on notions of 'Intertextuality':

---

12.  'Revelation', *Scripture Citing Scripture*, p. 330.
13.  'Trendy Intertextuality', *Intertextuality in Biblical Writings*, p. 47.

> First of all it is clear that the phenomenon text has been redefined. It has become a network of references to other texts (intertexts). Secondly it appears that more attention is to be given to text as a process of production and not to the sources and their influences. And thirdly it is apparent that the role of the reader is not to be neglected in this approach to the phenomenon of text.[14]

Each of these points suggests fruitful avenues of research. The first suggests that the reader is not addressed by a single voice (such as a single narrator) but a plurality of voices. How these are 'heard' and what the reader makes of them will differ from person to person. Secondly, the significance of an allusion or quotation is not limited to the specific source used. For example, an allusion to Isaiah. 6 is a gateway into all such 'throne visions', past, present and future. The use of infancy narratives in Matthew and Luke not only suggests particular Old Testament texts (such as Isa. 7.14) but makes use of the general 'intertext' of 'birth stories' (in which we all participate). Thirdly, the meaning of a text emerges through the interaction of text and reader. This was highlighted in Chapter 6, where it became clear that different interpretations of Revelation were largely the result of a (prior) choice concerning the book's hermeneutical key. It is highlighted in Fiorenza's introductory section on 'social location', which is not about first-century Asia (as expected) but the 'social location' of the reader:

> Competing interpretations of Revelation are not simply either right or wrong, but they constitute different ways of reading and constructing socio-historical and theo-ethical meaning. What is appropriate in such a rhetorical paradigm of biblical scholarship is not detached value-neutrality, but an explicit articulation of one's rhetorical strategies, interested perspectives, ethical criteria, theoretical frameworks, religious presuppositions, and sociopolitical locations for critical public discussion.[15]

### Biblical Stereotypes and Historical Allusions

During the course of this study, there have been several examples where it is unclear whether certain phrases are to be taken as historical references or allusions to the Old Testament. For example, phrases like 'flame of fire' and 'burnished bronze' are taken by Ramsay and Hemer

14. W. Vorster, 'Intertextuality and Redaktionsgeschichte', in *Intertextuality in Biblical Writings* (FS B. van Iersel; ed. S. Draisma; Kampen: Kok, 1989), p. 21.

15. E.S. Fiorenza, *Revelation: Vision of a Just World* (Edinburgh: T. & T. Clark, new edn, 1993), p. 3.

to refer to Thyatira's metal industry, whereas most scholars see an allusion to the book of Daniel. Are these contradictory explanations or can they both be true? In Chapter 5, it was noted that some scholars use the descriptions of the 'wicked priest' in the Qumran literature to try and identify him with a known individual, while others think they derive from the biblical text itself. Again, are these contradictory explanations, or can they co-exist together. The issue is of some importance since it affects

1.  *Historical Reconstructions.* Very often we know next to nothing about the circumstances of an ancient document. Historical allusions, if they exist, are sometimes the only evidence there is.

2.  *The Author's Exegesis.* Was it a serious attempt to interpret a text or a 'reading in' of one's own history?

3.  *Interpretation.* Much of the Bible is 'history-like', but is it to be taken literally? Did Matthew really believe that people came to life and walked into Jerusalem (Mt. 27.52-53) or is this his way of saying something about the significance of Jesus' death?

Surprisingly, however, the Scripture–history question has not received the theoretical treatment that it deserves. Callaway observes,

> when one searches the secondary literature for concrete arguments justifying the use of statements in the pesharim to reconstruct historical episodes involving members of the Qumran community and their enemies, one comes away rather perplexed, for a defense of this central assumption—that the pesher is a source of historical information about a particular historical community—can hardly be found.[16]

The discussion of local allusions in Chapter 2 was facilitated by the fact that a number of them had already occurred in the inaugural vision. Since most scholars accept that this is a scriptural composition, it is very difficult to accept that the allusions began life as historical references and were only later used to construct the vision. Nevertheless, the possibility that John modified Old Testament texts (cf. the word χαλκολίβανος) in order to allude to local circumstances cannot be ruled out.

Another example was the references to the Kittim in the DSS. Such references clearly have a definite group of people in mind (probably the

---

16. P.R. Callaway, *The History of the Qumran Community: An Investigation* (JSPSup 3; Sheffield: JSOT Press, 1988), p. 136.

Romans), and this must have affected the way that the community read the Scriptures (it is part of what they bring to the interpretative task). Further, since the words of the pesher frequently differ from the words of the lemma (e.g. 'quick and valiant in war' instead of Habakkuk's 'fierce and impetuous nation'), it is possible to argue that the author has the contemporary foe in mind. On the other hand, Brooke has shown that in the vast majority of cases the wording of the pesher can either be derived from the lemma by standard exegetical techniques or from a text that can be related to it. Thus differences from the lemma are not necessarily evidence for reconstructing the history of the Romans. It could be that by the use of recognized exegetical techniques, the ancient interpreter thinks he has discovered a fresh source of information about the Romans. Brooke says,

> We can learn little or nothing of the history of the Qumran community from these texts, and little enough about the Romans. Rather, the image of empire is controlled by biblical and non-biblical texts used intricately to show that the words of Habakkuk and others speak directly, if not always in great detail, to the author's contemporary and eschatological generation.[17]

The interactive approach that has been suggested in this book is not so much an answer to these issues as a way of posing the questions. By simply asking whether one side of an interaction has been forced into premature closure, fresh possibilities of interpretation emerge. Not all will be significant. Some echoes are rightly silenced because they fail to convince. This is the thrust of Fekkes's study. But it is often worth asking whether the less dominant voice has anything to contribute. It may be that traditions of interpretation have forced it into premature closure. The issues mentioned above certainly show that there can be a great deal at stake.

John's method is not to quote Scripture formally but to weave its 'words, images, phrases and patterns' into his own composition. Indeed, on many occasions, the language of the allusions is barely distinguishable from his own style and vocabulary. The argument of this book is that this requires a more interactive approach than traditional 'Use of the Old Testament' studies have followed. It is not attempting to devalue such studies. Focusing on one side of the interaction can often highlight areas that might be missed in a more general study. The emphasis of Ramsay

17. G.J. Brooke, 'The Kittim in the Qumran Pesharim', in *Images of Empire* (ed. L. Alexander; JSOTSup 122; Sheffield: JSOT Press, 1991), p. 159.

and Hemer on the local context and Beale on Daniel were both important in determining the need for a new approach. Likewise with Ezekiel. The significant parallels noted by Vanhoye and Goulder had to be related to the significant differences highlighted by Vogelgesang. This led to writers like Hollander and Greene, who have explored such interactions with respect to Milton and Renaissance poetry. The particular judgments offered in this book about John's use of the Old Testament are certainly open to further clarification, but the need for an interactive approach has, I believe, been established. As Ruiz says,

> to the extent that the 'interpreting subject' engages in an active reading of John's book, he or she engages in a dialogue with the text and with the texts within the text.[18]

---

18.  *Ezekiel in the Apocalypse*, p. 520.

# BIBLIOGRAPHY

Abbott-Smith, G., *A Manual Greek Lexicon of the New Testament* (Edinburgh: T. & T. Clark, 3rd edn, 1981).

Achtemeier, P.J., 'Revelation 5:1-14', *Int* 40 (1986), pp. 283-88.

Allegro, J.M., *DJD*, V (Oxford: Clarendon Press, 1968).

Anderson, H., 'The Old Testament in Mark's Gospel', in J.M. Efird (ed.), *The Use of the Old Testament in the New and other Essays* (*q.v.*), pp. 280-96.

—'A Future for Apocalyptic', in *Biblical Studies* (ed. J.R. McKay and J.F. Miller; London: Collins, 1976), pp. 56-71.

Arndt, W.F., and F.W Gingrich, *A Greek–English Lexicon of the New Testament and other Early Christian Literature* (Cambridge: Cambridge University Press, 1957).

Aune, D.E., 'The Social Matrix of the Apocalypse of John', *BR* 26 (1981), pp. 16-32.

—*Prophecy in Early Christianity and the Ancient Mediterranean World* (Grand Rapids: Eerdmans, 1983).

—'The Prophetic Circle of John of Patmos and the Exegesis of Revelation 22.16', *JSNT* 37 (1989), pp. 103-16.

—'The Form and Function of the Proclamations to the Seven Churches (Revelation 2–3)', *NTS* 36 (1990), pp. 182-204.

Aus, R.D., 'The Relevance of Isaiah 66:7 to Revelation 12 and 2 Thessalonians 1', *ZNW* 67 (1976), pp. 252-68.

Barclay, W., *The Revelation of St John* (2 vols.; Daily Study Bible; Edinburgh: Saint Andrew Press, rev. edn, 1976).

Barnett, P., 'Polemical Parallelism: Some Reflections on the Apocalypse', *JSNT* 35 (1989), pp. 111-20.

Barr, D.L., 'The Apocalypse as a Symbolic Transformation of the World: A Literary Analysis', *Int* 38 (1984), pp. 39-50.

—'The Apocalypse of John as Oral Enactment', *Int* 40 (1986), pp. 243-56.

Barr, J., 'Doubts about Homoeophony in the Septuagint', *Textus* 12 (1985), pp. 1-77.

Barrett, C.K., *The Epistle to the Romans* (BNTC; London: A. & C. Black, 1962).

—*The Gospel of John and Judaism* (London: SPCK, 1975).

—*The Gospel according to St John: An Introduction with Commentary* (London: SPCK, 1978).

Barth, M., 'The Old Testament in Hebrews. An Essay in Biblical Hermeneutics', in W. Klassen and G.F. Snyder (eds.), *Current Issues in New Testament Interpretation* (*q.v.*), pp. 53-78.

Barton, J., 'Should Old Testament Study be More Theological?', *ExpTim* 100 (1989), pp. 443-48.

Bauckham, R., *The Bible in Politics* (London: SCM Press, 1989).

—*The Climax of Prophecy: Studies on the Book of Revelation* (Edinburgh: T. & T. Clark, 1993).

—*The Theology of the Book of Revelation* (Cambridge: Cambridge University Press, 1993).

Beale, G.K., *The Use of Daniel in Jewish Apocalyptic Literature and in the Revelation of St John* (Lanham MD: University Press of America, 1984).

—'The Origin of the Title "King of Kings and Lord of Lords" in Revelation 17.14', *NTS* 31 (1985), pp. 618-20.

—'A Reconsideration of the Text of Daniel in the Apocalypse', *Bib* 67 (1986), pp. 539-43.

—'Revelation', in D.A. Carson and H.G.M. Williamson (eds.), *It is Written* (*q.v.*), pp. 318-36.

—'The Interpretative Problem of Rev. 1:19', *NovT* 34 (1992), pp. 360-87.

Beasley-Murray, G.R., *The Book of Revelation* (NCB; London: Marshall, Morgan & Scott, rev. edn, 1978).

Birdsall, J.N., 'The Georgian Version of the Book of Revelation', in E.A. Livingstone (ed.), *Studia Biblica 1978* (*q.v.*), pp. 33-45.

Black, M., 'The Recovery of the Language of Jesus', *NTS* 3 (1956–57), pp. 305-13.

—*An Aramaic Approach to the Gospels and Acts* (Oxford: Clarendon Press, 3rd edn, 1967).

—'The Christological Use of the Old Testament in the New Testament', *NTS* 18 (1971–72), pp. 1-14.

—'Some Greek Words with "Hebrew Meanings" in the Epistles and Apocalypse', in *Biblical Studies* (ed. J.R. McKay and J.F. Miller; London: Collins, 1976), pp. 135-46.

—'The "Two Witnesses" of Rev. 11:3-4 in Jewish and Christian Apocalyptic Tradition', in E. Bammel, C.K. Barrett and W.D. Davies (eds.), *Donum Gentilicium* (FS D. Daube; Oxford: Clarendon Press, 1978), pp. 227-37.

—'The Theological Appropriation of the Old Testament by the New Testament', *SJT* 39 (1986), pp. 1-18.

Blass, F., and A. Debrunner, *A Greek Grammar of the New Testament and other Early Christian Literature* (trans. and rev. R.W. Funk; Chicago: University of Chicago Press, 1961).

Bloom, H., *The Breaking of the Vessels* (Chicago: University of Chicago Press, 1982).

—*The Revelation of St John the Divine* (Modern Critical Interpretations; New York: Chelsea House, 1988).

Boccaccini, G., 'Jewish Apocalyptic Tradition: The Contribution of Italian Scholarship', in J.J. Collins and J.H. Charlesworth (eds.), *Mysteries and Revelations* (*q.v.*), pp. 33-50.

Boer, M.C. de, 'Jesus the Baptizer: 1 Jn 5:5-8 and the Gospel of John', *JBL* 107 (1988), pp. 87-106.

Boismard, M.E., '"L'Apocalypse" ou "Les Apocalypses" de St Jean', *RB* 56 (1949), pp. 507-41.

Boman, T., 'Hebraic and Greek Thought-Forms in the New Testament', in W. Klassen and G.F. Snyder (eds.), *Current Issues in New Testament Interpretation* (*q.v.*), pp. 1-22.

Bonsirven, J., *Exégèse rabbinique et exégèse paulinienne* (Paris: Beauchesne, 1939).

Borgen, P., *Bread from Heaven* (NovTSup 10; Leiden: Brill, 1965).

—'Response', *NTS* 23 (1976–77), pp. 67-75.

—'God's Agent in the Fourth Gospel', in *The Interpretation of John* (ed. J. Ashton; London: SPCK, 1986), pp. 67-98.

Boring, M.E., 'The Theology of Revelation. The Lord our God the Almighty Reigns', *Int* 40 (1986), pp. 257-69.

—*Revelation.* (Interpretation: A Bible Commentary for Teaching and Preaching; Louisville: John Knox Press, 1989).

Bowker, J.W., 'Prophetic Action and Sacramental Form', *Studia Evangelica* (vol. 3, part 2; ed. F.L. Cross; Berlin: Akademie-Verlag, 1964), pp. 129-37.

—'Speeches in Acts: A Study in Proem and Yelammedenu Form', *NTS* 14 (1977–78), pp. 96-111.

Boyarin, D. 'The Song of Songs: Lock or Key? Intertextuality, Allegory and Midrash', in *The Book and the Text* (ed. R. Schwartz; Cambridge, MA: Basil Blackwell, 1990), pp. 214-30.

Boyd, W.J.P., 'I am the Alpha and Omega (Rev. 1,8; 21,6; 22,13)', in *Studia Evangelica* (vol. 2, part 1; ed. F.L. Cross; Berlin: Akademie-Verlag, 1964), pp. 526-31.

Brewer, R.R., 'Revelation 4:6 and Translations Thereof', *JBL* 71 (1952), pp. 227-31.

Brock, S.P., 'Translating the Old Testament', in D.A. Carson and H.G.M. Williamson (eds.), *It is Written* (*q.v.*), pp. 87-98.

Brooke, G.J., *Exegesis at Qumran: 4Q Florilegium in its Jewish Context* (JSOTSup 29; Sheffield: JSOT Press, 1985).

—'The Kittim in the Qumran Pesharim', in *Images of Empire* (ed. L. Alexander; JSOTSup 122; Sheffield: JSOT Press, 1991), pp. 135-59.

—'Ezekiel in some Qumran and New Testament Texts', in *The Madrid Qumran Congress* (Proceedings of the International Congress on the Dead Sea Scrolls, Madrid 18–21 March, 1991; Leiden: Brill, 1992), pp. 317-37.

Brower, R., *Alexander Pope: The Poetry of Allusion* (Oxford: Clarendon Press, 1959).

Brown, R.E., *The Gospel according to John* (2 vols.; AB 29; Garden City: Doubleday, 1966, 1970).

Brown, S., 'The Hour of Trial (Rev. 3:10)', *JBL* 85 (1966), pp. 308-14.

—'Reader Response: Demythologising the Text', *NTS* 34 (1988), pp. 232-37.

Brownlee, W.H., 'Biblical Interpretation among the Sectaries of the Dead Sea Scrolls', *BA* 14 (1951), pp. 54-76.

—'Messianic Motifs of Qumran and the New Testament', *NTS* 3 (1956–57), pp. 12-30, 195-210.

—'The Priestly Character of the Church in the Apocalypse', *NTS* 5 (1958–59), pp. 224-25.

—*The Midrash Pesher of Habakkuk* (SBLMS 24; Missoula: Scholars Press, 1979).

Bruce, F.F., 'To the Hebrews or to the Essenes?', *NTS* 9 (1963–64), pp. 217-32.

—*Biblical Exegesis in the Qumran Texts* (London: Tyndale Press, 1960).

—'Biblical Exposition at Qumran', in *Gospel Perspectives*, III ed. R.T. France and D. Wenham; Sheffield: JSOT Press, 1983), pp. 77-98.

Brueggemann, W., 'At the Mercy of Babylon: A Subversive Rereading of the Empire', *JBL* 110 (1991), pp. 3-22.

Bruns, G.L., 'The Hermeneutics of Midrash', in *The Book and the Text* (ed. R. Schwartz; Cambridge, MA: Basil Blackwell, 1990), pp. 189-213.

Bultmann, R., *Theology of the New Testament* (2 vols.; London: SCM Press, 1952, 1955).

150     *The Old Testament in the Book of Revelation*

—*The Gospel of John: A Commentary* (Oxford: Blackwell, 1971).
Burney, C.F., *The Aramaic Origin of the Fourth Gospel* (Oxford: Clarendon Press, 1922).
Burrows, M., *The Dead Sea Scrolls of St Mark's Monastery*. I. *The Isaiah Manuscript and the Habakkuk Commentary* (New Haven: American Schools of Oriental Research, 1950).
Caird, G.B., *The Apostolic Age* (London: Duckworth, 1955).
—'Eschatology and Politics: Some Misconceptions', in *Biblical Studies* (ed. J.R. McKay and J.F. Miller; London: Collins, 1976), pp. 72-86.
—*The Language and Imagery of the Bible* (London: Duckworth, 1980).
—*The Revelation of St John the Divine* (BNTC; London: A. & C. Black, 2nd edn, 1984).
Callaway, P.R., *The History of the Qumran Community: An Investigation* (JSPSup 3; Sheffield: JSOT Press, 1988).
Cambier, J., 'Les images de l'Ancien Testament dans l'Apocalypse de Saint Jean', *NRT* 77 (1955), pp. 113-22.
Carroll, R.P., *When Prophecy Failed* (London: SCM Press, 1979).
Carson, D.A., and H.G.M. Williamson (eds.), *It is Written: Scripture Citing Scripture* (FS B. Lindars; Cambridge: Cambridge University Press, 1988).
Casey, J., 'Exodus Typology in the Book of Revelation' (PhD Dissertation, Southern Baptist Theological Seminary, 1981).
—'The Exodus Theme in the Book of Revelation against the Background of the NT', *Concilium* 189 (1987), pp. 34-43.
Casey, M., 'The Original Aramaic Form of Jesus' Interpretation of the Cup', *JTS* 41 (1990), pp. 1-12.
Charles, R.H., *Studies in the Apocalypse* (Edinburgh: T. & T. Clark, 2nd edn, 1915).
—*A Critical and Exegetical Commentary on the Revelation of St John* (2 vols.; ICC; Edinburgh: T. & T. Clark, 1920).
Charlesworth, J.H. (ed.), *The Old Testament Pseudepigrapha* (2 vols.; London: Darton, Longman & Todd, 1983, 1985).
—'The Jewish Roots of Christology: The Discovery of the Hypostatic Voice', *SJT* 39 (1986), pp. 19-41.
—'Folk Traditions in Jewish Apocalyptic Literature', in J.J. Collins and J.H. Charlesworth (eds.), in *Mysteries and Revelations* (*q.v.*), pp. 91-113.
Chernus, I., 'Visions of God in Merkabah Mysticism', *JSJ* 13 (1982), pp. 123-46.
Chilton, B.D., *The Glory of Israel: The Theology and Provenience of the Isaiah Targum* (JSOTSup 23; Sheffield: JSOT Press, 1983).
—(ed.), *The Kingdom of God in the Teaching of Jesus* (London: SPCK, 1984).
Coats, G.W., 'Balaam: Sinner of Saint?', *BR* 18 (1973), pp. 21-29.
Collins, A.Y., *The Combat Myth in the Book of Revelation* (Harvard Dissertations in Religion 9; Missoula: Scholars Press, 1976).
—'The Political Perspective of the Revelation of John', *JBL* 96 (1977), pp. 241-56.
—'The Early Christian Apocalypses', *Semeia* 14 (1979), pp. 61-121.
—'Revelation 18: Taunt Song or Dirge?', in J. Lambrecht (ed.), *L'Apocalypse johannique* (*q.v*), pp. 185-204.
—'Dating the Apocalypse of John', *BR* 26 (1981), pp. 33-45.
—*Crisis and Catharsis: The Power of the Apocalypse* (Philadelphia: Westminster Press, 1984).

—'Reading the Book of Revelation in the Twentieth Century', *Int* 40 (1986), pp. 229-42.

—Review of *The Use of Daniel in Jewish Apocalyptic Literature and in the Revelation of St John*, by G.K. Beale, *JBL* 105 (1986), pp. 734-35.

—'Vilification and Self-Definition in the Book of Revelation', *HTR* 79 (1986), pp. 308-20.

Collins, J.J., 'The Mythology of Holy War in Daniel and the Qumran War Scroll: A Point of Transition in Jewish Apocalyptic', *VT* 25 (1975), pp. 596-612.

—'The Jewish Apocalypses', *Semeia* 14 (1979), pp. 21-59.

— 'Introduction: Towards the Morphology of a Genre', *Semeia* 14 (1979), pp. 1-20.

—*Daniel: With an Introduction to Apocalyptic Literature* (FOTL 20; Grand Rapids: Eerdmans, 1984).

—*The Apocalytic Imagination: An Introduction to the Jewish Matrix of Christianity* (New York: Crossroad, 1984).

—'Genre, Ideology and Social Movements in Jewish Apocalyptism', in J.J. Collins and J.H. Charlesworth (eds.), *Mysteries and Revelations* (*q.v.*), pp. 11-32.

Collins, J.J., and J.H. Charlesworth (eds.), *Mysteries and Revelations: Apocalyptic Studies since the Uppsala Colloquium* (JSPSup 9; Sheffield: JSOT Press, 1991).

Collins, R.F., 'Tradition, Redaction and Exhortation in 1 Thess 4:13–5:11', in J. Lambrecht (ed.), *L'Apocalypse johannique* (*q.v*), pp. 325-43.

Colwell, E.C., *The Greek of the Fourth Gospel: A Study of its Aramaisms in the Light of Hellenistic Greek* (Chicago: University of Chicago Press, 1931).

— 'The Significance of Grouping of New Testament Manuscripts', *NTS* 4 (1957–58), pp. 73-92.

Cope, G., 'Throne Symbolism in the New Testament', in *Studia Evangelica* (vol. 3, part 2; ed. F.L. Cross; Berlin: Akademie-Verlag, 1964), pp. 178-82.

Court, J.M., *Myth and History in the Book of Revelation* (London: SPCK, 1979).

—*Revelation* (New Testament Guides; Sheffield: JSOT Press, 1994).

Crockett, L., 'Luke and the Jewish Lectionary', *JJS* 17 (1966), pp. 13-45.

Culpepper, R.A., *Anatomy of the Fourth Gospel: A Study in Literary Design* (Philadelphia: Fortress Press, 1983).

Daalen, D.H. van, *A Guide to the Revelation* (Theological Education Fund Study Guide 20; London: SPCK, 1986).

Dale, A., '4Q 403 Fragm. 1, Col.1, 38-46 and the Revelation to John', *RevQ* 12 (1986), pp. 409-14.

Dan, J., 'The Religious Experience of the Merkavah', in *Jewish Spirituality: From the Bible through the Middle Ages* (ed. A. Green; London: SCM Press, 1989), pp. 289-307.

Davidson, B., *The Analytical Hebrew and Chaldee Lexicon* (London: Bagster, 1956).

Davidson, H., *T.S. Eliot and Hermeneutics: Absence and Interpretation in the Waste Land* (Baton Rouge: Louisiana State University Press, 1985).

Davies, W.D., 'Paul and the People of Israel', *NTS* 24 (1977), pp. 4-39.

—*Paul and Rabbinic Judaism* (London: SPCK, 4th edn, 1981).

Dehandschutter, B., 'The Meaning of Witness in the Apocalypse', in J. Lambrecht (ed.), *L'Apocalypse johannique* (*q.v.*), pp. 283-88.

Deiana, G., 'Utilizzazione del libro di Geremia in alcuni brani dell'Apocalisse', *Lateranum* 48 (1982), pp. 125-37.

Delobel, J., 'Le texte de l'Apocalypse: Problèmes de méthode', in J. Lambrecht (ed.), *L'Apocalypse johannique* (*q.v*), pp. 151-66.

Deutsch, C., 'Transformation of Symbols: The New Jerusalem in Rev. 21:1–22:5', *ZNW* 78 (1987), pp. 106-26.

Dimant, D., and J.Strugnell, 'The Merkabah Vision in Second Ezekiel (4Q385 4)', *RevQ* 14 (1990), pp. 341–48.

Doble, P., 'The Son of Man saying in Stephen's Witnessing: Acts 6:8-8:2', *NTS* 31 (1985), pp. 68-84.

Dodd, C.H., *According to the Scriptures: The Substructure of New Testament Theology* (London: Collins, 1952).

—*The Parables of the Kingdom* (Glasgow: Fount, 1978).

Donfried, K.P., 'The Cults of Thessalonica and the Thessalonian Correspondence', *NTS* 31 (1985), pp. 336-56.

Downing, F.G., 'Revelation in the New Testament and among its Expounders', in *Studia Evangelica* (vol. 3, part 2; ed. F.L. Cross; Berlin: Akademie-Verlag, 1964), pp. 183-86.

—'Pliny's Prosecutions of Christians: Revelation and 1 Peter', *JSNT* 34 (1988), pp. 105-23.

Driver, G.R., 'Ezekiel's Inaugural Vision', *VT* 1 (1951), pp. 60-62.

Dugmore, C.W., 'Lord's Day and Easter', in *Neotestamentica et Patristica* (FS O. Cullmann NovTSup 6; Leiden: Brill, 1962), pp. 272-81.

Dumbrell, W.J., *The End of the Beginning: Revelation 21–22 and the Old Testament* (The Moore Theological Lectures; Homebush, West NSW: Lancer Books, 1985).

Dunn, J.D.G., 'Works of the Law and the Curse of the Law', *NTS* 31 (1985) pp. 523-42.

—*Romans 1–8* (WBC; Dallas: Word Books, 1988).

—*Unity and Diversity in the New Testament: An Inquiry into the Character of Earliest Christianity* (London: SCM Press, rev. edn, 1990).

Eakin, F.E., 'Spiritual Obduracy and Parable Purpose', in J.M. Efird (ed.), *The Use of the Old Testament in the New and other Essays* (*q.v.*), pp. 87-109.

Edgar, S.L., 'Respect for Context in Quotations from the Old Testament', *NTS* 9 (1962–63), pp. 55-62.

Efird, J.M. (ed.), *The Use of the Old Testament in the New and other Essays* (Durham NC: Duke University Press, 1972).

Eisenman, R., and M. Wise, *The Dead Sea Scrolls Uncovered* (London: Penguin Books, 1992).

Eliot, T.S., *Selected Essays* (London: Faber, 3rd edn, 1951).

Ellis, E.E., 'A Note on Pauline Hermeneutics', *NTS* 2 (1955–56), pp. 127-33.

—*Paul's Use of the Old Testament* (Edinburgh: T. & T. Clark, 1957).

Enroth, A.-M., 'The Hearing Formula in the Book of Revelation', *NTS* 36 (1990), pp. 598-608.

Evans, C.F., *Explorations in Theology,* II (London: SCM Press, 1977).

Evans, C.A., and J.A. Sanders (eds.), *Paul and the Scriptures of Israel* (JSNTSup 83; Sheffield: JSOT Press, 1993).

Farrer, A., *A Rebirth of Images* (Westminster: Dacre Press, 1949).

—*The Revelation of St John the Divine* (Oxford: Clarendon Press, 1964).

Fekkes, J., 'His Bride has Prepared Herself: Revelation 19–21 and Isaian Nuptial Imagery', *JBL* 109 (1990), pp. 269-87.

—*Isaiah and Prophetic Traditions in the Book of Revelation: Visionary Antecedents and their Development* (JSNTSup 93; Sheffield: JSOT Press, 1994).

Ferguson, D.S., *Biblical Hermeneutics: An Introduction* (London: SCM Press, 1987).

Ferris, S.C., 'On Discovering Semitic Sources in Luke 1–2', in *Gospel Perspectives,* II (ed. R.T. France and D. Wenham; Sheffield: JSOT Press, 1981), pp. 201-37.

Feuillet, A., 'Essai d'interprétation du chapitre XI de l'Apocalypse', *NTS* 4 (1957–58), pp. 183-200.

Fiorenza, E.S., 'Research Perspectives on the Book of Revelation', *Revelation: Justice and Judgment* (Philadelphia: Fortress Press, 1985), pp. 12-32.

—'History and Eschatology in Revelation', in *Revelation: Justice and Judgment,* pp. 35-67.

—'Redemption as Liberation', in *Revelation: Justice and Judgment,* pp. 68-81.

—'The Quest for the Johannine School: The Apocalypse and the Fourth Gospel', in *Revelation: Justice and Judgment,* pp. 85-113.

—'Apocalyptic and Gnosis in Revelation and in Paul', in *Revelation: Justice and Judgment,* pp. 114-32.

—'Apokalypsis and Propheteia: Revelation in the Context of Early Christian Prophecy', in *Revelation: Justice and Judgment,* pp. 133-56.

—'The Composition and Structure of Revelation', in *Revelation: Justice and Judgment,* pp. 159-80.

—'Visionary Rhetoric and Social-Political Situation', in *Revelation: Justice and Judgment,* pp. 181-203.

—*Revelation:Vision of a Just World* (Edinburgh: T. & T. Clark, new edn, 1993).

Fishbane, M., 'Revelation and Tradition: Aspects of Inner-Biblical Exegesis', *JBL* 99 (1980), pp. 343-61.

—'Use, Authority and Interpretation of Mikra at Qumran', in *MIKRA: Text, Translation, Reading and Interpretation of the Hebrew Bible in Ancient Judaism and Early Christianity* (ed. M.J. Mulder; Philadelphia: Fortress Press, 1988), pp. 339-77.

Fitzmyer, J.A., 'The Use of Explicit Old Testament Quotations in Qumran Literature and in the New Testament', *NTS* 7 (1960–61), pp. 297-333.

—'Further Light on Melchizedek from Qumran Cave 11', *JBL* 86 (1967), pp. 25-42.

Ford, J.M., *Revelation* (AB 38; Garden City: Doubleday, 1975).

—'The Heavenly Jerusalem and Orthodox Judaism', in E. Bammel, C.K. Barrett and W.D. Davies (eds.), *Donum Gentilicium* (FS D. Daube; Oxford: Clarendon Press, 1978), pp. 215-26.

—'The Structure and Meaning of Revelation 16', *ExpTim* 98 (1986), pp. 327-31.

France, R.T., 'Scripture, Tradition and History in the Infancy Narratives of Matthew', in *Gospel Perspectives,* II (ed. R.T. France and D. Wenham; Sheffield: JSOT Press, 1981), pp. 239-66.

Freed, E.D., *Old Testament Quotations in the Gospel of John* (NovTSup 11; Leiden: Brill, 1965).

Freyne, S., 'Reading Hebrews and Revelation Intertextually', in *Intertextuality in Biblical Writings* (FS B. van Iersel; ed. S. Draisma; Kampen: Kok, 1989), pp. 83-93.

Frost, S.B., 'Apocalyptic and History', in *The Bible in Modern Scholarship* (ed. J.P. Hyatt; London: Kingsgate Press, 1966), pp. 98-113.

Gangemi, A., 'L'utilizzazione del Deutero-Isaia nell'Apocalisse di Giovanni', *Euntes Docete* 27 (1974), pp. 109-44.

Gaylord, H.E., Review Article: 'Speculations, Visions, or Sermons', *JSJ* 13 (1982), pp. 187-94.

Gehman, H.S., 'The Relations between the Text of the J.H. Scheide Papyri and That of the other Gk MSS of Ez', *JBL* 57 (1938), pp. 281-87.

—'The Hebraic Character of Septuagintal Greek', *VT* 1 (1951), pp. 81-90.

Georgi, D., 'Who is the True Prophet?', *HTR* 79 (1986), pp. 100-26.

Gerhardsson, B., *Memory and Manuscript: Oral Tradition and Written Transmission in Rabbinic Judaism and Early Christianity* (Uppsula: CWK Gleerup, 1961).

—*The Origins of the Gospel Tradition* (London: SCM Press, 1979).

Giblin, C.H., 'Revelation 11.1-13: Its Form, Function and Contextual Integration', *NTS* 30 (1984), pp. 433-59.

Glasson, T.F., *The Revelation of John* (Cambridge: Cambridge University Press, 1965).

—'Schweitzer's Influence: Blessing or Bane?', *JTS* 28 (1977), pp. 289-302.

—'What is Apocalyptic?', *NTS* 27 (1981), pp. 98-105.

—'The Last-Judgment in Rev. 20 and Related Writings', *NTS* 28 (1982), pp. 528-39.

—'Theophany and Parousia', *NTS* 34 (1988), pp. 259-70.

—'The Temporary Messianic Kingdom and the Kingdom of God', *JTS* 41 (1990), pp. 517-25.

Goodman, M., 'Sacred Scripture and Defiling the Hands', *JTS* 41 (1990), pp. 99-107.

Gordon, R.P., 'Loricate Locusts in the Targum to Nahum III 17 and Revelation IX 9', *VT* 33 (1983), pp. 338-39.

Goulder, M.D., 'The Apocalypse as an Annual Cycle of Prophecies', *NTS* 27 (1981), pp. 342-67.

Grabbe, L.L., 'The Scapegoat Tradition: A Study in Early Jewish Interpretation', *JSJ* 18 (1987), pp. 152-67.

Grant, R.M., *A Historical Introduction to the New Testament* (London: Collins, 1963).

—*A Short History of the Interpretation of the Bible* (with D.Tracey; London: SCM Press, 2nd edn, 1984).

Greene, T.M., *The Light in Troy: Imitation and Discovery in Renaissance Poetry* (New Haven: Yale University Press, 1982).

Greenlee, J.H., *Introduction to New Testament Textual Criticism* (Grand Rapids: Eerdmans, 1964).

Grollenberg, L., *Unexpected Messiah* (London: SCM Press, 1988).

Guilding, A., *The Fourth Gospel and Jewish Worship* (Oxford: Oxford University Press, 1960).

Gundry, R.H., *The Use of the Old Testament in St Matthew's Gospel with Special Reference to the Messianic Hope* (NovTSup 18; Leiden: Brill, 1967).

—'The New Jerusalem: People as Place, not Place for People', *NovT* 29 (1987), pp. 254-64.

Guthrie, D., *The Relevance of John's Apocalypse* (Exeter: Paternoster, 1987).

Haak, R.D., *Habakkuk* (VTSup 44; Leiden: Brill, 1992).

Hall, R.G., 'Living Creatures in the Midst of the Throne. Another Look at Revelation 4:6', *NTS* 36 (1990), pp. 609-13.

Halperin, D.J., 'Merkabah Midrash in the Septuagint', *JBL* 101 (1982), pp. 351-63.

Halson, B.R., 'The Relevance of the Apocalypse', *Studia Evangelica* (vol. 2, part 1; ed. F.L. Cross; Berlin: Akademie-Verlag, 1964), pp. 388-92.

Hanhart, K., 'The Four Beasts of Daniel's Vision in the Night in the Light of Rev. 13:2', *NTS* 27 (1981), pp. 576-81.

Hanson, A.T., *Studies in Paul's Technique and Theology* (Grand Rapids: Eerdmans, 1974).

—*The New Testament Interpretation of Scripture* (London: SPCK, 1980).

—*The Living Utterances of God* (London: Darton, Longman & Todd, 1983).

—'The Origin of Paul's use of παιδαγωγός for the Law', *JSNT* 34 (1989), pp. 71-76.

Hanson, P.D., 'Old Testament Apocalyptic Re-Examined', in *Visionaries and their Apocalypses* (ed. P.D. Hanson; Philadelphia: Fortress Press, 1983), pp. 37-60.

Hartingsveld, L. van, *Revelation: A Practical Commentary* (Grand Rapids: Eerdmans, 1985).

Hartman, L.F. and A. DiLella, *The Book of Daniel* (AB 23; Garden City: Doubleday, 1978).

Hartman, L., *Prophecy Interpreted* (ConBNT Series 1; Lund: CWK Gleerup, 1966).

—'Form and Message. A Preliminary Study of "Partial Texts" in Rev. 1–3 and 22,6ff.', in J. Lambrecht (ed.), *L'Apocalypse* (*q.v.*), pp. 129-49.

Hatch, E., and H.A. Redpath, *A Concordance to the Septuagint and the other Greek Versions of the Old Testament* (2 vols. with Supplement; Oxford: Clarendon Press, 1887, 1906).

Hays, R.B., *Echoes of Scripture in the Letters of Paul* (New Haven: Yale University Press, 1989).

—'On the Rebound: A Response to Critiques of Echoes of Scripture in the Letters of Paul', in C.A. Evans and J.A. Sanders (eds.), *Paul and the Scriptures of Israel* (*q.v.*), pp. 70-96.

Heinemann, J., 'The Triennial Lectionary Cycle', *JJS* 19 (1968), pp. 41-48.

Hellholm, D., 'Methodological Reflections on the Problems of Definition of Generic Texts', in J.J. Collins and J.H. Charlesworth (eds.), *Mysteries and Revelations* (*q.v.*), pp. 135-63.

Hemer, C.J., *The Letters to the Seven Churches of Asia in their Local Setting* (JSNTSup 11; Sheffield: JSOT Press, 1986).

Hennecke, E., *New Testament Apocrypha* (2 vols.; Philadelphia: Westminster Press, 1963, 1965).

Hill, D., 'Prophecy and Prophets in the Revelation of Saint John', *NTS* 18 (1971–72), pp. 401-18.

Himmelfarb, M., 'Revelation and Rapture: The Transformation of the Visionary in the Ascent Apocalypses', in J.J. Collins and J.H. Charlesworth (eds.), *Mysteries and Revelations* (*q.v.*), pp. 79-90.

Hollander, J., *The Figure of Echo: A Mode of Allusion in Milton and After* (Berkeley: University of California Press, 1981).

Holm-Nielsen, S., *Hodayot: Psalms from Qumran* (Universitetsforlaget 1; Aarhus, 1960).

Holtz, T., 'Gott in der Apokalypse', in J. Lambrecht (ed), *L'Apocalypse johannique* (*q.v.*), pp. 247-65.

Hooker, M.D., *The Son of Man in Mark* (London: SCM Press, 1967).

—'Beyond the Things That are Written? St Paul's Use of Scripture', *NTS* 27 (1981), pp. 295-309.

Horgan, M.P., *Pesharim: Qumran Interpretations of Biblical Books* (CBQMS 8; Washington, DC: Catholic Biblical Association of America, 1979).

Howard, G., 'Hebrews and the Old Testament Quotations', *NovT* 10 (1968), pp. 208-16.

Hughes, G., *Hebrews and Hermeneutics* (SNTSMS 36; Cambridge: Cambridge University Press, 1979).

Hurtado, L.W., 'Revelation 4–5 in the Light of Jewish Apocalyptic Analogies', *JSNT* 25 (1985), pp. 105-24.

—*One God, One Lord:* Early *Christian Devotion and Ancient Jewish Monotheism* (London: SCM Press, 1988).

Jellicoe, S., *The Septuagint and Modern Study* (Oxford: Clarendon Press, 1968).

Jenkins, F., *The Old Testament in the Book of Revelation* (Grand Rapids: Eerdmans, 1972).

Jeske, R.L., 'Spirit and Community in the Johannine Apocalypse', *NTS* 31 (1985), pp. 452-66.

Jones, B.W., 'More about the Apocalypse as Apocalyptic', *JBL* 87 (1968), pp. 325–27.

Jonge, M. de, 'The Use of the Expression ὁ χριστός in the Apocalypse of John', in J. Lambrecht (ed.), *L'Apocalypse johannique* (*q.v.*), pp. 267-81.

—'11Q Melchizedek and the New Testament' (with A.S. van der Woude), *NTS* 12 (1965–66), pp. 301-26.

Juel, D., *Messianic Exegesis* (Philadelphia: Fortress Press, 1987).

Kallas, J., 'The Apocalypse—An Apocalyptic Book?', *JBL* 86 (1967), pp. 69-80.

—*Revelation: God and Satan in the Apocalypse* (Minneapolis: Augsburg, 1973).

Karrer, M., *Die Johannesoffenbarung als Brief* (FRLANT 140; Göttingen: Vandenhoeck & Ruprecht, 1986).

Käsemann, E., *Commentary on Romans* (London: SCM Press, 1980).

Kelsey, D.H., *The Uses of Scripture in Recent Theology* (London: SCM Press, 1975).

Kiddle, M., *The Revelation of St John* (MNTC; London: Hodder & Stoughton, 1940).

Kirby, J.T., 'The Rhetorical Situations of Revelation 1–3', *NTS* 34 (1988), pp. 197-207.

Klassen, W., and G.F. Snyder (eds.), *Current Issues in New Testament Interpretation* (London: SCM Press, 1962).

Knibb, M.A., *The Qumran Community* (Cambridge: Cambridge University Press, 1987).

Koch, K., *The Rediscovery of Apocalyptic* (London: SCM Press, 1972).

Kristeva, J., 'Word, Dialogue and Novel', in *The Kristeva Reader* (ed. T. Moi; Oxford: Columbia University Press, 1986), pp. 34-61.

Krodel, G.A., *Revelation* (Augsburg Commentary on the NT; Minneapolis: Augsburg, 1989).

Kummel, W., *Promise and Fulfilment* (SBT 23; London: SCM Press, 3rd edn, 1957).

—*Introduction to the New Testament* (London: SCM Press, rev. edn, 1975).

Kuhn, K.G., 'Γὼγ καὶ Μαγώγ', *TDNT*, I, pp. 789-91.

Kvanvig, H.S., 'An Akkadian Vision as Background for Dan 7?', *Studia Theologica* 35 (1981), pp. 85-89.

—'The Relevance of the Biblical Visions of the End. Hermeneutical Guidelines to the Apocalyptical Literature', *Horizons in Biblical Theology* 11 (1989), pp. 35-58.

Lacocque, A., 'Apocalyptic Symbolism: A Ricoeurian Hermeneutical Approach', *BR* 26 (1981), pp. 6-15.

Ladd, G.E., *A Commentary on the Revelation of St John* (Grand Rapids: Eerdmans, 1972).

Lambrecht, J., 'A Structuration of Revelation 4:1–22:5', in *idem* (ed.), *L'Apocalypse johannique* (*q.v.*), pp. 77-104.

Lambrecht, J. (ed), *L'Apocalypse johannique et l'apocalyptique dans le Nouveau Testment* (Leuven: Leuven University Press, 1980).

Lancellotti, A., 'L'Antico Testamento nell'Apocalisse', *RivB* 14 (1966), pp. 369-84.

Laws, S., 'Does Scripture Speak in Vain?', *NTS* 20 (1973–74), pp. 210-15.

—'The Blood-Stained Horseman: Revelation 19:11-13', in E.A. Livingstone (ed.), *Studia Biblica 1978* (*q.v.*), pp. 245-48.

Lee, J.A.L., 'Equivocal Renderings in the LXX', *RB* 87 (1980), pp. 104-17.

Leivestad, R., 'Exit the Apocalyptic Son of man', *NTS* 18 (1971–72), pp. 243-67.

Levey, S.H., *The Targum of Ezekiel Translated: With a Critical Introduction, Apparatus, and Notes* (The Aramaic Bible 13; Wilmington: Michael Glazier, 1987).

Liddell, H.G., and R. Scott, *A Greek–English Lexicon* (Rev. H.S. Jones and R. McKenzie; Oxford: Clarendon Press, 1940).

Lindars, B., *New Testament Apologetic* (London: SCM Press, 1961).

—*The Gospel of John* (NCB; London: Marshall, Morgan & Scott, 1972).

—'The Place of the Old Testament in the Formation of New Testament Theology', *NTS* 23 (1976–77), pp. 59-66.

Lohse, E., 'Die alttestamentliche Sprache des Sehers Johannes', *ZNW* 52 (1961), pp. 122-26.

Long, B.O., 'Reports of Visions among the Prophets', *JBL* 95 (1976), pp. 353-65.

Longenecker, B.W., 'The Nature of Paul's Early Eschatology', *NTS* 31 (1985), pp. 85-95.

—'Different Answers to Different Issues: Israel, the Gentiles and Salvation History in Romans 9–11', *JSNT* 36 (1989), pp. 95-123.

Longman, T., *Literary Approaches to Biblical Interpretation* (Foundations of Contemporary Interpretation 3; Grand Rapids: Academie; Leicester: Apollos, 1987).

Lovestam, E., 'The ἡ γενεὰ αὕτη Eschatology in Mk 13:30 parr', in J. Lambrecht (ed.), *L'Apocalypse johannique* (*q.v.*), pp. 403-13.

Lust, J., 'The Order of the Final Events in Revelation and Ezekiel', in J. Lambrecht (ed.), *L'Apocalypse johannique* (*q.v.*), pp. 170-83.

—'Ezekiel 36-40 in the Oldest Greek Manuscript', *CBQ* 43 (1981), pp. 517-33.

—'Messianism and Septuagint', in *Congress Volume, Salamamca 1983* (ed. J.A. Emerton; VTSup 36; Leiden Brill, 1985), pp. 174-91.

Macdonald, M.Y., *The Pauline Churches: A Socio-Historical Study of Institutionalization in the Pauline and Deutero-Pauline Writings* (SNTSMS 60; Cambridge: Cambridge University Press, 1988).

Mackay, T.W., 'Early Christian Exegesis of the Apocalypse', in E.A. Livingstone (ed.), *Studia Biblica 1978* (*q.v.*), pp. 257-63.

Malina, B.J., *The New Testament World: Insights from Cultural Anthropology* (London: SCM Press, 1983).

Marconcini, B., 'L'utilizzazione del T.M. nelle citazioni Isaiane dell'Apocalisse', *RivB* 24 (1976), pp. 113-36.

Marquis, G., 'Word Order as a Criterion for the Evaluation of Translation Technique in the LXX and the Evaluation of Word-Order Variants as Exemplified in LXX-Ezekiel', *Textus* 13 (1986), pp. 59-84.

Martin, R.A., 'Some Syntactical Criteria of Translation Greek', *VT* 10 (1960), pp. 295-310.

May, H.B., 'Some Cosmic Connotations of MAYIM RABBÎM ("Many Waters")', *JBL* 74 (1955), pp. 9-21.

Mayeda, G., 'Apocalyptic in the Epistle to the Romans—An Outline', in J. Lambrecht (ed.), *L'Apocalypse johannique* (*q.v.*), pp. 319-23.

Mazzaferri, F.D., *The Genre of the Book of Revelation from a Source-Critical Perspective* (BZNW 54; Berlin: de Gruyter, 1989).

McCullough, J.C., 'The Old Testament Quotations in Hebrews', *NTS* 26 (1980), pp. 363-79.

McGinn, B., 'Revelation', in *The Literary Guide to the Bible* (ed. A. Alter and F. Kermode; London: Collins, 1987), pp. 523-41.

McNamara, M., *Targum and Testament: Aramaic Paraphrases of the Hebrew Bible: A Light on the New Testament* (Grand Rapids: Eerdmans, 1972).

Mealy, J.W., *After the Thousand Years: Resurrection and Judgment in Revelation 20* (JSNTSup 70; Sheffield, JSOT Press, 1992).

Meeks, W.A., 'The Man from Heaven in Johannine Sectarianism', *JBL* 91 (1972), pp. 44-72.

Menken, M.J.J., 'The Provenance and Meaning of the Old Testament Quotations in John 6:31', *NovT* 30 (1988), pp. 39-56.

—'The Translation of Psalm 41.10 in John 13.18', *JSNT* 40 (1990), pp. 61-79.

Metzger, B.M., 'The Formulas Introducing Quotations of Scripture in the New Testament and the Mishnah', *JBL* 70 (1951), pp. 297-307.

—*The Text of the New Testament: Its Transmission, Corruption and Restoration* (Oxford: Oxford University Press, 2nd edn, 1968).

—*A Textual Commentary on the Greek New Testament* (Stuttgart: United Bible Societies, 1975).

Michael, J.H., 'East, North, South, West', *ExpTim* 49 (1937), pp. 141-42.

Michaels, J.R., *Interpreting the Book of Revelation* (Grand Rapids: Baker, 1992).

Milligan, W., *The Book of Revelation* (London: Hodder & Stoughton, 1889).

Minear, P.S., 'The Cosmology of the Apocalypse', in W. Klassen and G.F. Snyder (eds.), *Current Issues in New Testament Interpretation* (*q.v.*), pp. 23-37.

Moffatt, J., *Revelation of St John the Divine* (Expositor's Greek Testament 5; London: Hodder & Stoughton, 1910).

Montgomery, J.A., *The Book of Daniel* (ICC; Edinburgh: T. & T. Clark, 1927).

Morgan, R., and J. Barton, *Biblical Interpretation* (Oxford: Oxford University Press, 1988).

Morrice, W.G., 'John the Seer. Narrative Exegesis of the Book of Revelation', *ExpTim* 97 (1985–86), pp. 43-46.

Morris, L., *The Revelation of St John* (TNTC; London: Tyndale House, 1969).

Moule, C.F.D., *The Birth of the New Testament* (London: A. & C. Black, 1962).

—*An Idiom Book of NT Greek* (Cambridge: Cambridge University Press, 2nd edn, 1968).

Moulton, J.H., *A Grammar of New Testament Greek. I. Prolegomena* (Edinburgh: T. & T. Clark, 3rd edn, 1949).

Moulton, J.H., and G. Milligan, *The Vocabulary of the Greek New Testament: Illustrated from the Papyri and other Non-Literary Sources* (Grand Rapids: Eerdmans, 1974).

Moulton, W.F., and A.S. Geden, *A Concordance of the Greek Testament according to the Texts of Westcott and Hort, Tischendorf and the English Revisers* (Edinburgh: T. & T. Clark, 5th edn, 1906).

Mounce, R.H., *The Book of Revelation* (NICNT; Grand Rapids: Eerdmans, 1977).

Mowry, L., 'Revelation 4–5 and Early Christian Liturgical Usage', *JBL* 71 (1952), pp. 75-84.

Moyise, S., 'Intertextuality and the Book of Revelation', *ExpTim 104* (1993), pp. 295-98.

—'Does the New Testament Quote the Old Testament out of Context?', *Anvil* 11 (1994), pp. 133-43.

—'The Catena of Rom. 3:10-18', *ExpTim* (forthcoming).

Munck, J., *Paul and the Salvation of Mankind* (London: SCM Press, 1959).

Mussies, G., *The Morphology of Koiné Greek as Used in the Apocalypse of John: A Study in Bilinguilism* (NovTSup 27; Leiden: Brill, 1971).

—'The Greek of the Book of Revelation', in J. Lambrecht (ed.), *L'Apocalypse johannique* (*q.v.*), pp. 167-77.

Neusner, J., *What is Midrash?* (Philadelphia: Fortress Press, 1987).

Newman, C.C., *Paul's Glory-Christology* (NovTSup 69; Leiden: Brill, 1992).

Newsom, C.E., 'A Maker of Metaphors—Ezekiel's Oracles against Tyre', *Int* 38 (1984), pp. 151-64.

—*Songs of the Sabbath Sacrifice: A Critical Edition* (Harvard Semitic Studies 27; Atlanta: Scholars Press, 1985).

—'Merkabah Exegesis in the Qumran Sabbath Shirot', *JJS* 38 (1987), pp. 11-30.

Nickelsburg, G.W.E., 'The Apocalyptic Construction of Reality in 1 Enoch', in J.J. Collins and J.H. Charlesworth (eds.), *Mysteries and Revelations* (*q.v.*), pp. 51-64.

Orlinsky, H.M., 'The New Jewish Version of the Torah. Toward a New Philosophy of Bible Translation', *JBL* 82 (1963), pp. 249-64.

Ozanne, C.G., 'The Influence of the Text and Language of the Old Testament on the Book of Revelation' (PhD Thesis, University of Manchester, 1964).

Paulien, J., 'Elusive Allusions: The Problematic Use of the Old Testament in Revelation', *BR* 33 (1988), pp. 37-53.

Perrin, N., *The New Testament: An Introduction* (New York: Harcourt Brace Jovanovich, 1974).

Porter, S.E., 'The Language of the Apocalypse in Recent Discussion', *NTS* 35 (1989), pp. 582-603.

Preston, R.H., and A.T. Hanson, *The Revelation of Saint John the Divine* (Torch Bible Commentaries; London: SCM Press, 1968).

Prigent, P., 'Le Temps et le Royaume dans l'Apocalypse', in J. Lambrecht (ed.), *L'Apocalypse johannique* (*q.v.*), pp. 231-45.

Rabin, C., *The Zadokite Documents* (Oxford: Clarendon Press, 1954).

—'The Translation Process and the Character of the Septuagint', *Textus* 6 (1968), pp. 1-26.

Rahlfs, A. (ed.), *Septuaginta: Id est Vetus Testamentum graece iuxta LXX interpretes* (2 vols.; Stuttgart: Deutsche Bibelgesellschaft, 1935).

Ramsay, W.M., *The Letters to the Seven Churches of Asia and their Place in the Plan of the Apocalypse* (London: Hodder & Stoughton, 1904).

Reddish, M.G., 'Martyr Christology in the Apocalypse', *JSNT* 33 (1988), pp. 85-95.

Reim, G., *Studien zum alttestamentlichen Hintergrund des Johannesevangelium* (SNTSMS 22; Cambridge: Cambridge University Press, 1974).

Reinhartz, A., 'Jesus as Prophet: Predictive Prolepses in the Fourth Gospel', *JSNT* 36 (1989), pp. 3-16.

Rhoads, D., and D. Mitchie, *Mark as Story: An Introduction to the Narrative of a Gospel* (Philadelphia: Fortress Press, 1982).

Rissi, M., *The Future of the World: An Exegetical Study of Revelation 19:11–22:5* (London: SCM Press, 1972).

Roberts, B.J., *The Old Testament Text and Versions* (Cardiff: University of Wales Press, 1951).

Rowland, C., 'The Visions of God in Apocalyptic Literature', *JSJ* 10 (1979), pp. 137-54.

—'The Vision of the Risen Christ in Rev. 1.13ff: The Debt of an Early Christology to an Aspect of Jewish Angeology', *JTS* 31 (1980), pp. 1-11.

—*The Open Heaven: A Study of Apocalypticism in Judaism and Christianity* (London: SPCK, 1982).

—'Apocalyptic Literature', in D.A. Carson and H.G.M. Williamson (eds.), *It is Written* (*q.v.*), pp. 170-89.

—*Radical Christianity* (Oxford: Polity Press, 1988).

Royse, J.R., '"Their Fifteen Enemies": The Text of Rev. 11:12 in 𝔓47 and 1611', *JTS* 31 (1980), pp. 78-80.

Ruiz, J.-P., *Ezekiel in the Apocalypse: The Transformation of Prophetic Language in Revelation 16:17–19:10* (European University Studies 23; Frankfurt: Peter Lang, 1989).

Russell, D.S., *The Method and Message of Jewish Apocalyptic* (London: SCM Press, 1964).

—*The Old Testament Pseudepigrapha: Patriarchs and Prophets in Early Judaism* (London: SCM Press, 1987).

Sanders, E.P., *Paul and Palestinian Judaism* (London: SCM Press, 1977).

—*Paul, the Law and the Jewish People* (London: SCM Press, 1983).

Sanders, H.A., 'The Beatty Papyrus of Revelation and Hoskier's Edition', *JBL* 53 (1934), pp. 371-80.

Sanders, J.A., 'Paul and Theological History', in C.A. Evans and J.A. Sanders (eds.), *Paul and the Scriptures of Israel* (*q.v.*), pp. 52-57.

Sanders, J.N., 'St John on Patmos', *NTS* 9 (1962–63), pp. 75-85.

Sandmel, S., 'Parallelomania', *JBL* 81 (1962), pp. 1-13.

Schlatter, A., *Das alte Testament in der johanneischen Apokalypse* (BFCT 16.6; Gütersloh: Bertelsmann, 1912).

Schmid, J., *Studien zur Geschichte des Griechischen Apokalypse-Textes. I. Der Apokalypse-Kommentar des Andreas von Kaisareia* (Munchen: Karl Zink, 1955).

Schmidt, D.D., 'Semitisms and Septuagintalisms in the Book of Revelation', *NTS* 37 (1991), pp. 592-603.

Scholem, G.G., *Major Trends in Jewish Mysticism* (New York: Schocken, 1961).

Schweizer, E., 'The Son of Man Again', *NTS* 10 (1964), pp. 256-61.

Scobie, C.H.H., 'Local References in the Letters to the Seven Churches', *NTS* 39 (1993), pp. 606-24.

Scott, R.B.Y., 'Behold, he Cometh with Clouds', *NTS* 5 (1958–59), pp. 127-32.

Silberman, L.H., 'Unriddling the Riddle: A Study in the Structure and Language of the Habakkuk Pesher (1QpHab.)', *RevQ* 3 (1961–62), pp. 323-64.

—'Farewell to "'O AMHN". A Note on Rev. 3,14', *JBL* 82 (1963), pp. 213-15.

Sinclair, L., 'A Qumran Biblical Fragment 4Q Ezek$^a$ (Ezek.10,17–11,11)', *RevQ* 14 (1989), pp. 99-105.

Slomovic, E., 'Toward an Understanding of the Exegesis in the Dead Sea Scrolls', *RevQ* 7 (1969), pp. 3-15.

Smith, C.R., 'The Portrayal of the Church as the New Israel in the Names and Order of the Tribes in Revelation 7.5-8', *JSNT* 39 (1990), pp. 111–18.

Smith, D.M., 'The Use of the Old Testament in the New', in J.M. Efird (ed.), *The Use of the Old Testament in the New and other Essays* (*q.v.*), pp. 3-65.

—*Johannine Christianity: Essays on its Setting, Sources and Theology* (Edinburgh: T. & T. Clark, 1987).

Staniforth, M. (ed.), *Early Christian Writings: The Apostolic Fathers* (London: Penguin Classics, 1968).

Stanley, C.D., *Paul and the Language of Scripture: Citation Technique in the Pauline Epistles and Contemporary Literature* (SNTSMS 74; Cambridge: Cambridge University Press, 1992).

Stanton, G. (ed.), *The Interpretation of Matthew* (London: SPCK, 1983).

Stendahl, K., 'The Apocalypse of John and the Epistles of Paul in the Muratorian Fragment', in W. Klassen and G.F. Snyder (eds.), *Current Issues in New Testament Interpretation* (*q.v.*), pp. 239-45.

—*The School of St Matthew and its Use of the Old Testament* (Philadelphia: Fortress Press, 2nd edn, 1968).

—*Paul among Jews and Gentiles and other Essays* (Philadelphia: Fortress Press, 1976).

Stenning, J.F. (ed.), *The Targum of Isaiah* (Oxford: Clarendon Press, 1953).

Stibbe, M.W.G., *John* (Readings: A New Biblical Commentary; Sheffield: JSOT Press, 1993).

Stockhausen, C.K., '2 Corinthians 3 and the Principles of Pauline Exegesis', in C.A. Evans and J.A. Sanders (eds.), *Paul and the Scriptures of Israel* (*q.v.*), pp. 143-64.

Stone, M.E., 'On Reading an Apocalypse', in J.J. Collins and J.H. Charlesworth (eds.), *Mysteries and Revelations* (*q.v.*), pp. 65-78.

Stott, W., 'A Note on the Word KYPIAKH in Rev 1:10', *NTS* 12 (1965), pp. 70-75.

Strand, K.A., 'Another Look at "Lord's Day" in the Early Church and in Rev.1.10', *NTS* 13 (1966), pp. 174-81.

Strugnell, J., 'The Angelic Liturgy at Qumran', in *Congress Volume, Oxford 1959* (ed. J.A. Emerton; VTSup 7; Leiden: Brill, 1960), pp. 318-45.

Strugnell, J., and D. Dimant, '4Q Second Ezekiel', *RevQ* 13 (1988), pp. 45-58.

Surridge, R., 'Redemption in the Structure of Revelation', *ExpTim* 101 (1990), pp. 231-35.

Sweet, J.P.M., *Revelation* (TPI New Testament Commentaries; London: SCM Press, 2nd edn, 1990).

Swete, H.B., *Introduction to the Old Testament in Greek* (Cambridge: Cambridge University Press, 2nd edn, 1902).

—*The Apocalypse of St John* (London: Macmillan, 3rd edn, 1911).

Talmon, S., *The World of Qumran from Within* (Jerusalem: Magnes Press, 1989).

Tasker, R.V.G., *The Old Testament in the New Testament* (London: SCM Press, 1946).

Tengbom, L.C., 'Studies in the Interpretation of Revelation Two and Three' (PhD Dissertation, Hartford Seminary Foundation, 1976).

Thackeray, H.St.-J., *A Grammar of the Old Testament in Greek according to the Septuagint* (Cambridge: Cambridge University Press, 1909).

Theissen, G., *The Shadow of the Galilean* (London: SCM Press, 1987).

Thiselton, A.C., *New Horizons in Hermeneutics* (London: HarperCollins, 1992).

Thomas, K.J., 'The Old Testament Citations in Hebrews', *NTS* 11 (1964–65), pp. 303-25.

Thompson, L.L., *The Book of Revelation: Apocalypse and Empire* (Oxford: Oxford University Press, 1990).

Thomson, S., *The Apocalypse and Semitic Syntax* (SNTSMS 52; Cambridge: Cambridge University Press, 1985).

Thornton, T.C.G., 'Christian Understanding of the Birkath Ha-Minim in the Eastern Roman Empire', *JTS* 38 (1987), pp. 419-31.

Topham, M., ' "A Human Being's Measurement, Which is an Angel's"', *ExpTim* 100 (1989), p. 217.

—'The Dimensions of the New Jerusalem', *ExpTim* 100 (1989), pp. 417-19.

Torrey, C.C., *The Apocalypse of John* (New Haven: Yale University Press, 1958).

Tov, E., 'Three Dimensions of LXX words', *RB* 83 (1976), pp. 529-44.

—'Computer-Assisted Study of the Criteria for Assessing the Literalness of Translation Units in the LXX' (with B.G. Wright), *Textus* 12 (1985), pp. 149-87.

—'The Unpublished Qumran Texts from Caves 4 and 11', *BA* (June 1992), pp. 94-104.

Trebilco, P., *Jewish Communities in Asia Minor* (SNTSMS 69; Cambridge: Cambridge University Press, 1991).

Trevett, C., 'The other Letters to the Churches of Asia: Apocalypse and Ignatius of Antioch', *JSNT* 37 (1989), pp. 117-35.

Trudinger, L.P., 'The Text of the Old Testament in the Book of Revelation' (ThD Dissertation, Boston University, 1963).

—'Some Observations concerning the Text of the Old Testament in the Book of Revelation', *JTS* 17 (1966), pp. 82-88.

—'O AMHN (Rev III.14) and the Case for a Semitic Original of the Apocalypse', *NovT* 14 (1972), pp. 277-79.

Turner, N., 'The Greek Translators of Ezekiel', *JTS* 7 (1956), pp. 12-24.

Ulrich, E., 'Daniel Manuscripts from Qumran. Part 1: A Preliminary Edition of 4QDan$^c$', *BASOR* 268 (1987), pp. 17-37.

Unnik, W.C. van, 'A Formula Describing Prophecy', *NTS* 9 (1963), pp. 86-94.

Vanhoye, A., 'L'utilisation du livre d'Ezéchiel dans l'Apocalypse', *Bib* 43 (1962), pp. 436-76.

Vanni, U., 'L'Apocalypse johannique. Etat de la question', in J. Lambrecht (ed.), *L'Apocalypse johannique* (q.v.), pp. 21-46.

—'Liturgical Dialogue as a Literary Form in the Book of Revelation', *NTS* 37 (1991), pp. 348-72.

Vermes, G., *Jesus the Jew* (London: SCM Press, 2nd edn, 1983).

—(ed.), *The Dead Sea Scrolls in English* (London: Penguin, 3rd edn, 1990).

Vogelgesang, J.M., 'The Interpretation of Ezekiel in the Book of Revelation' (PhD dissertation, Harvard University, Cambridge, MA, 1985).

Vorster, W., 'Intertextuality and Redaktionsgeschichte', in *Intertextuality in Biblical Writings* (FS B. van Iersel; ed. S. Draisma; Kampen: Kok, 1989), pp. 15-26.

Vos, L.A., *The Synoptic Traditions in the Apocalypse* (Kampen: Kok, 1965).

Walker, N., 'The Origin of the "Thrice-Holy"', *NTS* 5 (1958–59), pp. 132-33.

Whale, P., 'The Lamb of John: Some Myths about the Vocabulary of the Johannine Literature', *JBL* 106 (1987), pp. 289-95.

Wilcock, M., *I Saw Heaven Opened: The Message of Revelation* (Bible Speaks Today; Leicester: IVP, 1975).

Wilcox, M., 'Tradition and Redaction of Rev 21,9–22,5', in J. Lambrecht (ed.), *L'Apocalypse johannique* (*q.v.*), pp. 205-15.

Wilder, A.N., 'Eschatological Imagery and Earthly Circumstance', *NTS* 5 (1958–59), pp. 229-45.

—'New Testament Hermeneutics Today', in W. Klassen and G.F. Snyder (eds.), *Current Issues in New Testament Interpretation* (*q.v.*), pp. 38-52.

Wilken, R.L., 'Early Christian Chiliasm, Jewish Messianism and the Idea of the Holy Land', *HTR* 79 (1986), pp. 298-307.

Wilkinson, R.H., 'The ΣΤΥΛΟΣ of Revelation 3:12 and Ancient Coronation Rites', *JBL* 107 (1988), pp. 498-501.

Williamson, H.G.M., 'History', in D.A. Carson and H.G.M. Williamson (eds.), *It is Written* (*q.v.*), pp. 25-38.

Wilson, R.R., 'Prophecy in Crisis: The Call of Ezekiel', *Int* 38 (1984), pp. 117-30.

Winter, B.W., 'The Public Honouring of Christian Benefactors: Romans 13:3-4 and 1 Peter 2:14-15', *JSNT* 34 (1989), pp. 87-103.

Wintermute, O., 'A Study of Gnostic Exegesis of the Old Testament', in J.M. Efird (ed.), *The Use of the Old Testament in the New and other Essays* (*q.v.*), pp. 241-70.

Wolde, E. van, 'Trendy Intertextuality', in S. Draisma (ed.), *Intertextuality in Biblical Writings* (FS B. van Iersel; ed. Kampen: Kok, 1989), pp. 43–49.

Worten, M., and J. Still, 'Introduction', in *Intertextuality: Theories and Practices* (ed. M. Worten and J. Still; Manchester: Manchester University Press, 1990), pp. 1-44.

Woude, A.S. van der, 'Wicked Priest or Wicked Priests? Reflections on the Identification of the Wicked Priest in the Habakkuk Commentary', *JJS* 33 (1982), pp. 349-59.

—*Aramaic Texts from Qumran* (with C.J. Labuschagne and B. Jongeling; Semitic Study Series 4, vol. 1; Leiden: Brill, 1976).

Wright, A., 'The Literary Genre Midrash', *CBQ* 28 (1966), pp. 105-38, 417-57.

Würthwein, E., *The Text of the Old Testament* (London: SCM Press, 1980).

Yadin, Y., *The Message of the Scrolls* (With a New Introduction by J.H. Charlesworth; New York: Crossroad, 1992).

Young, F.W., *Sacrifice and the Death of Christ* (London: SCM Press, 1975).

—*Meaning and Truth in 2 Corinthians* (with D. Ford; London: SPCK, 1987).

Zimmerli, W., *Ezekiel* (2 vols.; Hermeneia Series; Philadelphia: Fortress Press, 1979, 1983).

# INDEXES

## INDEX OF REFERENCES

### OLD TESTAMENT

| Genesis | | | | | |
|---|---|---|---|---|---|
| 1 | 137 | 5.4-5 | 122 | 89 | 117, 118, |
| 17.2 | 105 | 5.31 | 38, 44, 127 | | 126 |
| 49.9 | 128, 129 | | | 89.1 | 117 |
| | | *1 Samuel* | | 89.2 | 117 |
| | | 4.8 | 105 | 89.5 | 117 |
| *Exodus* | | | | 89.8 | 117 |
| 6.6 | 105 | *2 Samuel* | | 89.14 | 117 |
| 9.18-26 | 123 | 7.11-14 | 92 | 89.20 | 117 |
| 9.18 | 122 | 7.11 | 91 | 89.24 | 117 |
| 10.6 | 122 | 7.12 | 91 | 89.27 | 116, 117 |
| 11.6 | 122 | 7.13 | 91 | 89.27 (NRSV) | 116 |
| 15.2 | 103 | 7.14 | 11, 92 | 89.29 | 117 |
| 18.21 | 101 | 22.9 | 105 | 89.33 | 117 |
| 19.16-18 | 123 | | | 89.37 | 116, 117 |
| | | *1 Kings* | | 89.46 | 105, 117 |
| *Leviticus* | | 19 | 90, 106, 107 | 89.49 | 117 |
| 19.18 | 19 | 19.11-12 | 90 | | |
| 25 | 94, 95 | 20.41 | 71 | *Proverbs* | |
| 25.10 | 95 | 22 | 68 | 8.22 | 35 |
| 25.13 | 94 | | | 14.5 | 116 |
| 27.24 | 94 | *1 Chronicles* | | 30.15-16 | 103 |
| | | 5.2 | 103 | | |
| *Numbers* | | | | *Isaiah* | |
| 24.17 | 86 | *Esther* | | 1.10 | 105 |
| 25.12 | 105 | 9.19 | 105 | 5.14 | 103 |
| | | | | 6 | 57, 68-70, |
| *Deuteronomy* | | *Psalms* | | | 143 |
| 1.5 | 97 | 2.9 | 133 | 6.3 | 70 |
| 6.4 | 19 | 5.11 | 105 | 7.14 | 143 |
| 8.6 | 105 | 68.29 | 57 | 9.6 | 88 |
| 10.17 | 95 | 74.9 (LXX) | 123 | 11 | 39, 133 |
| 15.2 | 94 | 75.9 | 123 | 11.4 | 31, 35, 36, |
| | | 82.1 | 94, 95, 107 | | 38, 54, 127, |
| *Judges* | | 88.28 (LXX) | 116 | | 133 |
| 5 | 39 | 88.38 (LXX) | 116 | | |

NEW TESTAMENT

## PSEUDEPIGRAPHA

# JOURNAL FOR THE STUDY OF THE NEW TESTAMENT

## Supplement Series

## DATE DUE

| | | | |
|---|---|---|---|
| | | | |
| | | | |
| | | | |
| | | | |
| | | | |
| | | | |
| | | | |
| | | | |
| | | | |
| | | | |
| | | | |
| | | | |
| | | | |
| | | | |
| | | | |
| | | | |
| | | | |
| | | | |
| | | | |
| | | | |
| | | | Printed in USA |